1995

SPSS[×] MADE SIMPLE

OTHER TITLES OF RELATED INTEREST IN SOCIOLOGY

Research Methods and Statistics

Earl Babbie, THE PRACTICE OF SOCIAL RESEARCH, 4TH
Earl Babbie, OBSERVING OURSELVES: ESSAYS IN SOCIAL RESEARCH
Earl Babbie, SURVEY RESEARCH METHODS
Margaret Jendrek, THROUGH THE MAZE: STATISTICS WITH COMPUTER APPLICATIONS
John Lofland/Lyn Lofland, ANALYZING SOCIAL SETTINGS: A GUIDE TO QUALITATIVE
     OBSERVATION AND ANALYSIS, 2D
Joseph Healey, STATISTICS: A TOOL FOR THE SOCIAL SCIENCES
June True, FINDING OUT: CONDUCTING AND EVALUATING SOCIAL RESEARCH

Computer Software for the Social Sciences

Cognitive Development Company, SHOWCASE: DEMONSTRATING SOCIOLOGY LIVE IN
     THE CLASSROOM with demonstration scripts by Rodney Stark

SPSS[×] MADE SIMPLE

JOHN HEDDERSON
University of Texas at El Paso

Wadsworth Publishing Company
Belmont, California
A Division of Wadsworth, Inc.

To Monique and Shanti

Sociology Editor: Sheryl Fullerton
Editorial Associate: Cynthia Haus
Production: Stacey C. Sawyer, Montara, Calif.
Design: MaryEllen Podgorski
Copy Editor: Tricia Cain
Chapter 1 Illustration: Bob Haydock
Compositor: G & S Typesetters, Austin, Texas
Cover: Al Burkhardt

SPSS^X, SPSS, and SCSS are the trademarks of SPSS Inc. for proprietary software.

Printed in the United States of America

1 2 3 4 5 6 7 8 9 10—90 89 88 87

ISBN 0-534-07458-8

Library of Congress Cataloging in Publication Data

Hedderson, John.
  SPSSx made simple.

  On t.p. "x" is superscript.
  Bibliography: p.
  Includes index.
  1. SPSS X (Computer system)   2. Social sciences—
Data processing.   I. Title.
HA32.H43   1986   005.3'29   86-22458
ISBN 0-534-07458-8

CONTENTS

PREFACE

After ten years of teaching first SPSS and currently SPSS^X, I am convinced that SPSS^X is not easy for the average college student to learn. I am also convinced that the program manuals are not easy to teach from. Students who are experienced with statistics and programming or students with a high aptitude for this type of work will learn SPSS^X easily. The rest suffer. Typically, my students have scant training in statistics or programming and have average or less-than-average aptitude for this work. Often they are not comfortable with mathematics, computers, and "that sort of thing." I wrote *SPSS^X Made Simple* to help this type of student and his or her instructor.

Organization

As the title implies, my book does not attempt to present all the intricacies and capacities of SPSS^X. In Part 1, I have tried to put only what is essential for a student with little background in statistics and no background in programming to do successful analyses with SPSS^X. Being able to produce interesting output quickly is a tremendous morale booster. In Part 1 of the text, my objectives are

- to minimize student errors
- to teach the student to think in terms of coding data into cases, variables, and formatted records

- to introduce the student to basic data file cleaning through the LIST command
- to introduce the student to univariate analysis through the use of the FRE-QUENCIES command
- to teach the student how to focus on subsets of his or her cases using the SELECT IF command
- to teach the student how to transform variables and create new variables with the commands, RECODE, COMPUTE, and IF
- to introduce the student to bivariate analysis through the commands CROSSTABS, BREAKDOWN, PEARSON CORR, and SCATTERGRAM

Part 2 covers multivariate statistical techniques that, in themselves, are not simple. Although I present simple approaches to using SPSS^x to produce analyses, my discussion of the meaning of the statistics is unavoidably more challenging and less complete than the discussion in Part 1. Part 2 includes chapters on using tapes from the Bureau of the Census and on using SPSS/PC+.

Advantageous Features

Throughout this book I have tried to proceed step by step without making implicit leaps in logic or sneaking in new terms without definitions.

A single topic, the correlates of happiness, is used for examples throughout the text to illustrate the various procedures as they are introduced. This extended example elaborates chapter by chapter how happiness corresponds with gender, education, income, health, marital status, and parenthood.

An easily conducted research project is incorporated into the text. This project gives the student the experience of being involved in an analysis from data collection to final product.

Data from a National Opinion Research Center General Social Survey is available from Wadsworth Publishing Company to instructors who adopt the book, so that analyses paralleling those in the text can be done as exercises.

Each chapter has Review Questions with answers that enable the students to test their comprehension of the chapter. Each chapter also has Assignment Questions with answers provided only to the instructor to test the students' comprehension.

Outputs discussed in the nucleus of the manual are simplified to facilitate the learning of key statistics. At the end of each chapter, there are replications of SPSS^x outputs; these enable the student to see the context in which the statistics appear and provide the instructor the option of discussing additional statistics.

A glossary of examples enables the student to quickly look up command keywords and specifications.

Finally and very significantly, this manuscript condenses into one book the most essential material covered in six expensive SPSS[x] manuals.

Acknowledgments

Anyone who has worked on a textbook appreciates that the end product is a collective effort. That is why, outside the preface, I use the plural "we" in my writing, even though I am sole author. This project began in the summer of 1983 as a text for SPSS, before the appearance of the X version. The draft manuscripts produced in subsequent summers have benefited from the labor of many people.

Special thanks go to the questioning students who sought clarification and examples and applications in their classes.

I am also grateful to the people at Wadsworth Publishing Company for their willingness to tackle the task of developing the first draft and their continuing assistance, encouragement, and confidence. In particular, I wish to thank Sheryl Fullerton and the other editors listed in the front of this book: The final writing and production benefited immensely from their contributions. My first communication with Wadsworth was through marketing representatives Nancy Tandberg and Tamy Stenquist, who have shared their thoughts over the years on textbooks, education, and the cosmos while ably representing Wadsworth up and down the Continental Divide from Anchorage to El Paso.

I also benefited from the patient work of the Department of Sociology and Anthropology staff at the University of Texas at El Paso, especially Bea Ogaz and Irene Casas, who weathered the production of ever longer manuscripts, including the one that disabled the department's best printer.

Invaluable service was done by the guinea pigs who "volunteered" at my behest to serve as test readers. Their willingness to plunge through material admittedly less entrancing than a best-selling novel and point out confusing pages and errors have been invaluable. Foremost among these have been my daughter Shanti, my brother Mark, and my friends Gregory Van Boom and Sarah Ray.

My colleague Howard Daudistel served as a more statistically sophisticated reader and advisor.

Finally, I appreciate the numerous constructive comments of the following reviewers whose work improved this book substantially: Ken Berry, Colorado State University; David Chilson, Bowling Green State University; Scott Feld, State University of New York at Stony Brook; Larry Felice, Baylor University; Richard Harris, University of Texas at San Antonio; Jeff Jacques, Florida A&M; David Marshall, Texas Woman's University; and Dave Thissen, University of Kansas.

Note to the Student

SPSS^x is a computer program for doing statistical analyses. A program is a set of instructions to the computer. This manual will show you how to use SPSS^x. The SPSS^x acronym stands for the Statistical Package for the Social Sciences, version X. Pronounce each letter of the acronym separately—S-P-S-S-X—or call it X for short when people know you are talking about an SPSS program.

If you are unfamiliar with statistics or computers, you may be a little nervous—perhaps very nervous. Relax. You do not have to be a genius to do statistical analysis or to use a computer. Step by step, this book will explain how to do statistical analyses with SPSS^x. After studying it, you still will not be an expert on statistics or computers. You will, however, be able to do the procedures used most often in academic, government, and business work.

The SPSS^x material is most easily learned by studying examples. We will study happiness as a learning example using data gathered from a sample survey of the United States. In particular, we will study how happiness is affected by gender, education, income, health, marital status, and parenthood. We challenge you to venture a guess right now as to which of these variables will be most strongly associated with happiness.

We begin with "An Introduction for Beginners." The rest of Part 1 proceeds gradually through basic statistical analyses. Part 2 introduces some of the more sophisticated statistical procedures of SPSS^x. Part 2 also covers how to use tapes from the U.S. Bureau of the Census and how to use SPSS/PC+, a version of SPSS designed for use on microcomputers.

PART 1

LEARNING THE BASICS

If you have never used a computer or the SPSS^x program before, Part 1 is the place to begin. Part 1, consisting of seven chapters, discusses using computers, preparing data files for computers, saving and retrieving SPSS system files, and using the most basic SPSS^x commands. If you have experience using SPSS^x, you can go directly to the chapters that discuss whatever commands you need more information about.

- In Chapter 1 you are introduced to computers and SPSS^x.
- In Chapter 2 you learn to code data for computer analysis and to save and retrieve SPSS system files.
- In Chapter 3 you learn to examine your data for errors and to obtain the distribution of cases by variable categories.
- In Chapter 4 you learn to transform variables into new categories, to compute new variables, and to label your output clearly.
- In Chapter 5 you learn to use the command CROSSTABS to examine the association between two variables. You also learn to use control variables with CROSSTABS.
- In Chapter 6 you learn to use the command BREAKDOWN to compare group means on variables.
- In Chapter 7 you learn to use the commands PEARSON CORR and SCAT-TERGRAM, two more ways of examining the association between two variables.

Part 1 also provides practice in using an SPSS^x system file. As an example, we use the National Opinion Research Center's 1984 General Social Survey, discussed in Appendix B. The text examples focus on the characteristics of respondents that are associated with happiness. However, the file contains many other variables covering a broad range of attitudes and background information.

Part 1 also provides class assignments that involve the gathering and coding of data, using the Happiness Questionnaire in Appendix C. This research project involves collecting information about people and their level of happiness. You will be instructed chapter by chapter on how to treat the information you collect, so it can be analyzed with SPSS^X. Finally, you will be guided through several sample analyses of the information. This project will give you a more complete understanding of the research process. It also will enable you to compare the people in your sample with the respondents to the 1984 General Social Survey.

1

INTRODUCTION: WHAT HAVE YOU GOTTEN YOURSELF INTO?

Many people hate working with computers or statistics, and you are now in the position of having to do both. Hatred of a task is often grounded in an unspoken fear that "I won't be able to do it right." To become an expert at programming or statistics is a long, difficult learning process, but you need not be an expert to do useful statistical analysis with computers. *Learning to do basic statistics with SPSS^X is no more difficult than learning to read. You learned to read, and you can learn to use SPSS^X correctly.*

The best way to learn to use SPSS^X is by example. As a learning example, we will analyze how various types of people differ in their likelihood of being happy. Are men happier than women? Are college graduates happier than people who end their education with high school? Are the affluent or the poor happier than the middle class? Are single people happier than married people? Are people with children happier than people without children? In the coming chapters, you will learn how SPSS^X can help you answer these and a wide range of other questions.

This book's primary goal is to teach you to use SPSS^X. Although we review many statistical concepts when they first appear in the text, we presume that you have some knowledge of statistics. Take the Background Test at the end of this chapter to check whether your statistical knowledge is at the expected level. If your grasp of statistics concepts is shaky, you may wish to have handy an introductory statistics text for reference. An easy introduction is *Statistics without Tears* by Derek Roundtree (New York: Charles Scribner's Sons, 1981). A more advanced introduction is Hubert Blalock's *Social Statistics: Revised Second Edition* (New York: McGraw-Hill, 1979). A statistics text that also discusses SPSS[x] commands is *Through the Maze: Statistics with Computer Applications* by Margaret Jendrek (Belmont, Calif.: Wadsworth, 1985).

1.1 About SPSS[x]: Friend or Foe?

We now provide some basic background about SPSS[x], computer programs, and data. These beginning terms are like your car tires. They are not the most exciting part of the vehicle, but you cannot go anywhere without them.

What Is SPSS[x]?

SPSS[x] is a set of computer programs that enable researchers to do many types of statistical analyses. Sometimes researchers analyze data they have collected; other times they analyze data sets acquired from other researchers. With SPSS[x] you can

- count the number of cases in each category of a variable
- compute score means for variables
- do crosstabulations to examine associations between variables
- compute correlations between variables
- do multiple regressions, analyses of variance, discriminant function analyses, log-linear analyses, factor analyses, and other sophisticated multivariate analyses
- display data in a variety of report and graphic formats

Although other statistics programs are available, SPSS[x] is easier to learn than most programs and is available at more installations than any other program package.

What Are Data and What Data Will We Use?

Broadly defined, **data** are any kind of information; however, the term often is used to refer particularly to information that is organized for computer processing. The word *data* is the plural form of *datum,* so we use *data* with the plural form of verbs, which may sound peculiar at first.

SPSS^X is a tool that can analyze all sorts of data about a countless variety of topics. What you use it for depends on your interests. SPSS^X has been used in studies of such diverse subjects as

- business payrolls
- school registrations
- earthquakes
- income distributions
- death rates
- population growth
- unemployment trends
- attitudes about nuclear weapons
- which kinds of people are most likely to be very happy or very unhappy

The subject of happiness is one we will use for examples throughout this book. For these examples, we employ data gathered by the National Opinion Research Center (NORC), a nonprofit research branch of the University of Chicago. Founded in 1941, NORC is one of the oldest national survey research facilities in the country and does work for a wide range of clients. Academic researchers, marketing managers, city planners, and political campaigners are some of the variety of people involved in survey research who have utilized the services or data of NORC.

Among its many research projects, NORC has conducted a General Social Survey almost every year since 1964. (The exceptions were in 1979 and 1981, when government funding for the project was insufficient.) This survey measures people's social, psychological, and political attitudes. The NORC General Social Survey also gathers information about age, sex, income level, level of education, ethnicity, race, marital status, and other social characteristics.

Our examples use data from the 1984 survey (see Appendix B). We also give assignments involving this data file as you progress chapter by chapter. Appendix B lists the questions used by NORC in their data collection. (Assignment Question 1.1 at the end of this chapter will begin preparing you to use this file.)

You can also collect data of your own using the Happiness Questionnaire in Appendix C. These data can be compared with the data from the NORC survey. Look at Appendix C now to get an idea of what the course research project entails. (The Research Project Work at the end of this chapter begins the research project.)

Perhaps you have already collected your own data on a question of interest to you. If so, this book will take you step by step through what you need to know to analyze them.

What Is a Program?

A **program** is a set of instructions to a computer to make it perform tasks that the user wants done.

A common mistake of beginning students is to think that a computer program already has the data and that they need only ask their questions. This is not true. For example, if you want to know the mean length of employment at Wadsworth, Inc., a statistics program can calculate the mean only if you supply employment data about the individuals working for Wadsworth. Unless someone has already stored the necessary data set in the system's memory and your program makes reference to its location, you must provide the data along with your commands.

The following is an example of an SPSS[x] "job" that includes the data (the lines of numbers between BEGIN DATA and END DATA). A **job** or **run** is the submission of a program to a computer for execution.

```
DATA LIST   ID 1-2   EDUC 3-4   SEX 5   HAPPY 6
BEGIN DATA
010912
021223
031521
041222
050611
061612
071522
081612
091821
101412
111321
121611
130922
141212
151221
161821
170821
181222
191613
20142
END DATA
FREQUENCIES   VARIABLES=EDUC SEX HAPPY
```

There is nothing magical about this (or any) program. Preceding the commands in the example there would have to be operating system commands.

These commands, which differ slightly for each computer installation, indicate the user's name, what account is to be billed, and where the output is to be sent. If the user were going to use data on a memory device within the system, other operating system commands and subcommands might be needed. You will need to learn from local people the operating system commands used at your installation. When the user gives a command like DATA LIST, certain procedures are carried out according to the instructions in the SPSS^X program. (The work done by the DATA LIST command is explained in Chapter 2.) The commands are merely a shorthand to activate the more complete instructions contained in the SPSS^X program, which is stored in the computer's memory. The lines in bold print in the example are the SPSS^X commands.

Each space in a line represents a column. All SPSS^X commands begin in column 1. If the command will not fit on one line, it is continued on the following line, but after column 1. If by mistake you begin the continuation of a command in column 1, SPSS^X will try to read the line as a new command and an error will probably result. You must not split any words or variable names when you continue on a new line. At most installations, the SPSS^X commands normally cannot extend beyond column 72. (If you enter the command UN-NUMBERED as the first SPSS^X command, however, your SPSS^X commands can extend through column 80.)

Most SPSS^X commands have two parts: (1) a command keyword beginning in column 1 and (2) a specification field, which provides details of the command. In our example, FREQUENCIES is a command keyword calling for a frequencies analysis. (FREQUENCIES is explained in Chapter 3.) Following the command keyword is the specification field VARIABLES=EDUC SEX HAPPY, which names the specific variables for which the frequencies are to be produced. Most SPSS^X commands begin with a command keyword, followed by specifications. However, some commands use a command phrase containing two keywords—for example, DATA LIST—and a few command keywords do not require specifications—for example, BEGIN DATA. (DATA LIST and BEGIN DATA are discussed in Chapter 2.)

How Do You Learn to Use SPSS^X?

You learn SPSS^X step by step, just as you learned to read. Our book takes you through the process of learning to use SPSS^X to analyze social science data. For further reference see the *SPSS^X User's Guide, Second Edition* (New York: McGraw-Hill, 1986). All our references to the *SPSS^X User's Guide* are to the second edition. This large, intimidating volume is an encyclopedic reference tool for the SPSS^X user. A section at the end of each chapter, entitled "Where to Look in the *SPSS^X User's Guide*," will cite where in the *SPSS^X User's Guide* to find more discussion of the material covered in the chapter. A copy of the *SPSS^x User's Guide* should be available at your installation for reference, and it is sold in most college bookstores.

1.2 About Using Computers

If you have no experience with a computer, learning to use a computer may be the hardest part of learning to use SPSS^x. Just remember that you cannot break a computer by using it, even if you make mistakes. A deliberate attack, perhaps with an axe or a sledgehammer, can damage a computer. (Sometimes you will feel like destroying it. Don't!) Dropping a computer down a flight of stairs or pouring coffee into it can damage it, but making errors while using a computer will not damage it. So don't be nervous about hurting it.

What Is a Computer?

What is usually called a **computer** is actually a system of machines that can receive, process, store, and send out information. Remember that you are deal-ing with a mindless system of machines that does only what it is instructed to do and holds in memory only what it is told to store. (Human and mechanical malfunctions can mess up the ideal state of operation.) We use computers be-cause, once programmed correctly, they perform tasks very quickly and accu-rately. What we hate about computers are the difficulties encountered in pro-gramming them correctly. User-friendly (easy to use) programs like SPSS^x reduce the difficulties.

What Are the Basic Parts of a Computer System?

The basic parts of a computer system are the input devices, the central pro-cessing unit, the storage devices, and the output devices (see Figure 1.1).

At most computer installations, the input device you will use is a **terminal** that consists of a **keyboard** (similar to that of a typewriter) and a **video display screen** (similar in appearance to a television screen). Different types of termi-nals have small differences in how they are used. Computer installations will also differ in the program that operates the terminal. To give you a rough idea of what happens, we describe in Section 1.3 how information is entered at a TELEX terminal at UTEP (University of Texas at El Paso).

We presume in this text that you will not use an optical scanner, which can extract the information for the computer directly from questionnaires or an-swer sheets. We also presume that you will not conduct computer-assisted in-terviews in which the questions are displayed on a screen and the responses

FIGURE 1.1 Typical components of a mainframe computer system

entered directly into the computer's memory. Both these techniques can expedite the work of entering data.

Another input device is a **card reader** into which cards with punched holes are fed. The punched holes are a code for letters, numbers, and other characters. The holes are made by a **keypunch machine,** which can make entries in 80 numbered columns on the card. The card devices have been almost completely superseded by more efficient electronic devices.

The **central processing unit** (CPU) of the computer coordinates the parts of the system, processes data, and has a memory core for storing data and instructions.

Programs and data must be stored in such a way that the computer can access them when so instructed. The most common **storage devices** are punched cards, magnetic tapes and disks, and the memory core of the CPU. To store or retrieve information on a tape requires a machine called a tape drive that is linked with the computer's CPU. Disks usually come in packs; some are permanently mounted on a disk drive, whereas others are removable.

Often the output from the computer will be on the same video display screen that indicates your input. For example, if you make a typing error when entering a command, you may receive an error message on the screen. Or, if your output is stored in a file in the computer's memory, you may be able to have the file displayed on your video screen.

Another option is to have your output printed on paper as a **hard copy.** This requires a **printer** and instructions, in the system language, telling the computer to print the output at a particular printer. A common practice is to send the output to a file, examine it on a video screen to ensure that it is correct, and then, if it is correct, have it printed. The commands to perform this operation vary from one computer installation to another.

You may never see all the parts of the computer system with which you are working. Often the user sits at a terminal that can exchange information with the system's CPU. The CPU may be in another room, in another building, or even thousands of miles away. The communication is like talking over a telephone. In fact, with the help of devices called **modems,** phone lines usually can be used to communicate between the terminal and the CPU. All that matters is that the electronic signals you are entering at the keyboard are being sent to the CPU and its responses are being sent back to you.

SPSS^x is normally run with a mainframe computer. **Mainframe** is a term used to describe a powerful CPU that works quickly and has a large memory core. A mainframe computer is capable of running more than one job at a time and capable of communicating with more than one input or output device simultaneously. Usually a mainframe computer is linked to tape drives and disks.

SPSS/PC$^+$ is an interactive version of SPSS for **microcomputers** like the IBM PC (see Chapter 14). A microcomputer has a small CPU with less speed and memory than a mainframe. A "micro" fits on a desk, usually contained in a rectangular case under the display screen.

As the speed and memory core of computers continue to increase, micros become more powerful and capable of performing more of the traditionally mainframe functions such as operating a network of terminals. At the same time, smart terminals and interactive programs are making mainframes more like micros in how they are used. **Smart terminals** have data processing and storage capacities independent of the mainframe to which they are linked. **Interactive programs** are those in which the computer responds with output to individual commands as they are entered. (The output may be merely an acknowledgment that a legitimate command has been entered.) This method contrasts with the **batch entry** method, in which a complete set of commands is submitted at one time, and then, after processing all the commands, the computer gives one set of output.

Taking the Computer Plunge: What Do You Do First?

A good first step is to visit your computer installation and learn how it works. What are the input and output devices? Who is available to provide help when you need it? What are the hours of operation? What operating system commands are needed at the beginning of a job? Where will your hard copy output be sent? (If you submit a program and receive no output, your system language commands probably contain an error.)

1.3 Example of a Session at a Terminal

The description that follows is to give you some preparation for using a terminal. Remember, however, that systems will differ. Even within the UTEP system, procedures may vary depending on what type of terminal is being used. Life is full of little trials, one of them being to learn the idiosyncrasies (individual characteristics) of your particular computer system. Although tricky at first, operating your system will become old hat, and you'll wonder how it ever could have been a problem.

At each terminal at UTEP, the screen usually displays a UTEP logo or a message that the last user has signed off. (If a screen is totally blank and dark, make sure the machine is switched on and the brightness is turned up high enough. At many installations, the power is switched off or the brightness turned down when the machine is not in use.) Press the ENTER key, and a message will appear on the screen instructing you to enter your account number. (Information is **entered** by typing it and then pressing the ENTER key.) After entering your account number, you are asked to enter your password. After you have entered your password, the system indicates that you are signed on by printing some preliminary messages and the word *GO. At this point you can call up many programs, including one named **EDIT,** which is used to create, change, or store a file. This type of program is called an **editor.**

To use EDIT at UTEP, you type the word EDIT followed by the name of the file you are creating. For example, to begin a file named PROJECT, you would enter the line EDIT PROJECT. The computer would respond with a screen that is mostly blank. At the top is the name of the file (PROJECT). A line at the bottom of the screen indicates the cursor position and what mode the editor is in.

(These details will be explained shortly.) Above the bottom line is a command line for entering commands to the editor.

Commands entered at the command line will be executed immediately. Above the command line is an area for entering or editing information in a file. Your entries in this area will be stored but not executed at the time of entry.

The information-entry area of the screen is a grid like graph paper in which each position can be identified by two numbers: a line number and a column number. Think of each position as being a seat in a concert hall. The line number indicates the location of a row of seats (or positions). The column number indicates the location of a particular seat (or position) in that row. A light marker called a **cursor** shows where you are. The cursor is usually a rectangular patch of light about the size of one position. As mentioned, the final line displayed on the screen indicates the line number and column number of the cursor's position. You can move the cursor by using keys with arrows on them. Press the Up arrow and the cursor moves up. Press the Down arrow and the cursor moves down. Similarly, the Left arrow moves the cursor to the left, and the Right arrow moves the cursor to the right.

When the editor is in the Insert mode, what you type appears in the space by the cursor without deleting any of the surrounding characters. When the editor is in the Replace mode, what you type replaces the character in the cursor position. You can switch the editor back and forth between the Insert mode and the Replace mode by pressing the INSERT key.

When you press a key on the keyboard, that key's character will appear on the video display screen. You can make changes when in the Insert mode by using the DELETE key to erase what is incorrect and then inserting what is desired. You can make changes when in the Replace mode by simply typing over the error with the correct character. The arrow keys allow you to position the cursor for deletion of unwanted characters and insertion of new characters.

When you finish and want to store the file, you move the cursor to the command line and type the command FILE PROJECT. The file named PROJECT will be stored, and the message *GO will appear on the screen, indicating that the system is ready for you to call up another program.

If your file named PROJECT is an SPSS^x program that you are now ready to run, you enter the command SEND PROJECT. The system will respond with a message indicating that the program PROJECT has been sent to be executed. Then the *GO message will appear on the screen.

If you are finished working with the computer, after receiving the *GO message, you enter the word OFF. The OFF command causes your account to be logged off (signed off) the machine, and a message appears confirming the log off. If you press the ENTER key again, the UTEP logo will appear on the screen and you will be back where you started when you sat down at the terminal.

1.4 Summary

In this chapter you've learned that

- *SPSS^x* is a program that enables researchers to organize data sets, transform variables, and do many types of statistical analysis.
- *Programs* are sets of instructions that the user gives to a computer to command desired operations.
- *Data* are information to be stored or processed.
- A *job* or *run* is the submission of a program to a computer for execution.
- *Computers* receive, store, process, and transmit information.
- *Terminals* transmit information to and receive information from computers.
- *Printers* produce computer output on paper.
- *Video display screens* produce visual images of computer output.
- *Computer cards* are paper cards that have 80 columns in which holes are punched to indicate characters.
- *Keypunch machines* are devices used to punch holes in computer cards.

RESEARCH PROJECT WORK FOR CHAPTER 1

Administer the Happiness Questionnaire in Appendix C to a sample of 20 people.

REVIEW QUESTIONS FOR CHAPTER 1

(Answers to Review Questions are given at the back of the book.)

1.1   In which column do SPSS^x commands begin?

1.2   In which column do continuations of SPSS^x commands begin?

1.3   Which is the highest numbered column that can be used by an SPSS^x command if the UNNUMBERED command is not used?

1.4   Which is the highest numbered column that can be used by an SPSS^x command if the UNNUMBERED command is used?

1.5   Which is the highest numbered column that can be used for operating system commands at most computer installations?

1.6   Can the operating system commands from another computer installation be used at your computer installation?

1.7   Can the SPSS^x commands used in this chapter's example be used at your computer installation?

1.8   What are the various storage devices used by computer systems?

1.9   When you use SPSS^X, is the machine at which you enter data a self-contained computer?

1.10 What is the difference between program commands and data?

ASSIGNMENT QUESTION FOR CHAPTER 1

(Solutions to the Assignment Questions are given in the Instructor's Manual.)

1.1   Look through the questions in Appendix B and make a list of the variable names that relate to
      (a) family background,
      (b) satisfaction with aspects of one's life,
      (c) attitudes toward freedom of speech.

BACKGROUND TEST

This book assumes you are familiar with basic statistical terms and concepts. To check your knowledge and refresh your memory, fill in the blanks in the statements below using the terms provided. (The answers are provided after the final question.)

(a) case
(b) central tendency
(c) Pearson correlation coefficient
(d) interval measure
(e) N
(f) nominal measure
(g) mean
(h) median
(i) mode
(j) ordinal measure
(k) population
(l) range
(m) sample
(n) score
(o) standard deviation
(p) statistical significance
(q) t-test
(r) unit of analysis
(s) variable
(t) Z score

1.   One specific example of what is being studied is called a _____.

2.   The number of cases in your study is called the _____.

3.   The type of entity being studied is termed the _____.

4.   The total set of what you are studying is called the _____.

5.   A smaller number of the total set of what you are studying is termed a _____.

6.   A set of mutually exclusive attributes that can be used to classify cases according to a characteristic (for example, income) is a _____.

7.   The measure of a particular case on a variable is its _____ for that variable.

8.   The point in a distribution around which other scores tend to cluster is the _____.

9.   The _____ is a measure of central tendency that is the point in a distribution above which and below which half the scores fall.

10.   A measure of central tendency that is the average—that is, the sum of scores divided by the number of cases—is called the _____.

11.   The score that occurs most frequently is called the _____.

12.   A measure that has categories that can be ranked but are not of equal size is termed _____.

13.   A measure that has categories of equal size that can be ranked is called _____.

14.   A measure that has distinct categories that cannot be ranked is called _____.

15.   The difference between the highest score and the lowest score is called the _____.

16.   The _____ is a measure of the typical distance from the mean score in a distribution. It is the square root of the sum of the deviations from the mean squared divided by the number of cases. $\sqrt{\dfrac{\Sigma\,(X - \bar{X})^2}{N}}$

17.   A score minus the mean divided by the standard deviation $(X - \bar{X})/s$ is a _____.

18.   The probability that a given result could be caused by sampling error is called the _____.

19.   One test of the statistical significance of the distance between the means of two sets of scores is the _____.

20.   A measure of the strength of association between two interval variables is the _____.

Answers to Background Test

1. a
2. e
3. r
4. k
5. m
6. s
7. n
8. b
9. h
10. g
11. i
12. j
13. d
14. f
15. l
16. o
17. t
18. p
19. q
20. c

2

GETTING STARTED

New SPSS[X] Commands:

```
DATA LIST
BEGIN DATA
END DATA
MISSING VALUES
SAVE
GET
```

After the NORC researchers interviewed 1473 people for the 1984 General Social Survey and recorded their answers, they needed to feed the data into the computer in a form it could use. If you have collected responses to the Happiness Questionnaire in Appendix C, you are in the same boat. What you need to know now is how to code data and how to tell that code to the computer.

2.1 Coding Your Data to Be Computer Readable

In this section we discuss how to prepare information so that it can be analyzed with a computer. Suppose you did the Research Project Work in Chapter 1, which involved administering the Happiness Questionnaire to 20 people. Now you have data from 20 people marked on questionnaires. What is the next step?

Because computers store information in columns, we usually convert verbal responses to numbers that will require fewer columns. For example, in our Happiness Questionnaire, one question is: "Would you say that you are very happy, pretty happy, or not too happy?" The person is asked to choose from three answers:

1	2	3
Very happy	Pretty happy	Not too happy

To store the verbal responses in columns, we would need to reserve as many columns as there are letters and spaces in the longest response—that would be 13 columns for "not too happy." Instead of this approach, we can have each response correspond to the number above it. Fantastic! Now we need only one column reserved for the number that corresponds to the response for that case.

At first, converting the responses to numbers may seem odd; however, this convention saves a tremendous amount of column space. An equally important reason to use numbers is that we often are dealing with variables for which we want to calculate the mean (average of all scores) and other statistics. In the above example, we might like to know the mean of the responses. If it were 1.6, we would know that in our sample the average of the responses was between "pretty happy" and "very happy."

There may be times when you want to work with words instead of numbers. For example, you may be conducting a study for which you want to be able to make a directory of respondents with names and addresses. To work with words you need to use string variables, which are discussed in Appendix A.

Once we have coded the data, we must store them in a way that enables the computer to find them. Think of your data for each case as being stored on a line. These lines are called **records.** Every column in a line of data is numbered sequentially starting with 1. Each **column** can hold one character—a number, letter, or other symbol. If columns 1 and 2 hold the case identification numbers for case 1, columns 1 and 2 will hold the case identification numbers for all other cases as well. This setup, known as a **fixed format,** is the formatting we will use in this book. Other types of formats are available, but the fixed format is most commonly used for statistical data. (See Appendix A for a discussion of free format.)

The number of columns in each line is the **record length.** The most common record length is 80 columns. What if you need to enter more data for this

TABLE 2.1 Example Data Set

Name	Years of Education	Sex	Happiness Level
Acuna	09	male	pretty happy
Adams	12	female	not too happy
Bates	15	female	very happy
Beall	12	female	pretty happy
Cunningham	06	male	very happy
Dunham	16	male	pretty happy
Estrada	15	female	pretty happy
Franklin	16	male	pretty happy
Graham	18	female	very happy
Hadi	14	male	pretty happy
Hedgepeth	13	female	very happy
Jordan	16	male	very happy
Kim	09	female	pretty happy
Lawrence	12	male	pretty happy
MacKenzie	12	female	very happy
Morrison	18	female	very happy
Palafox	08	female	very happy
Practor	12	female	pretty happy
Razkowski	16	male	not too happy
Zirl	14	female	no answer

case? You go to the next record—the next line—and use two or more records for each case.

The concepts of cases, columns, and records will be more clear if we go through an example of coding data for a set of cases. Table 2.1 shows a small data file before it is coded. The data in this file, except the names, are real cases taken from the NORC 1984 General Social Survey, described in Appendix B. This data set will be used throughout Part I to provide examples of SPSS^x procedures. We will refer to it as our "example data set."

There are many ways to code a data set, so the researcher has to make some decisions. We could code this data file as follows:

- Case number: The first two columns will be for the case number code; each individual will be given a unique code number to identify who the data are for.
- Education: The third and fourth columns will be education, coded in years.
- Sex: The fifth column will indicate the respondent's sex (1 = male, 2 = female).
- Happiness: The sixth column will be happiness level (1 = very happy, 2 = pretty happy, 3 = not too happy).

We also need codes to indicate missing information. The simplest approach is to leave columns blank to indicate missing data. For example, the last case above, Zirl, did not answer the question about happiness, so the column for that variable will be left blank on the line for Zirl. If you want to distinguish between different types of missing data, you need to use the MISSING VALUES command discussed in Section 2.4.

The coding system described above would result in the following data file:

```
010912
021223
031521
041222
050611
061612
071522
081612
091821
101412
111321
121611
130922
141212
151221
161821
170821
181222
191613
20142
```

Each line above is one record and represents the variable codings for one person. Thus the first line of numbers, 010912, represents the responses of Acuna, the first case in our data file. The first two digits, 01, are the case number that identifies Acuna. The second two digits, 09, indicate that Acuna has 9 years of formal education. The 1 following the 9 shows that Acuna is male. The 2 following the 1 shows that Acuna responded that he was pretty happy.

The second line, 021223, is the coded information for Adams, our second case. The digits 02 beginning the line are Adams' identification number. The 12 following the 02 indicates that Adams has 12 years of education. The 2 following the 12 indicates that Adams is female. The 3 following the 2 indicates that Adams is not too happy.

Likewise, each following line is for a subsequent case. Note that the eighth column for Zirl, the last case, is blank because the information was missing for that variable, and we are using blanks to indicate missing data. Having carefully coded and entered your data, you need to explain these codes and data locations to the SPSS[X] program. This communication with the SPSS[X] program is done via the DATA LIST statement, which is discussed in the next section.

2.2 Telling the Computer How Your Data Are Organized: DATA LIST

The **DATA LIST** command tells the SPSS[X] program the name of each variable that you intend to use and the location of the columns being used for each of these variables. (You do not need to use all of your variables on every run.) Variable names must not be over eight characters long and must begin with a letter. Using variable names that are too long or that do not begin with a letter is a common error made by beginners. Blanks, commas, and periods are not permitted in a variable name, but numbers and other symbols are okay. There are several words that SPSS[X] reserves in its programming that the user cannot employ as a variable name. The **reserved words** are: ALL, AND, BY, EQ, GE, GT, LE, LT, NE, NOT, OR, THRU, TO, and WITH. A good practice is to give your variables names that will remind you of the nature of the variable. For instance, we gave the name HAPPY to the variable containing the responses to the question about happiness.

Normally the DATA LIST command is positioned immediately after the operating system commands (discussed in Chapter 1). However, the UNNUM-BERED command, if used, goes between the operating system commands and the DATA LIST command. By itself, the DATA LIST command does not produce any output. It simply provides the SPSS[X] program with information needed to perform other commands. (If your data are in an SPSS[X] system file, you will not use DATA LIST. See Section 2.5.)

Let's consider an example of a DATA LIST command:

```
DATA LIST    ID 1-2
```

The words DATA LIST alert the SPSS[X] program that the rest of the command will describe the names and locations of the variables for this run. The words DATA LIST must begin in column 1 of the command and there must be one space and only one space between DATA and LIST.

The expression ID 1-2 indicates that the first variable name is ID and that the ID information is located in columns 1 and 2.

There must be at least one space between the variable name and the column numbers—in this example, between ID and 1-2. If the data span two or more columns, enter the number of the first column, a hyphen, and then the number of the second column—in this example, 1-2.

Usually you will be concerned with more than one variable. The following DATA LIST command contains information for the four variables described in the coding example at the beginning of this chapter:

```
DATA LIST   ID 1-2   EDUC 3-4   SEX 5   HAPPY 6
```

In this longer DATA LIST command, the EDUC 3-4 indicates the name of the second variable and the location of the education responses in columns 3 and 4.

In the command, two spaces separate ID 1-2 from EDUC 3-4. Each variable name must be separated from the column numbers of the preceding variable by one or more commas or spaces. The same convention for separating a list of variable names is followed in other SPSS[x] commands. In this text, we will sometimes use two spaces where one would suffice or use a comma instead of a space. We do so for the sake of clarity. Writing commands that can be read easily, quickly, and correctly is as important as writing commands as compactly as possible.

The third variable is SEX; its data are located in column 5. The fourth variable is named HAPPY; its data are located in column 6.

The DATA LIST command is one of two places where you can indicate whether your data contain decimal points. Indicate the number of digits that are to the right of the decimal point in parentheses following the column location information. For example, if you had a variable named WAGE (hourly wages) in columns 11-15 and you wanted a decimal point to the left of the last two columns, your code would be:

```
DATA LIST   WAGES 11-15  (2)
```

You could also simply enter the wage data with a decimal point before the last two digits; the (2) would then be unnecessary. For example, if an hourly wage of $7.50 were entered as 7.50, the decimal would not have to be indicated on the DATA LIST command. However, the practice of including decimal points in the data uses up more columns than indicating the decimal place in the DATA LIST command.

Two more examples of coding are provided by the NORC84 Codebook in Appendix B and the Happiness Questionnaire in Appendix C. (If you are still unclear about coding, take time to look at these appendices now.) Throughout Part I we will refer to the example data set in this chapter, the NORC84 Codebook in Appendix B, and the Happiness Questionnaire in Appendix C. They will be used in the Review Questions, the Assignment Questions, and the Research Project Work because they are realistic examples of the types of data sets researchers collect and analyze.

2.3 Indicating Where Your Data Records Begin and End: BEGIN DATA and END DATA

Before doing a statistical procedure in SPSS^X, you need to instruct the computer to begin reading data. This is done with the BEGIN DATA command:

BEGIN DATA

   This command is followed by the data records—the lines of data. After all the data are entered, instruct the computer to stop reading data with the command

END DATA

The DATA LIST, BEGIN DATA, and END DATA commands, as well as the data themselves, are all omitted from your commands when you use an SPSS system file. (We discuss SPSS system files in Section 2.5 below.)

2.4 Indicating Where Data Are Missing: MISSING VALUES

As we explained earlier in this chapter, the easiest way to handle missing data is to leave the columns for that variable blank when entering data. The blanks signal the SPSS^X program that the data are missing.

   At times, however, the researcher will want to distinguish among different types of missing data. The **MISSING VALUES** command enables us to do this. As an example, information on education might be missing because the interviewer forgot to ask that question or because the respondent refused to answer. We could code the education variable -9 to indicate that the interviewer forgot to ask the question and 99 when the respondent refused to answer. The choice of values -9 and 99 is arbitrary. We could have used 98 and 99 or any numbers that would not be confused with an actual response to the education question. We could not use 09 as a missing value because some respondents might have had nine years of formal education.

Now we can distinguish between a respondent's refusal—which we code as 99—and an interviewer's forgetfulness—which we code as -9. We might want to distinguish between these two types of missing data because the person who refuses to answer is showing some reluctance about the interview. This information may be significant in evaluating other answers of that respondent. The following example shows the SPSS[x] command necessary to give the EDUC variable two missing values: -9 and 99.

MISSING VALUES   EDUC(-9,99)

This command indicates that, if the code in the EDUC columns is -9 or 99, then the response is missing for that case. In the MISSING VALUES command, the two missing values must be separated by at least one comma or space.

We are limited to specifying individually three missing values per variable; however, two values can be used with the keyword THRU to specify a range such as (90 THRU 99). Also the RECODE command (discussed in Chapter 4) allows us to change the code value given to a response to one of the missing values.

If no numbers appear within parentheses immediately after a variable, the missing values will be the same as those for the first variable following on the MISSING VALUES command that does have missing value information. In the example below, HAPPY is not followed by a number in parentheses, whereas SEX, the variable after HAPPY, is followed by a missing value of 0. Thus, the missing value for HAPPY is also 0.

MISSING VALUES   HAPPY SEX(0)

Not all the variables in the DATA LIST command need to be listed in the MISSING VALUES command, nor does the order of variable names in the MISSING VALUES command need to be the same as the order in the DATA LIST command.

A nice convention is to give all the variables the same missing values, but sometimes this practice is awkward. For income or years of education, for example, one would not use the number 0 to designate missing data because 0 could be a legitimate response. Often a negative number is used for variables that have 0 as a response category. A negative number takes up two columns, however, and you would not want to use it universally if your data set has many variables that can be fit in one column. The use of blanks to indicate missing values is not only convenient, because it will not require a MISSING VALUES command; it also is efficient because it does not require two columns like a negative number.

Procedures are available in some of the SPSS[x] analyses for giving missing values another value, such as the mean for the variable, so that those cases may be included in the analysis. (See the *SPSS^x User's Guide* where it discusses the OPTIONS available for the technique you want to use.) This reassignment of values is often done when an analysis includes so many variables that the number of cases with missing data on one or more variables is quite high. It is possible, especially in an analysis with many variables, for every case to have missing data on one or more of the variables. Under these circumstances, the analysis is impossible unless new values are assigned to the cases missing data or unless some of the variables are dropped from the analysis.

Where in the program you place the MISSING VALUES command is important. This command must be placed somewhere after the DATA LIST command and before the first statistical procedure command for which the specified values are to be treated as missing. The missing values will stay in effect for the entire run following the MISSING VALUES command unless the command is superseded by a second MISSING VALUES command. Below we have added a MISSING VALUES command to our example:

```
DATA LIST   ID 1-2   EDUC 3-4   SEX 5   HAPPY 6
BEGIN DATA
010912
021223
031521
041222
050611
061612
071522
081612
091821
101412
111321
121611
130922
141212
151221
161821
170821
181222
191613
20142
END DATA
MISSING VALUES   EDUC(-9,99)   HAPPY SEX(0)
FREQUENCIES   VARIABLES=EDUC SEX HAPPY
```

As you can see from this example, when the data and commands are on one file, the file can soon become very bulky. SPSS system files, which we discuss in the next section, provide a solution to this problem.

2.5 Using SPSS System Files

You can think of an **SPSS system file** as a data file that is saved along with the DATA LIST and MISSING VALUES commands. This type of file is a great convenience because you need not enter all this information every time you want to do an analysis of the file. If you use an SPSS system file, DATA LIST, MISSING VALUES, BEGIN DATA, the data themselves, and END DATA are omitted from your commands.

SPSS system files can be combined easily, which is useful when you have a set of related data files that you use in different combinations. For example, you may have a file for each census tract in a city and want to do a series of analyses using different groupings of tracts.

Creating an SPSS System File

In creating an SPSS system file, you need to place information in the operating system commands about where this file will be stored.

The SPSS^x command you use to create an SPSS system file is **SAVE.** This command must be accompanied by the specification field **FILE=** followed by the name under which to store the file. To create a system file with the name PROJECT, you would use the command

```
SAVE    FILE=PROJECT
```

Normally this command is placed at the end of your program so that any transformations and variables created during the program will be saved as well. The SPSS^x commands and data needed to create an SPSS system file from our learning example data set are:

```
DATA LIST    ID 1-2    EDUC 3-4    SEX 5    HAPPY 6
BEGIN DATA
010912
021223
031521
041222
050611
```

```
061612
071522
081612
091821
101412
111321
121611
130922
141212
151221
161821
170821
181222
191613
20142
END  DATA
SAVE   FILE=PROJECT
```

Note that you need DATA LIST, BEGIN DATA, END DATA, and the data themselves among your commands when you create an SPSS file. Once the file is
created, however, you need not include these commands or the data when you
use the file. In the run to create the system file PROJECT, statistical procedure
commands such as FREQUENCIES could have followed after END DATA.

Accessing a System File

You would use the **GET** command to access the system file named PROJECT
that we saved in the preceding example. A **FILE =** specification field is also necessary, so the entire GET command would be:

```
GET   FILE=PROJECT
```

To produce the frequency distributions (see Section 3.2) for all the variables in the SPSS system file PROJECT, the SPSS[x] commands would be:

```
GET   FILE=PROJECT
FREQUENCIES   VARIABLES=ALL
```

2.6 Summary

In this chapter we explain how to code information into numbers.

We explain how to use the DATA LIST command to tell the computer what our variables are and what columns contain each variable's information.

We show how to set off data with the BEGIN DATA and END DATA commands.

We explain how to indicate missing data with blanks or with the MISSING VALUES command.

Finally, we explain how to create and access SPSS system files using the SAVE and GET commands.

2.7 Where to Look in the SPSS^x User's Guide

- The information on coding that is presented in this chapter is not given in the *SPSS^x User's Guide.*
- DATA LIST is discussed on pages 29–40.
- BEGIN DATA and END DATA are discussed on pages 45–46.
- MISSING VALUES is discussed on pages 40–41.
- SPSS system files are discussed on pages 80–99.

RESEARCH PROJECT WORK FOR CHAPTER 2

1. Enter into a memory device at your installation the data you gathered doing the Chapter 1 research project work. For all but the final question, you can use the codes provided for each response on the Happiness Questionnaire. The final question is not precoded, however, so you will have to decide how to categorize the answers and what code value to give each category.

2. Write DATA LIST and MISSING VALUES commands for the data file you have stored.

REVIEW QUESTIONS FOR CHAPTER 2

(Answers to Review Questions are given at the back of the book.)

Hint: The variables in these problems can be coded in more than one way.

2.1   Using the variables and the coding system from our example data set, what would be the data record for the following case: Hedderson, whose identification number is 25, whose sex is male, who has 21 years of formal education, and who states that he is very happy.

2.2 How would you code the variable *age?*

2.3 How would you code the variable *political affiliation?*

2.4 How would you code the variable *annual salary?*

REVIEW USING DATA LIST

2.5 Write a DATA LIST command that would allow you to use the education variable from our example data set presented in this chapter.

2.6 Do you need to use a DATA LIST command if the file you are using is an SPSS system file?

2.7 For the file that would be created from the Happiness Questionnaire discussed in Appendix C, write a DATA LIST command that would allow you to use variables named INCOME and SEX.

REVIEW USING MISSING VALUES

2.8 Write a MISSING VALUES command that would assign a missing value of -9 to the variable EDUC.

2.9 Write a MISSING VALUES command that would assign missing values of -9 and -8 to the variable INCOME.

2.10 Write a MISSING VALUES command that would assign a missing value of 0 to the variables SEX, RELIGION, and PARTY.

2.11 What must be done in order for a blank to be treated as a missing value?

ASSIGNMENT QUESTIONS FOR CHAPTER 2

(Solutions to the Assignment Questions are given in the *Instructor's Manual.*)

2.1 Using the variables and the coding system from our example data set, what would be the data record for the following case: Foster, whose identification number is 33, whose sex is female, who has 18 years of formal education, and who states that she is very happy.

2.2 How would you code the variable *number of months* employed by Wadsworth?

2.3 How would you code the variable *number of dependents?*

2.4 How would you code the variable *religious affiliation?*

2.5 Write a DATA LIST command that would allow you to use the happiness variable from our example data set.

2.6   Would a DATA LIST command be needed to use the variables AGE and INCOME on the SPSS system file NORC84, discussed in Appendix B?

2.7   Write a DATA LIST command for the variables in the Happiness Questionnaire given in Appendix C.

2.8   Write a MISSING VALUES command that would assign a missing value of -9 to INCOME.

2.9   Write a MISSING VALUES command that would assign missing values of -8 and -9 to a variable named AGE.

2.10   Write a MISSING VALUES command that would assign a missing value of 0 to the variables MARITAL, STATE, and RELIGION.

TAKING A FIRST LOOK AT YOUR DATA

New SPSS[x] Commands:

LIST
FREQUENCIES
SELECT IF

When you analyze your data for the first time, one of your obvious concerns will be the general distribution of cases for each variable. For instance, in considering the example data set presented in Chapter 2, you might ask what percent of the cases were "very happy," "pretty happy," and "not too happy," respectively. The answer would be the frequency distribution of cases for the variable HAPPY. In this chapter we learn how to produce frequency distributions with SPSS[x].

Less obvious concerns, however, that should take precedence over analyzing the distribution of cases for each variable are to ensure: (1) that the data were entered correctly into memory and (2) that your program is reading them correctly.

It is very important to check your data for errors in coding and data entry. If the data set is given to you on cards, tapes, or disks by someone who has already checked it extensively, it may be "clean"—that is, free of errors. However, if you or someone else types in the data from a coding sheet, questionnaires, or your scribbled class notes, errors in data entry are likely to occur.

The LIST command, covered in this chapter, allows you to list by case the values entered for each variable.

The FREQUENCIES command, which we also cover in this chapter, allows you to learn about the frequency distribution of the cases for each variable. Interesting in itself, the frequency distribution is also useful for revealing errors in data entry.

The SELECT IF command, the final command introduced in this chapter, allows us to limit an analysis to whatever types of cases we choose to specify.

Together, the LIST, FREQUENCIES, and SELECT IF commands provide you with tools for tracking down errors in data entry and for taking a first look at the distribution of your cases by variable category.

3.1 Printing Out Data for Cases of Interest: LIST

Perhaps you have received a data set on a tape and want to see if it matches an accompanying codebook that explains the variable codings. Perhaps a data set has just been entered onto a storage device and you want to check each case's data to be sure they were entered correctly. Perhaps a statistical analysis has led you to suspect that the data were entered incorrectly for a particular case and you want to list all the data entries for that case. You can accomplish these types of tasks with the **LIST** command.

A listing is an output that gives the values that have been entered in your data file. You may want to list the scores for some or all of your cases or for some or all of your variables. If you want to see all the data entries for all your cases, the command is simply

```
LIST
```

For example, to list all the data entries for our example data set from Chapter 2, the data and necessary SPSS^x commands would be as follows. (Once again, you must first use the operating system commands for your installation.)

```
DATA LIST    ID 1-2    EDUC 3-4    SEX 5    HAPPY 6
BEGIN DATA
010912
021223
031521
041222
050611
061612
```

071522
081612
091821
101412
111321
121611
130922
141212
151221
161821
170821
181222
191613
20142
END DATA
LIST

The output produced by this set of commands is given in Table 3.1. Note that a period is printed for the final case, which has missing data in the column

TABLE 3.1 Output from the LIST Command

ID	EDUC	SEX	HAPPY
1	9	1	2
2	12	2	3
3	15	2	1
4	12	2	2
5	6	1	1
6	16	1	2
7	15	2	2
8	16	1	2
9	18	2	1
10	14	1	2
11	13	2	1
12	16	1	1
13	9	2	2
14	12	1	2
15	12	2	1
16	18	2	1
17	8	2	1
18	12	2	2
19	16	1	1
20	14	2	.

for HAPPY. Preceding and following the output will be many lines summarizing what operations were done by the computer system during execution of the program. The operating system commands and the SPSS^x commands that you submitted will also be printed. If the job did not run properly, you may see an error message. An **error message** is a statement produced by the SPSS^x program when it encounters something amiss in trying to read or execute your commands. The message will be a statement that tries to explain what went wrong. It will normally be printed in the output immediately after the command with the error.

If your data file has a large number of variables and you do not want to print them all, you can specify which ones to print with the **VARIABLES =** subcommand. Adding the subcommand VARIABLES=ID HAPPY would cause only those two values to be listed for each case. The command at the end of our example would then be

```
LIST   VARIABLES=ID HAPPY
```

If your data file is very large and you do not want to list all the cases, you can specify the number of cases you want listed. If we substituted the following command in our example, the program would list the scores for ID and HAPPY for the first 25 cases.

```
LIST   VARIABLES=ID HAPPY/
       CASES=25
```

(The full output generated by this command appears in Table 3.6 at the end of the chapter.)

CASES = is a subcommand to indicate how many cases you want to list. For example, CASES=25 will list 25 cases. CASES=ALL would list all the cases, and this is also what would happen by default if CASES= was omitted. We recommend placing the CASES= subcommand on its own line starting after column 1. In our example, we aligned CASES= with VARIABLES to improve readability. (It can be placed on the same line as the last variable name following VARIABLES= if a slash (/) is used to separate the CASES= subcommand from the last variable name. However, placing it on the same line as the VARIABLES= subcommand makes it more difficult for a user to find CASES= in the program.)

3.2 Learning the Distribution of Cases: FREQUENCIES

The **FREQUENCIES** command instructs the computer to print out all the code numbers that occur for each variable and the number of cases in each of the code-number categories. For example, the variable SEX in our example data set has the code numbers 1 for males, 2 for females, and a blank if the information is missing. The FREQUENCIES command would print out that there was a category coded 1 and the number of cases in this category; it would also print out that there was a category coded 2 and the number of cases in this category. Similarly, it would print out the number of cases for which the data are missing.

In addition to giving the distribution of cases by variable, the FREQUENCIES command is an excellent way to check the validity (accuracy) of your data file. If a value that is impossible appears to have cases, we can be sure that the data were entered incorrectly for those cases or that the DATA LIST command contains an error. Thus, if for some case the value of SEX is listed as 3, when only code values 1, 2, and blank are being used, you would know an error occurred in data entry for that case.

The FREQUENCIES output will not catch errors that are realistic in appearance. For example, if, for the variable SEX, a 1 were entered instead of a 2, nothing would look wrong. One would assume that the case was a male and not realize that it was a female whose gender data had been entered incorrectly. (The LIST command, covered in the previous section, must be used to detect less obvious errors by checking the printout against the original data.)

To do a FREQUENCIES procedure for the variable HAPPY in our example data set, you would use the following command:

```
FREQUENCIES   VARIABLES=HAPPY
```

FREQUENCIES must begin in column 1, as with all SPSS^x commands. Leave at least one blank space between FREQUENCIES and the VARIABLES= subcommand. There can be spaces before or after the equals (=) symbol. Variable names must be separated by at least one comma or space.

Placed in the context of the operating system commands, other SPSS^x commands, and the data for our example data set described in Chapter 2, the preceding FREQUENCIES command would instruct SPSS^x to produce the frequencies for the variable HAPPY. In the following display we have provided an example omitting operating system commands. Notice that the FREQUENCIES command follows directly after the END DATA command. As we will illustrate later in this chapter, more than one SPSS^x command may be placed after END DATA.

```
DATA LIST    ID 1-2   EDUC 3-4   SEX 5   HAPPY 6
BEGIN DATA
010912
021223
031521
041222
050611
061612
071522
081612
091821
101412
111321
121611
130922
141212
151221
161821
170821
181222
191613
20142
END DATA
```
FREQUENCIES   VARIABLES=HAPPY

These commands and data would produce the output in Table 3.2. The column headed VALUE indicates what the code categories are for the variable HAPPY. The numbers under FREQUENCY indicate the number of cases in each category. The numbers under PERCENT indicate the percent of all cases that are in each category.

Recall from the coding we did in Chapter 2 that, in our example data set,

TABLE 3.2 Simplified Output from a FREQUENCIES Command

HAPPY

VALUE	FREQUENCY	PERCENT
1	8	42.1
2	9	47.4
3	2	10.5
.	1	MISSING
TOTAL	20	100.0

the value 1 stands for "very happy," the value 2 stands for "pretty happy," and the value 3 stands for "not too happy." In our sample of 20 people, 42 percent responded that they were very happy, 47 percent responded that they were pretty happy, and 10 percent responded that they were not too happy.

To produce a table that presents the number of cases in each category for all variables, you would substitute the following FREQUENCIES command in the preceding example:

```
FREQUENCIES   VARIABLES=ALL
```

The **ALL** in this example is a specification keyword that has the same meaning in SPSS^x and in everyday usage. (Specification **keywords** are words used in commands and subcommands to facilitate the expression of what must be done. Their meaning is generally apparent, and we will cover them as we introduce the SPSS^x commands and subcommands.) In this example, ALL calls for FREQUENCIES to be done for all the variables in the DATA LIST command. ALL can be used with many SPSS^x commands.

Before doing a FREQUENCIES run, review your variables to be certain that none of them contains more categories than you want printed out. Otherwise your printout may be far bulkier than you want. For example, family income to the nearest dollar might have as many categories as the number of cases, and for a large data set the frequencies for family income would be an enormous table. The best way to solve this problem is to combine many values into fewer large categories. This combining of values is done with the RECODE command, discussed in Chapter 4.

3.3 Doing FREQUENCIES with an SPSS System File

The use of FREQUENCIES with an SPSS system file differs from the example in the previous section. The GET command replaces the DATA LIST, MISSING VALUES, BEGIN DATA, and END DATA commands, and you do not enter the data with your commands. (The program will go to the memory device where you stored the file referred to in your GET command. SPSS^x will know the location from the directions in the operating system commands.) To do a FREQUENCIES run of all the variables in the SPSS system file NORC84, you would use the following commands. (Again the operating system commands for your installation must precede the SPSS^x commands.)

```
GET FILE=NORC84
FREQUENCIES   VARIABLES=ALL
```

TABLE 3.3 Partial Output of FREQUENCIES Using the NORC84 SPSS System File

HAPPY

VALUE LABEL	VALUE	FREQUENCY	PERCENT
VERY HAPPY	1	502	34.7
PRETTY HAPPY	2	756	52.3
NOT TOO HAPPY	3	187	12.9
DK	8	1	MISSING
NA	9	27	MISSING
	TOTAL	1473	100.0

Part of the output produced by the preceding commands is replicated in Table 3.3. In this table for the 1473-case NORC84 file, we can see a few differences in format from Table 3.2. First, there are value labels for the values, because NORC84 was saved with the VALUE LABELS command. (Creation of value labels is discussed in Chapter 4.) Second, there are some cases with data missing. A check of the NORC84 Codebook in Appendix B will show that DK stands for "don't know" and NA stands for "no answer."

There are also very noticeable differences in the distribution of HAPPY for this sample. The frequency of "very happy" is 35 percent instead of 45 percent (we will round off to the nearest percent in the text), the frequency of "pretty happy" is 52 percent instead of 45 percent, and the frequency of "not too happy" is 13 percent instead of 10 percent. The NORC84 sample is much larger than our 20-case example, so we presume that it more accurately reflects what the percentages would be if we surveyed the entire population of the United States.

From Table 3.3 we learn that about half the respondents in the NORC84 sample reported being pretty happy, another third reported being very happy, and the remaining 13 percent were not too happy. (In Chapter 4 we will begin to investigate how various types of people differ in their likelihood of being in each of these categories.)

3.4 Producing More with FREQUENCIES: Subcommand STATISTICS

Using the subcommand **STATISTICS** in a FREQUENCIES command will produce the high score, low score, mean, and standard deviation for each variable named. (Other statistics can be produced as well. See Section 18.18 of the

SPSS^x User's Guide.) The format to obtain frequencies and statistics on the variable HAPPY from the NORC84 system file would be:

FREQUENCIES   VARIABLES=HAPPY/
              STATISTICS

Note that the subcommand STATISTICS is separated from the previous subcommand, VARIABLES=HAPPY, by a slash. For greater visual separation, we have placed the STATISTICS subcommand on a separate line. A good practice is to make it as easy as possible to pick out the various parts of your SPSS^x commands. Any continuation of an SPSS^x command on a subsequent line must be indented at least one column; therefore, we have indented STATISTICS, a continuation of the FREQUENCIES command. (We indented more than one space for clarity.) Note, however, that following some commands, STATISTICS is used as a command itself, beginning in column 1 (see Section 5.4).

The output from the preceding commands for the variable HAPPY in the NORC84 SPSS system file is given in Table 3.4. This table replicates all the output produced by FREQUENCIES for HAPPY. Note that it includes a variable label, GENERAL HAPPINESS, and valid percent and cum percent (cumulative percent) columns.

For a simple description of the characteristics of a set of cases, the information provided by FREQUENCIES will often be sufficient. But what if you

TABLE 3.4 Actual Output from the Command
FREQUENCIES   VARIABLES=HAPPY/
              STATISTICS

HAPPY   GENERAL HAPPINESS

VALUE LABEL	VALUE	FREQUENCY	PERCENT	VALID PERCENT	CUM PERCENT
VERY HAPPY	1	502	34.1	34.7	34.7
PRETTY HAPPY	2	756	51.3	52.3	87.1
NOT TOO HAPPY	3	187	12.7	12.9	100.0
DK	8	1	.1	MISSING	
NA	9	27	1.8	MISSING	
	TOTAL	1473	100.0	100.0	

MEAN   1.782   STD DEV   .655   MINIMUM   1.000
MAXIMUM   3.000

VALID CASES   1445   MISSING CASES   28

want to focus on a subset of your cases? For example, your employer's personnel department may have assigned you the task of describing the salaries, positions, and length of employment of all female personnel. Or you may want to select those cases with invalid data and print the frequencies of the ID variable. This output would give you the identification number of all cases that need corrections in their data. The SELECT IF command, presented in the next section, will allow you to focus on such subsets of your set of cases.

3.5 Focusing on Cases of Interest: SELECT IF

Often in an analysis you will not want to include all the cases in your data file. Perhaps you want to obtain a description of only the women in your sample. The **SELECT IF** command allows you to select certain cases. Study the following command (remembering that female is coded 2 for the SEX variable):

```
SELECT IF   SEX EQ 2
```

There must be one space and only one space separating SELECT and IF; otherwise the spacing on this command is flexible. The reserved word **EQ** symbolizes "equal," hence this command selects only the women in the data file.

The SELECT IF command must be placed after the DATA LIST command and before any commands for which you want it to apply. The following example illustrates the normal placement of the SELECT IF command:

```
DATA LIST   ID 1-2   EDUC 3-4   SEX 5   HAPPY 6
BEGIN DATA
010912
021223
031521
041222
050611
061612
071522
081612
091821
101412
111321
121611
130922
141212
```

```
151221
161821
170821
181222
191613
20142
END DATA
SELECT IF   SEX EQ 2
FREQUENCIES   VARIABLES=EDUC SEX HAPPY/
        STATISTICS
```

To do the same procedures for our SPSS system file NORC84, the SPSS[x] commands would be:

```
GET   FILE=NORC84
SELECT IF   SEX EQ 2
FREQUENCIES   VARIABLES=ALL/
        STATISTICS
```

If we did two jobs, one selecting for females and the other selecting for males, we would obtain on separate outputs one frequencies distribution for females and one for males. Pooling the information from these outputs, we could put together Table 3.5. (In Chapter 4 we will learn how the TEMPORARY

TABLE 3.5 Table Constructed for HAPPY from FREQUENCIES Outputs

MALES		
VALUE LABEL	FREQUENCY	PERCENT
VERY HAPPY	186	31.8
PRETTY HAPPY	315	53.8
NOT TOO HAPPY	84	14.4
TOTAL	585	100.0
FEMALES		
VALUE LABEL	FREQUENCY	PERCENT
VERY HAPPY	316	36.7
PRETTY HAPPY	442	51.4
NOT TOO HAPPY	102	11.9
TOTAL	860	100.0

command enables us to select for females and then later select for males in the same job.) In the table, the numbers in the first row under the word PERCENT indicate that 32 percent (rounding to the nearest percent) of the males are very happy. (Recall that the response "very happy" has the value 1.) The second part of the table concerns females, and the first row of that part indicates that 37 percent of the females report being very happy.

We can see then that females are slightly more likely than males to report being very happy. We will look at this relationship more closely in later chapters, as we examine how other variables are associated with the likelihood of being happy.

Perhaps you want to do an analysis using only the people with over 15 years of education among your cases. The following command would select that subset:

SELECT IF   EDUC GT 15

The reserved word **GT** symbolizes "greater than," so GT 15 indicates that only those cases with an EDUC value greater than 15 will be used in this analysis. If **LT** were used in place of GT, only those whose EDUC value was less than 15 would be used. If EQ were used in place of GT, only those whose EDUC value equaled 15 would be used. The following abbreviated expressions (called *relational operators*) may be used with SELECT IF:

EQ   equal

NE   not equal

LT   less than

GT   greater than

LE   less than or equal to

GE   greater than or equal to

What if you want to select cases in a certain range of values? For example, you want to study only adults with 13 to 16 years of education. No problem. Note the following example (with double spaces for clarity between the parts of the command):

SELECT IF   EDUC GT 12   AND   EDUC LT 17

The EDUC GT 12   AND   EDUC LT 17 part of this command means that only cases with an EDUC value that is both above 12 and below 17 will be selected.

You can also select people from two or more of the categories on one variable. For example, the following command would select both those who had 13 years of education and those who had 14 years of education:

```
SELECT IF   EDUC EQ 13   OR   EDUC EQ 14
```

If you want to use two or more variables in your selection process, you can combine them as follows:

```
SELECT IF   EDUC GT 12   AND   SEX EQ 2
```

This command would select only those respondents whose EDUC value was greater than 12 and whose SEX value was 2; in our data set, these would be women with more than 12 years of education.

You may want to select people who are in a particular category in either of two variables. That, too, is no problem. For example, to select people who have less than 16 years of education *or* are not too happy, one would use the following command:

```
SELECT IF   EDUC LT 16   OR   HAPPY EQ 3
```

SELECT IF commands can become quite convoluted. Often you will want to place your conditions in several commands, rather than have one complex command. Be careful! A series of SELECT IF commands will be interpreted as if they are linked by AND. In other words, only those cases that meet all the specifications of all the commands will be selected for the analysis. For example, the two commands

```
SELECT IF   EDUC GT 16
SELECT IF   SEX EQ 1
```

together would dictate that only those with both a value over 16 on EDUC *and* a value of 1 on SEX will be included in the analysis.

SELECT IF can also be used to examine cases for which the data seem incorrect. This cleaning operation is done using SELECT IF together with the LIST command. For example, you might want to list the ID numbers of cases that obviously have false data entered. Suppose you have a variable named SEX coded 1 for males, 2 for females, and blank for missing. Any other value entered in the SEX data column of the data file would be an error that you would want to discover and correct. The following command would list the ID numbers of cases for which SEX had not been coded as either blank, 1, or 2:

```
SELECT  IF   SEX NE 1   OR   SEX NE 2
LIST
```

The first line of these commands selects cases that have not been coded as missing, 1 (male), or 2 (female). The second command instructs SPSS^x to print all the variable codings for these cases. This list will include the ID number of each case so you can go back to the file or questionnaire to see what error occurred when the datum for SEX was entered. Having the values of the other variables may also help you detect the error. Perhaps a variable was omitted so that the positions of all the other variables after it were offset by the number of columns in the missed variable.

   To select missing value cases, such as those coded blank, the specification MISSING is used followed by the variable name in parentheses. For example,

```
SELECT  IF   MISSING(SEX)
```

This command would select the cases coded blank for missing on the variable SEX.

3.6 Summary

In this chapter we explain the LIST command, which produces the data entered by case. LIST can be used for all the variables or for a subset of them; it can be used for all the cases or for a subset of the cases.

   The FREQUENCIES command produces the distribution of cases by categories of a variable. It can be used for all the variables or for a subset of the variable set. STATISTICS is a subcommand that causes particular statistics to be added to or deleted from the output. Most SPSS^x procedure commands allow tailoring of output by STATISTICS.

   The SELECT IF command causes SPSS^x to focus its analyses on subsets of the cases in the data file. The cases kept in the analyses following SELECT IF are those that meet the conditions specified in the SELECT IF command. If more than one SELECT IF command is used, a case must meet the conditions specified by all the commands to be kept in the analysis.

3.7 Where to Look in the SPSS^x User's Guide

- FREQUENCIES is discussed on pages 315–327.
- SELECT IF is discussed on pages 181–183.

RESEARCH PROJECT WORK FOR CHAPTER 3

1. Produce a listing and the frequencies for all the variables in the data set you created from the Happiness Questionnaire.

2. Clean the data set of any errors that were made in entering the data.

REVIEW QUESTIONS FOR CHAPTER 3

(Answers to Review Questions are given at the back of the book.)

LIST

3.1 Write a set of commands that will output the data entries for all variables for all cases of our example data set.

3.2 Write a set of commands that will output the data entries for all variables for the first 20 cases of the SPSS system file NORC84, presented in Appendix B.

3.3 Write a set of commands that will list all the data entries for the variable INCOME from the SPSS system file NORC84.

FREQUENCIES

3.4 Write all the commands necessary to produce the frequencies for all the variables in our example data set.

3.5 Write all the commands necessary to produce the frequencies for the variables AGE, SEX, and MARITAL from the SPSS system file NORC84 (Appendix B).

3.6 What would you need to do before using a FREQUENCIES command for a variable named INCOME, which is the annual income of the respondent to the nearest dollar?

3.7   What would be the meaning of the following output?

NEIGHBOR

VALUE	FREQUENCY	PERCENT
1	3	30.0
2	5	50.0
3	2	20.0

MISSING CASES 1

SPSS System File

3.8   Write the commands necessary to produce a FREQUENCIES procedure for all the variables in the NORC84 file.

3.9   Write the command necessary to print out the frequencies for variables in the NORC84 file that concern attitudes toward abortion.

3.10   Write the commands necessary to produce frequencies for the variables concerning the respondent's education, health, and happiness in the NORC84 file.

SELECT IF

3.11   Write a SELECT IF command that will select only those cases that are coded 1 on the variable SEX.

3.12   Write a SELECT IF command that will choose only those cases that have a value of 65 or greater on the variable AGE.

3.13   Write a SELECT IF command that will choose only those cases that are over 16 on the EDUC value or over 30000 on the INCOME value.

3.14   Write a SELECT IF command that will choose only those cases that have a value greater than 15 and less than 66 on the variable AGE.

3.15   Write a SELECT IF command that will choose only those cases that are coded 2 on the variable SEX and also coded between 14 and 45 on the variable AGE.

3.16   Write a set of commands that will list the data entries for all the variables for the first 25 cases that are coded above 15 on EDUC and coded 2 on SEX from the SPSS system file NORC84, presented in Appendix B.

ASSIGNMENT QUESTIONS FOR CHAPTER 3

(Solutions to the Assignment Questions are given in the *Instructor's Manual*.)

3.1 Write all the commands necessary to produce all the frequencies for the variable named EDUC in our example data set (given in Chapter 2).

3.2 Write all the commands necessary to produce the frequencies for the variables AGE, INCOME, and TVHOURS from the SPSS system file NORC84, described in Appendix B.

3.3 What would you need to do before using a FREQUENCIES command for a variable named SQFEET, which is the area of housing units to the nearest square foot?

3.4 What would be the meaning of the following output?

POLPARTY

VALUE	FREQUENCY	PERCENT
1	7	35.0
2	9	45.0
3	4	20.0

MISSING CASES 1

(You need to be familiar with the SPSS system file NORC84, explained in Appendix B, to work the following problems.)

3.5 Write the SPSS[x] commands necessary to produce a FREQUENCIES procedure for all the variables in the NORC84 file. We know you did this task before as a Review Question, but you will want to perform this task frequently and we want to be sure you remember. Besides, this is one of the easy questions.

3.6 Write the SPSS[x] commands necessary to print out the frequencies for variables in the NORC84 file that concern anomie.

3.7 For the NORC84 file, write the commands necessary to produce frequencies for the variables concerning whether the respondent has been unemployed any time in the past 10 years and concerning his or her current employment.

3.8 Write a SELECT IF command that will select only those cases coded 1 on the variable named RACE.

3.9 Write a SELECT IF command that will choose only those cases that have a value of 40 or less on the variable AGE.

3.10 Write a SELECT IF command that will choose only those cases coded below 12 on EDUC or under 10000 on INCOME.

3.11 Write a SELECT IF command that will choose only those cases that have a value less than 16 or greater than 65 on the variable AGE.

3.12 Write a SELECT IF command that will choose only those cases that are coded 2 on the variable RACE and are also coded between 21 and 65, inclusive, on the variable AGE.

3.13 Write a LIST command that will output the data entries for all the variables for the first 20 cases.

3.14 Write a LIST command that will output the data entries for the variable ID for all the cases in the file.

3.15 Write a set of commands that will list the data entries for the variable ID for all the cases coded above 3 on the variable RACE.

3.16 Write a set of commands that will list the data entries for all the variables for the first 20 cases that are coded above 15 on EDUC and coded 2 on SEX.

TABLE 3.6 Actual Output from Command:
LIST   VARIABLES=ID HAPPY/CASES=25

ID HAPPY

ID	HAPPY
1	3
2	1
3	3
4	2
5	2
6	2
7	1
8	3
9	3
10	1
11	9
12	1
13	2
14	2
15	3
16	1
17	1
18	1
19	1
20	2
21	1
22	2
23	2
24	2
25	2

NUMBER OF CASES READ = 25   NUMBER OF CASES LISTED = 25

4

TRANSFORMING VARIABLES AND LABELING OUTPUT

New SPSS^x Commands:

RECODE
COMPUTE
IF
TEMPORARY
VARIABLE LABELS
VALUE LABELS

In Chapter 3 we used the FREQUENCIES and SELECT IF commands to find that, in the NORC84 data file, 35 percent of the respondents reported they were very happy and that women were more likely than men to report being very happy. In this chapter we will learn whether the likelihood of being very happy is affected by the variable AGE. Before we begin, we need to cover some of the data transformation commands available in SPSS^x. A problem frequently encountered is that your data are coded differently than you want them coded for a particular analysis. This annoyance can be remedied using the RECODE, COMPUTE, and IF commands described in this chapter. The TEMPORARY command, also covered in this chapter, allows you to confine the effects of the data transformation commands to the statistical procedure immediately following TEMPORARY instead of being in effect for all following procedures.

Finally, we explain how to use the VARIABLE LABELS and VALUE LABELS commands to make the output easier to read.

4.1 Changing Variable Categories Where Necessary: RECODE

Suppose you coded information on education that ranged from 0 to 22 years of formal education, and now you need to do an analysis using only three education categories: respondents who did not complete high school, those who completed high school but not college, and those who completed college. The data you enter for a variable can be reclassified using the **RECODE** command. Carefully study the following example:

RECODE   EDUC (0 THRU 11=1) (12 THRU 15=2) (16 THRU 30=3)

The RECODE command indicates that some changes follow in one or more variable codings. EDUC indicates that the first data to be recoded will be for the variable named EDUC. THRU is a reserved keyword in SPSS^x that can be used to indicate a range of values in many commands. (0 THRU 11=1) indicates that the numbers 0, 1, 2, 3, 4, 5, 6, 7, 8, 9, 10, and 11 will now all be treated as though they have the value 1. (12 THRU 15=2) indicates that the numbers 12, 13, 14, and 15 will all be treated as though they have the value 2. (16 THRU 30=3) indicates that the numbers 16 through 30 will all be treated as though they have the value 3. A statistical procedure done after the RECODE command changes the values of EDUC will use the new values. Thus, a new FREQUENCIES of the EDUC variable would now reveal that the case scores have a range of from 1 to 3 instead of from 0 to 22.

For a variable that is being recoded, if some of the numbers fall outside the range of the RECODE command, these numbers will keep their original values. For example, if someone had 31 years of education, that value in the data columns for education would remain unchanged, because the command recoded only values up to 30. Although someone could have more than 30 years of education, you should verify the data for that case before adjusting the RECODE command.

RECODE allows the use of two terms—**HI** and **LO**—to encompass extreme scores. Using these terms, our previous example would read:

RECODE   EDUC (LO THRU 11=1) (12 THRU 15=2) (16 THRU HI=3)

A hazard of using the LO and HI terms, however, is that you might accidentally encompass your MISSING VALUES. In the above example, if 99 were the missing value for refusing to answer for EDUC, all the cases with missing values would be recoded from 99 to 3 and no longer treated as cases with missing data. Likewise, if -9 were the missing value for EDUC, it would be recoded to 1.

The RECODE command must follow the DATA LIST command and appear somewhere before any command for which you want to use the recoded information. However, the RECODE command need not *immediately* precede commands for which you want to use the recoded information. The data will stay recoded throughout the run, unless a TEMPORARY command is placed before the RECODE command. The TEMPORARY command, which we discuss in Section 4.4, would keep the recoding in effect for only the first statistical procedure following the RECODE command.

The following set of commands illustrates the file placement of the RECODE command using our example data set:

```
DATA LIST    ID  1-2    EDUC  3-4    SEX  5    HAPPY  6
BEGIN DATA
010912
021223
031521
041222
050611
061612
071522
081612
091821
101412
111321
121611
130922
141212
151221
161821
170821
181222
191613
20142
END DATA
MISSING VALUES    EDUC (-9, 99)
RECODE    EDUC  (0  THRU  11=1) (12  THRU  15=2) (16  THRU  30=3)
FREQUENCIES    ID EDUC SEX HAPPY
```

4.2 Making New Variables from Old Variables: COMPUTE

At times you will want to create new variables from variables already in your data file. For example, you may have a variable for family income named IN-COME and a variable for family size named FAMSIZE. In addition to these two variables, you might want to have a variable for family income per capita—that is, the family income divided by the number of persons in the family.

We can create a new variable for income per capita, INCOMPER, with the COMPUTE command as follows. (Note how a slash is used to indicate division.)

```
COMPUTE   INCOMPER=INCOME/FAMSIZE
```

Anywhere in your program following this COMPUTE command, you can refer to the INCOMPER variable just as you refer to any variable contained in your DATA LIST command.

The SPSS^x equivalents of the basic arithmetic operators are as follows:

- **+**   addition
- **−**   subtraction
- **/**   division
- **∗**   multiplication
- **∗∗**   exponentiation (raising to a power)
- **SQRT** taking the square root

These operations can be done with actual numeric values, with variables, or with a mixture of both. First we will give examples of doing the arithmetic operations with numbers. Then we will give examples of doing the arithmetic operations with variables.

COMPUTE Commands with Numbers

Addition—Example 1:

```
COMPUTE   ANSWER1=450+200
```

In this example, after the COMPUTE command ANSWER1 would equal 650.

Subtraction—Example 2:

```
COMPUTE   ANSWER2=450−200
```

In this example, after the COMPUTE command ANSWER2 would equal 250.

Multiplication—Example 3:

COMPUTE   ANSWER3=450*2

In this example, after the COMPUTE command ANSWER3 would equal 900.

Division—Example 4:

COMPUTE   ANSWER4=450/50

In this example, after the COMPUTE command ANSWER4 would equal 9.

Exponentiation—Example 5:

COMPUTE   ANSWER5=5**3

In this example, after the COMPUTE command ANSWER5 would equal 125—that is, 5^3.

Square Root—Example 6:

COMPUTE   ANSWER6=SQRT(81)

In this example, after the COMPUTE command ANSWER6 would equal 9.

COMPUTE Commands with Variables

The previous operations were done with numbers. The following examples illustrate each of these operations with variables.

Addition—Example 7: To compute a new variable, total income (TINC), equal to Wife's Income (WINC) plus husband's income (HINC):

COMPUTE   TINC=WINC+HINC

Subtraction—Example 8: To compute a new variable, years until retirement (RETIRE), equal to 65 minus age (AGE):

COMPUTE   RETIRE=65−AGE

Multiplication—Example 9: To compute a new variable, total pay (TPAY), equal to daily salary (DSALARY) multiplied by number of days worked (DAYS):

COMPUTE   TPAY=DSALARY*DAYS

Division—Example 10: To compute a new variable, average salary (AVESAL), equal to payroll (PAYROLL) divided by number of employees (NEMPLOYS):

COMPUTE   AVESAL=PAYROLL/NEMPLOYS

Exponentiation—Example 11: To compute a new variable, the deviation from the mean squared (DEVSQ), equal to income minus the mean of income (INC−MINC) squared:

COMPUTE   DEVSQ=(INC−MINC)**2

Square Root—Example 12: To compute a new variable, absolute deviation (ABDEV), equal to the square root of the deviation from the mean squared (DEVSQ):

COMPUTE   ABDEV=SQRT(DEVSQ)

Many other functions can be used with the COMPUTE command—nearly 50 in all. (See the *SPSS^x User's Guide,* pages 105–125, for a more complete description of these functions.)

COMPUTE Commands and Missing Values

What happens if a variable you use in a COMPUTE command has missing values? For example, you may want to COMPUTE the household's income per person, but for some of the households the income variable is missing. SPSS^x will assign the **system missing value** (usually blanks) for the variable being computed to any case that has a missing value for any variable used in the computation. The system missing value will be displayed as a period in the output. For example, if you do a FREQUENCIES procedure for a variable and the value for one of the categories appears as a period, then the category of cases has missing data on that variable.

The system missing value will also be assigned to cases for which the computation is mathematically impossible. For example, you cannot divide by zero or take the square root of a negative number. If you gave the command COMPUTE INCOMPER=INCOME/CHILDS, the system missing value would be assigned to all cases for which the value of CHILDS was 0.

4.3 The IF Statement

At times you will want to compute new variables for some cases but not for others. The **IF** command allows this type of operation. You can think of it as a combination of a SELECT IF command and a COMPUTE command. The first part of the command selects the cases for which the procedure is to be done; the second part computes the new variable. For example, you may want to use an individual's income for a person not living with his or her parents but use the parents' income if the person lives with them. To do so, the following SPSS[x] commands could be used. Assume we have a variable named LPARENT, for "living with parent(s)," coded 1 for yes. Assume also that we have a variable named PARENT$, income of parent(s). The following command would make INCOME equal to PARENT$ when the individual lives with his or her parent(s) (two spaces are inserted between the parts of the command to improve readability):

IF   LPARENT EQ 1   INCOME=PARENT$

Notice the similarity in syntax between each of the two parts of this command and the SELECT IF and COMPUTE commands, respectively:

(like SELECT IF)   (like COMPUTE)

IF   LPARENT EQ 1   INCOME=PARENT$

All the relational operators used in the SELECT IF command can be used in the IF command. They are:

EQ   equal

NE   not equal

LT   less than

GT   greater than

LE   less than or equal to

GE   greater than or equal to

All the functions used in the COMPUTE command can be used in the second part of the IF command. (These functions are explained in Section 4.2)

Parentheses can be used where necessary to clarify the command. For example, we can rewrite the preceding example as:

```
IF    (LPARENT EQ 1)    INCOME=PARENT$
```

Another example using IF would be to create a new variable AGEGROUP, which groups age into 10-year categories, from AGE, which records an individual's actual age. (Note that the IF command must be used instead of the RECODE command in this case, if you want to retain the original values for AGE.)

Grouping AGE into new categories for the variable AGEGROUP could be accomplished with the following commands:

```
IF    AGE LE 9    AGEGROUP=1
IF    AGE GT 9 AND AGE LE 19    AGEGROUP=2
IF    AGE GT 19 AND AGE LE 29    AGEGROUP=3
IF    AGE GT 29 AND AGE LE 39    AGEGROUP=4
IF    AGE GT 39 AND AGE LE 49    AGEGROUP=5
IF    AGE GT 49 AND AGE LE 59    AGEGROUP=6
IF    AGE GT 59 AND AGE LE 69    AGEGROUP=7
IF    AGE GT 69 AND AGE LE 79    AGEGROUP=8
IF    AGE GT 79    AGEGROUP=9
```

The treatment of missing data and impossible computations for the IF command is the same as for the COMPUTE command (discussed in Section 4.2). For example, if a case was coded 99 for AGE, which has 99 as one of its missing values, then AGEGROUP would be assigned the system missing value.

In Appendix A we discuss the DO IF-END IF structure. For further discussion of complex IF commands and DO IF-END IF, see the *SPSS^x User's Guide*, pages 149–161.

4.4 Making a Transformation for Only One Procedure: TEMPORARY

The TEMPORARY command signals SPSS^x to do the data transformations that follow it only for the next statistical procedure. For example, this useful command allows you to do separate FREQUENCIES for different subsets on the same run. To do two FREQUENCIES—one for males and one for females—on the same run, the following procedure could be used. After the TEMPORARY command, use SELECT IF for males (code 1) and then do a FREQUENCIES procedure. Following this FREQUENCIES, add another TEMPORARY command, use SELECT IF for females (code 2), and do another FREQUENCIES. The result will be two FREQUENCIES outputs, one for males and one for females:

```
DATA LIST   ID 1-2   EDUC 3-4   SEX 5   HAPPY 6
BEGIN DATA
010912
021223
031521
041222
050611
061612
071522
081612
091821
101412
111321
121611
130922
141212
151221
161821
170821
181222
191613
20142
END DATA
TEMPORARY
SELECT IF   SEX EQ 1
FREQUENCIES   VARIABLES=ALL/
              STATISTICS
TEMPORARY
SELECT IF   SEX EQ 2
FREQUENCIES   VARIABLES=ALL/
              STATISTICS
```

The first SELECT IF would select only males for the first FREQUENCIES. Because this selection is for only the first statistical procedure after the TEMPORARY command, following the FREQUENCIES procedure we have our entire sample back. The second SELECT IF would select the female cases, and they would be used for the second FREQUENCIES. Combining the output from these two FREQUENCIES commands, we can compare men and women in our sample data. The second TEMPORARY command is not necessary because only one command follows it. We included it in the program to remind our-selves that the SELECT IF following it is meant to be temporary.

For the same procedures with our SPSS system file NORC84, the SPSS^x commands would be:

```
GET   FILE=NORC84
TEMPORARY
SELECT IF   SEX EQ 1
FREQUENCIES   VARIABLES=ALL/
              STATISTICS
TEMPORARY
SELECT IF   SEX EQ 2
FREQUENCIES   VARIABLES=ALL/
              STATISTICS
```

Pooling the information from the two frequency distributions these commands produce, we could construct tables for all the variables like Table 3.5 for the variable HAPPY. However, by using TEMPORARY only one job is needed in-stead of two.

As another example, we could select first the respondents in the SPSS system file NORC84 who are under age 40 (respondents had to be at least 18) and then the respondents age 40 and over. (In NORC84, ages 98 and older were coded 97, because 98 and 99 were used as missing values and the vari-able AGE had only 2 columns for data.) Then we will do a separate FREQUEN-CIES for each group and find whether being in either group increases the like-lihood of being happy. The SPSS^x commands required would be:

```
GET FILE=NORC84
RECODE   AGE  (18 THRU 39=1) (40 THRU 97=2)
TEMPORARY
SELECT IF   AGE EQ 1
FREQUENCIES   VARIABLES=HAPPY
TEMPORARY
SELECT IF   AGE EQ 2
FREQUENCIES   VARIABLES=HAPPY
```

The output from the preceding commands would include the information in Table 4.1.

The combined total of younger and older persons is 1467 instead of the NORC84 total of 1473 because 6 cases missing age data were removed by the SELECT IF commands.

The first set of percents is for the under-40 respondents. Rounding to the

TABLE 4.1 Happiness by Age for the NORC84 File

PERSONS AGE 18-39

VALUE LABEL	FREQUENCY	PERCENT
VERY HAPPY	210	29.4
PRETTY HAPPY	415	58.0
NOT TOO HAPPY	90	12.6
NA	12	MISSING
TOTAL	727	100.0

PERSONS AGE 40 AND OVER

VALUE LABEL	FREQUENCY	PERCENT
VERY HAPPY	289	39.9
PRETTY HAPPY	340	47.0
NOT TOO HAPPY	95	13.1
DK	1	MISSING
NA	15	MISSING
TOTAL	740	100.0

nearest percent, we can see that 29 percent of them report being very happy. The second set of percents is for respondents 40 and over. We can see that 40 percent of these respondents report being very happy. Hence the likelihood of being very happy appears to be greater for the older respondents. So those of you under 40 can take some comfort in the thought that your likelihood of being very happy will increase when you pass 40.

So far we have seen that one's likelihood of being very happy is improved slightly by being female and by being over 40. You might complain that you have no control over these variables. Fair enough. In the next chapter and beyond, we will consider the effects of some variables that you can control: education, income, marital status, and number of children.

4.5 Identifying Variables: VARIABLE LABELS

In SPSS^x variable names are limited to eight or fewer characters. At times you will want to give a variable a longer label in order to express more clearly what it is. The **VARIABLE LABELS** command enables the user to attach a label of 40 characters or less to a variable. (Starting with Release 2.1, up to 120 characters can be used. However, most procedures will truncate long labels in the output.) The label may contain more than one word; it may also contain punctuation.

The label is placed after the variable name and must be enclosed in quotation marks. Either single or double quotation marks may be used. If you use double quotation marks, do not place double quotation marks within the label. If you use single quotation marks, do not place single quotation marks within the label.

The following command would give the label YEARS OF EDUCATION to the variable named EDUC:

```
VARIABLE LABELS   EDUC "YEARS OF EDUCATION"
```

The VARIABLE LABELS command must begin in column 1 and there must be one space and only one space between the word VARIABLE and the word LABELS.

Two or more variables can be given labels with the same VARIABLE LABELS command. The variables' specifications are separated by one or more spaces or commas. The following example gives labels to EDUC, HEALTH, and INCOME:

```
VARIABLE LABELS   EDUC "YEARS OF EDUCATION"
                  HEALTH "SELF-ASSESSMENT OF HEALTH"
                  INCOME "TOTAL FAMILY INCOME"
```

Although more than one variable label can be put on a line, the program is easier to read if each label is on a separate line. This setup also keeps the user from splitting a label across two lines, which cannot be done without additional special punctuation. (For a discussion of how to split a label across two lines, see the *SPSS* *User's Guide,* page 43.)

4.6 Identifying Codings: VALUE LABELS

With the **VALUE LABELS** command, you can label the categories of a variable in the output with more than the number code in the data file. The format for this command is as follows, where labels are being given to categories of the variable SEX:

```
VALUE LABELS   SEX 1"MALE" 2"FEMALE"
```

The VALUE LABELS command is similar to the VARIABLE LABELS command with one important exception: if the VALUE LABELS command contains more than one variable, the variables' specifications must be separated by a slash (/). For example, the following command would create value labels for the categories of EDUC, HEALTH, and INCOME:

```
VALUE LABELS
    EDUC    1"0 TO 11 YEARS" 2"12 TO 15 YEARS"
            3"16 YEARS AND OVER"/
    HEALTH 1"EXCELLENT" 2"GOOD" 3"FAIR" 4"POOR"/
    INCOME 1"UNDER $5,000"        2"$5,000 TO $9,999"
            3"$10,000 TO $14,999" 4"$15,000 TO $19,999"
            5"$20,000 TO $24,999" 6"$25,000 TO $34,999"
            7"$35,000 TO $49,999" 8"OVER $50,000"
```

VALUE LABELS cannot exceed 20 characters in releases preceding Release 2.1, after which they can have up to 60 characters. As with long variable labels, long value labels will be truncated in the output of many statistical procedures.

If you create an SPSS system file, the labels you define before saving the file will be saved with it. (Saving SPSS system files is described in Chapter 2.)

The next two chapters describe the CROSSTABS and BREAKDOWN statistical procedures. These procedures have great utility in themselves, and they also are the preliminary steps for doing more advanced statistical analyses.

4.7 Summary

The RECODE, COMPUTE, IF, and TEMPORARY commands covered in this chapter enable us to transform data.

The RECODE command allows us to regroup categories of a variable and change their coded values.

COMPUTE enables us to calculate new variables from our old variables.

IF allows us to restrict the recoding or computation of variables to cases that meet specified conditions.

TEMPORARY enables us to make transformations for one statistical procedure without changing the data set for the balance of the job.

The VARIABLE LABELS and VALUE LABELS commands enable us to make our output easier to interpret.

4.8 Where to Look in the SPSS^x User's Guide

- RECODE is discussed on pages 102–105.
- COMPUTE is discussed on pages 105–108.
- IF, DO IF, and END IF are discussed on pages 149–161.
- TEMPORARY is discussed on pages 128–129.
- The VARIABLE LABELS and VALUE LABELS commands are discussed on pages 43–45.

RESEARCH PROJECT WORK FOR CHAPTER 4

1. Write a VARIABLE LABELS command for your research project data file.

2. Write a VALUE LABELS command for your research project data file.

REVIEW QUESTIONS FOR CHAPTER 4

(Answers to Review Questions are given at the back of the book.)

RECODE

Hint: Before you can do a RECODE command for a variable, you need to know its missing values.

4.1   For a variable named MARITAL, married people were coded 1, never-married people were coded 2, divorced people were coded 3, and widowed people were coded 4. Recode MARITAL so that all three types of unmarried people are coded 2. The missing value for MARITAL was a blank.

4.2   A variable named HEIGHT has each respondent's height coded in inches. Recode HEIGHT so that people under 60 inches are coded 1, people 60 to 70 inches are coded 2, and people over 70 inches are coded 3. The missing value for HEIGHT is blanks.

4.3   A variable named CARS was coded 0 if the family had no car, 1 if the family had one car, 2 if the family had two cars, 3 if the family had three cars, and so on. Recode CARS so that any families with two or more cars will be coded 2. The missing value for CARS is -1.

4.4   A variable named AGE has been coded in one-year intervals; that is, someone who is 20 years old was given a value of 20, someone who is 66 years old was given a value of 66. The missing value for this variable is -9. Recode AGE into three categories: those under 16, those 16 to 65, and those over 65.

COMPUTE and IF

4.5   Write a command that will compute a variable named FAMILY$, which is to be WIFE$ (wife's income) plus HUSBAND$ (husband's income).

4.6   Write a command that will divide a variable named SALARY (monthly salary) by 160 to make an estimate of HOURLY$ (average hourly salary of the subjects).

4.7   Create a new variable named NEWEXEC (new executives) that will be coded 1 when an executive's TENURE with the company, measured in months, is less than 12.

4.8   Write a command that will place a family in category 1 of a variable named IN-COME if the value on a variable named FAMINCOM is greater than the value of a variable named AVEINCOM.

TEMPORARY

4.9   Using the TEMPORARY, SELECT IF, and FREQUENCIES commands, write the commands necessary to compare the FREQUENCIES output for women on the variable INCOME with the FREQUENCIES output for men on the same variable for the file NORC84, discussed in Appendix B.

4.10   Using the TEMPORARY, SELECT IF, and FREQUENCIES commands, write the SPSS^x commands necessary to compare the education of persons age 50 and over with the education of persons age 25 to 49 in the file NORC84, discussed in Appendix B.

VARIABLE LABELS and VALUE LABELS

4.11   Write a command that would assign to a variable named CHILDS the variable label NUMBER OF CHILDREN.

4.12   Write a command that would assign to a variable named INCOME the variable label GROSS INCOME and to a variable named NET the variable label NET INCOME.

4.13   Write a command for the variable POLVIEWS that would give the category coded 1 the value label LIBERAL, give the category coded 2 the label MIDDLE OF THE ROAD, and give the category coded 3 the label CONSERVATIVE.

4.14   Write a command for the variable named OVERDUE that will create the value label LESS THAN 60 DAYS for the category coded 1 and MORE THAN 60 DAYS for the category coded 2. As part of the same command, for a variable named MILITARY, create the label MILITARY PERSONNEL for category 1 and the label CIVILIAN PERSONNEL for category 2.

ASSIGNMENT QUESTIONS FOR CHAPTER 4

(Solutions to Assignment Questions are given in the *Instructor's Manual.*)

4.1 RECODE the variable CHILDS in the SPSS system file NORC84 so that any families with more than two children will be coded 3.

4.2 RECODE the variable AGE in the SPSS system file NORC84 into three categories: those under 16, those 16 to 65, and those over 65.

4.3 Write a command that will compute a variable named RELATIVE, which is CHILDS (number of children) plus SIBS (number of siblings).

4.4 Write a command that will divide a variable named INCOME (annual income) by PERSONS (number of persons in the family) to make a new variable named INCOMPER.

4.5 Create a new variable named GRAD that will be coded 1 when EDUC is greater than 15 and 0 otherwise.

4.6 Using the variable INCOME in the SPSS system file NORC84, create a variable named UPPER that will be coded 1 for a family with an income of $25,000 or more and 0 for a family with an income below $25,000.

4.7 For a variable named AGED, assign the variable label NUMBER OF PERSONS AGE 65 AND OLDER.

4.8 Using the TEMPORARY, SELECT IF, and FREQUENCIES commands, write the commands necessary to compare the FREQUENCIES output for blacks on the variable EDUC with the FREQUENCIES output for whites on the same variable for the SPSS system file NORC84, discussed in Appendix B.

4.9 Using the TEMPORARY, SELECT IF, and FREQUENCIES commands, write the commands necessary to compare the income of persons age 40 and over with the income of persons between ages 18 and 39, inclusive, in the system file NORC84, discussed in Appendix B.

4.10 For a variable named GRASS, write the variable label FAVOR LEGALIZING MARIJUANA, and in the same command give a variable named CUTSPEND the label FAVOR LESS SPENDING ON EDUCATION.

4.11 For the variable named RELIG, label category 1 PROTESTANT, category 2 CATHOLIC, category 3 JEWISH, category 4 NONE, category 5 OTHER, and category 9 NO ANSWER.

4.12 For the variable named UNEMPLOY, label category 1 YES, category 2 NO, category 8 DO NOT REMEMBER, and category 9 NO ANSWER. In the same command, for the variable named CLASS, label the categories as follows: 1 LOWER, 2 WORKING, 3 MIDDLE, 4 UPPER, and 9 NO ANSWER.

5

CROSSTABULATIONS OF TWO OR MORE VARIABLES

New SPSS[x] Command:

CROSSTABS

We often begin an analysis suspecting that one variable affects another. For example, students invest time, energy, and money for each additional year of education. One might ask whether this effort pays off in happiness. Are people with more education happier than their less-educated peers? This question is "bivariate," which means that it concerns the association between two variables. (The prefix is the Latin word *bi,* meaning *two.*)

One way to investigate a bivariate question is by doing a crosstabulation. If we "crosstabulate" a happiness variable with an education variable, the output will reveal the percentage of people in each education category who are in each happiness category. We can then look for differences in happiness levels among the educational categories. Such differences would indicate an association between education and happiness. For example, if the percentage of highly educated people in the high-happiness category is greater than the percentage of less-educated people in the same category, increasing one's education would seem to increase the likelihood of being happy.

Described verbally, crosstabulations sound confusing. The example we present next will clarify what we mean.

TABLE 5.1 Crosstabulation of Happiness by Education

		EDUC		
		1	2	3
HAPPY	1	50.0	33.3	50.0
	2	50.0	55.6	33.3
	3		9.1	16.6
COLUMN TOTAL		4	9	6

5.1 An Introduction to Crosstabulations

Consider the crosstabulation presented in Table 5.1. It is an analysis of the association between happiness and education using our example data set from Chapter 2.

The three columns in Table 5.1 represent the coding categories for the education variable. (Recall that we have recoded the values as 1 to mean 0–11 years of education, 2 to mean 12–15 years of education, and 3 to mean 16 or more years of education.) Column 1 represents the people coded 1 on education. Column 2 represents the people coded 2 on education. Column 3 represents the people coded 3 on education. The total for column 1 is 4, which means that 4 respondents were coded 1 on education.

The row numbers under HAPPY correspond to the categories of that variable. Row 1 represents the people who responded "very happy," coded 1. Row 2 represents those who responded "pretty happy," coded 2. Row 3 represents those who responded "not too happy," coded 3.

The upper left-hand cell of the table (row 1, column 1) is the conjunction of people who were coded 1 on both EDUC and HAPPY. The 50.0 in that cell indicates that 50.0 percent of the people with 0–11 years of education stated they felt very happy. The middle cell of column 1 (that is, in row 2) is the conjunction of people who were coded 1 on EDUC and 2 on HAPPY. The 50.0 in that cell indicates that 50.0 percent of the people with 0–11 years of education stated they felt pretty happy. The bottom cell of column 1 is blank, which means that none of the people with 0–11 years of education responded that they were not too happy.

It is easy to become confused when reading a crosstabulation table, especially one that shows more than two variables. You must think carefully about:

(1) what the percents represent, and (2) what comparisons are meaningful. In our example, each percent has as a base the number of people in that column, and each column is an education category. (Note that for each column the sum of the percents equals 100.)

We can compare up and down the columns. In our example, the percent of people in the top cells is greater than the percent of people in the bottom cells, which means that the percent of people who are very happy is greater than the percent of people who are not too happy.

We can also compare across rows. In our example, if we compare across the top row, we find that 50.0 percent of those with less than 12 years of education (column 1) or more than 16 years of education (column 3) are very happy, whereas 40 percent of those with 12 to 15 years of education (column 2) are very happy. Thus we have no clear pattern here. Among both those with the least education and those with the most education, 50.0 percent stated they were very happy; however, the sample size of our example is small. The association between variables will be clear when we replicate this crosstabulation in Section 5.4 using the larger sample in the NORC84 SPSS system file.

5.2 The CROSSTABS Command

In SPSS[x], crosstabulations are produced by the CROSSTABS command. The following CROSSTABS command, using two of its OPTIONS, produced the output in Table 5.1:

```
CROSSTABS   HAPPY BY EDUC
OPTIONS   4,13
```

The CROSSTABS command must begin in column 1. We recommend placing the variable you think is being affected (the dependent variable) before the BY and the variable you think is causing an effect (the independent variable) after the BY. This way the dependent variable will always appear as row categories along the side of your table.

An OPTIONS command can be used with most procedural commands to select alternatives to the default operations and output (see the *SPSS[x] User's Guide,* pages 307–308). The OPTIONS command must also begin in column 1. For the CROSSTABS command, OPTIONS 4 produces column percents for each cell, which makes the table easier to interpret. OPTIONS 13 omits the cell frequencies, which makes the table easier to read. OPTIONS 4,13 will put into effect both options.

The number of cases in each cell can be obtained when OPTIONS 13 is employed by multiplying the cell percent by the number of cases in that column. For example, in Table 5.1 the upper left cell (row 1, column 1) is the conjunction of people who have 0–11 years of education and are very happy. The percent in this cell, 50.0 percent, multiplied by the column total, 4, gives the number of cases in that cell: $0.5 \times 4 = 2$. Thus two cases are represented in the upper-left cell. Following these procedures, the total cases for each cell can be calculated.

Placed with the other SPSS[x] commands necessary to produce a run with our example data set, the commands needed to generate the CROSSTABS output in Table 5.1 would be:

```
DATA LIST    ID 1-2    EDUC 3-4    SEX 5    HAPPY 6
RECODE    EDUC  (0 THRU 11=1) (12 THRU 15=2) (16 THRU 30=3)
BEGIN DATA
010912
021223
031521
041222
050611
061612
071522
081612
091821
101412
111321
121611
130922
141212
151221
161821
170821
181222
191613
20142
END DATA
MISSING VALUES    EDUC (-9, 99)    HAPPY SEX (0)
CROSSTABS    HAPPY BY EDUC
OPTIONS    4, 13
```

A problem arises when we do CROSSTABS with a small number of cases. Some of the cells are empty and, more importantly, the results are not likely to be generalizable. For example, when we have only 4 individuals with less than 12 years of education, we are not confident that they are likely to be typical of all people with less than 12 years of education.

5.3 Using CROSSTABS with an SPSS System File

To illustrate the problem of representativeness and to give you a more accurate impression of the relationship between education and happiness, we now do an identical CROSSTABS for the entire SPSS system file NORC84, described in Appendix B. The commands needed to do a crosstabulation of the variables HAPPY and EDUC in the NORC84 file are as follows:

```
GET   FILE=NORC84
RECODE   EDUC  (0 THRU 11=1) (12 THRU 15=2) (16 THRU 30=3)
CROSSTABS   HAPPY BY EDUC
OPTIONS   4,13
```

Table 5.2 is constructed from the output produced by these commands. The entire sample size is 1473 cases. Consequently we now have no empty cells and the percents, based on a much larger sample, are more likely to portray accurately the relationship between education and happiness in the United States.

TABLE 5.2 Crosstabulation of Happiness by Education Using the NORC84 System File

| | EDUC | | |
	1	2	3
HAPPY			
VERY HAPPY	32.3	31.4	41.0
PRETTY HAPPY	48.5	57.1	52.8
NOT TOO HAPPY	19.2	11.5	6.1
COLUMN TOTAL	408	772	262

NUMBER OF MISSING OBSERVATIONS = 31

Along the top of Table 5.2 are the education categories; each column under an education value corresponds to the people in that category. Along the left side of the table are the happiness categories; each row corresponds to the people in that category.

Look at the percent of less-educated people in the very happy category—the upper-left cell (row 1, column 1). The 32 percent (rounded) demonstrates that about one-third of the people with less than 12 years of education are very happy. Compare this figure with the percent of highly educated people who report being very happy—41 percent. We see that more education appears to increase the likelihood of being very happy.

Interpretation of what causes what, however, is tricky. Perhaps people who are happy tend to stay in school longer. If this statement is true, then happiness increases the likelihood of high educational attainment rather than educational attainment's increasing the likelihood of being happy. Perhaps both effects are at work: higher education increases the likelihood of being happy and being happy increases the likelihood of high educational attainment. We should also remember that associations in society are usually far from absolute. Fifty-nine percent of the highly educated people are *not* very happy (100 percent minus 41 percent), so we would conclude that obtaining more education is far from a good guarantee that one will be very happy.

5.4 Multivariate Analysis with CROSSTABS

We have seen that the probability of respondents' reporting that they are very happy is linked to their sex and educational achievement. Another question we might ask is whether the association of happiness with education is the same for women and men. When two or more independent variables are present, the analysis is called *multivariate*.

To add a third variable to a CROSSTABS analysis, we simply add the word BY and the name of the third variable. For our example with the NORC84 system file, the CROSSTABS and accompanying SPSS^x commands would be:

```
GET   FILE=NORC84
RECODE   EDUC (0 THRU 11=1) (12 THRU 15=2) (16 THRU 30=3)
CROSSTABS   HAPPY BY EDUC BY SEX
OPTIONS   4,13
STATISTICS   1,2
```

In this analysis SEX is called the *control variable* because we will see the effects of education controlling for SEX. Note that the control variable is the last in the command sequence. If the positions of EDUC and SEX were reversed in the command, we would see the effects of SEX controlling for EDUC.

Note also that we have added the command STATISTICS 1,2. (Unfortunately in SPSS[x] the term STATISTICS sometimes is a command beginning in column 1 and sometimes is a specification beginning after column 1.) This command, when following CROSSTABS, will produce two statistics: chi-square and Cramer's *V*. Cramer's *V* is easy to interpret. It ranges from 0.0, when there is absolutely no association between two variables, to 1.0, when there is a perfect association.

χ^2 (chi-square, pronounced "kai square") is another useful statistic, because it has a known sampling distribution and its significance level is included in the output. In calculating chi-square, the value expected for each cell (if the variables were not associated) is compared to the actually observed values through a somewhat complex formula. The resulting chi-square statistic does not have a simple range such as 0.0 to 1.0; hence it is not easy to assess its importance immediately. Cramer's *V* is a transformation of χ^2 that standardizes for the number of cells in the crosstabulation table so that the range becomes 0.0 to 1.0 and easier to interpret. Consequently, the significance level of Cramer's *V* is the same as the significance level of χ^2.

The output will be on different pages for each category of the control variable. In our example the output will be spread over two pages. The first page will contain the HAPPY BY EDUC table for men (SEX value = 1) and the second will contain the HAPPY BY EDUC table for women (SEX value = 2).

Table 5.3 is the simplified output produced by the preceding commands. Notice how the addition of the STATISTICS 1,2 command has produced the chi-square and Cramer's *V* statistics at the bottom of each portion of the table. Actual output is like Table 5.4 at the end of this chapter.

Looking at the percentages in the two portions of the table, we can see that for females the difference in percent between the least educated and the most educated who are very happy is greater than for males. For females the difference in the top row (the very happy respondents) between the respondents with 16 or more years of education (47.7) and the respondents with less than 12 years of education (31.5) is 16.2 percent. The corresponding difference for males is 6.2 percent. This result suggests that a higher level of education improves the likelihood of being very happy more for females than for males.

TABLE 5.3 Output from Multivariate Crosstabulation

CROSSTABULATION OF HAPPY BY EDUC CONTROLLING FOR SEX
SEX   VALUE=1

HAPPY	COL PCT	EDUC 1	2	3
VERY HAPPY	1	33.5	27.1	38.8
PRETTY HAPPY	2	45.9	58.9	53.7
NOT TOO HAPPY	3	20.6	13.9	7.5
COLUMN TOTAL		170	280	134	584

CHI-SQUARE   SIGNIFICANCE
  16.5   0.002

        STATISTIC   VALUE
CRAMER'S V   0.12

CROSSTABULATION OF HAPPY BY EDUC CONTROLLING FOR SEX
SEX   VALUE=2

HAPPY	COL PCT	EDUC 1	2	3
VERY HAPPY	1	31.5	36.4	47.7
PRETTY HAPPY	2	50.0	53.3	46.9
NOT TOO HAPPY	3	18.5	10.4	5.5
COLUMN TOTAL		238	492	128	858

CHI-SQUARE   SIGNIFICANCE
  21.0   0.000

        STATISTIC   VALUE
CRAMER'S V   0.11

NUMBER OF MISSING OBSERVATIONS = 31

5.5 Summary

In this chapter we explain how CROSSTABS can be used to produce the crosstabulations of two or more variables. These crosstabulations are useful for examining the associations between variables. We show how chi-square is used to assess the statistical significance of associations in a crosstabulation. We describe Cramer's *V*, which is a transformation of chi-square that ranges on a scale from 0.0 to 1.0. Crosstabulations can be very simple and easy to interpret; they can likewise be very complex and arduous to interpret. Some of the techniques we cover in Part II are methods of searching through complex crosstabulations for the most important associations.

We now know that we can increase our likelihood of being happy by being more educated. This variable is the first we have examined over which individuals have any control. By now we hope your curiosity is aroused as to why certain variables are associated with happiness. Are more-educated people generally happier because they generally have more money? Are older people generally happier because they are more likely to be parents? We will be better able to tackle these multivariate questions using the techniques presented in Part II of this text. The researcher's never-ending task is to try to push our understanding a bit further, knowing full well that answering one question leads immediately to asking more questions.

5.6 Where to Look in the SPSS^X User's Guide

- CROSSTABS is discussed on pages 336–353.

RESEARCH PROJECT WORK FOR CHAPTER 5

1. (a) For the data set you gathered, replicate the crosstabulations of HAPPY BY EDUC and HAPPY BY EDUC BY SEX done in this chapter.

    (b) Describe any differences between the results in your sample and the results for the NORC84 file given in Tables 5.2 and 5.3.

    (c) If there are differences, what do you think caused them?

2. (a) Produce a crosstabulation of HAPPY by another variable in the data set that you think might affect happiness.

    (b) Discuss whether the results are as you expected.

REVIEW QUESTIONS FOR CHAPTER 5

(Answers to Review Questions are given at the back of the book.)

5.1 Write the CROSSTABS and OPTIONS commands that would crosstabulate a variable named INCOME with a variable named SEX. Your hypothesis is that the SEX variable is causing differences in INCOME. Remember that whether the variables are independent or causal affects the order of the variables on the command.

5.2   Write the CROSSTABS and OPTIONS commands that would crosstabulate a variable named DAY with a variable named SALES. Your hypothesis is that the DAY variable is affecting the SALES variable.

5.3   Write all the commands necessary to crosstabulate EDUC with SEX in our example data set. Assume that SEX is the causal variable and recode EDUC into the categories specified in Section 5.1

5.4   Write the commands that are needed to demonstrate through a crosstabulation the effects of the variable RELIGION on the variable POLITICS for the SPSS system file NORC84, described in Appendix B.

5.5   Write the CROSSTABS and OPTIONS commands that would produce three crosstabulations demonstrating the association of the independent variable named EDUC with the variables HAPPY, HEALTH, and INCOME for the SPSS system file NORC84, described in Appendix B.

5.6   Write the CROSSTABS and OPTIONS commands that would produce a crosstabulation demonstrating the association of the dependent variable HAPPY with the variable MARITAL, controlling for the variable SEX.

5.7   What command must be added to the CROSSTABS and OPTIONS commands to produce the chi-square and Cramer's V statistics?

5.8   Explain the difference between chi-square and Cramer's V.

ASSIGNMENT QUESTIONS FOR CHAPTER 5

(Solutions to the Assignment Questions are given in the *Instructor's Manual*.)

5.1   Write the CROSSTABS and OPTIONS commands that would crosstabulate a variable named AGE with a variable named SEX. Your hypothesis is that there are differences between the sexes in death rates and, therefore, in age distribution.

5.2   Write the CROSSTABS and OPTIONS commands that would crosstabulate a variable named HEALTH with a variable named EDUC. Your hypothesis is that the education level of respondents affects the likelihood of good health.

5.3   Write all the commands necessary to crosstabulate HAPPY by SEX in our example data set. Assume that SEX is the causal variable.

5.4   Write the commands that are needed to demonstrate through a crosstabulation the effects of the variable named INCOME on the variable named ATTEND for the SPSS system file NORC84, described in Appendix B.

5.5   Write the commands needed to produce three crosstabulations demonstrating the effects of the variable named INCOME on the variables SATFAM, SATFRND, and SATJOB for the SPSS system file NORC84, described in Appendix B.

5.6   Write all the commands necessary to crosstabulate INCOME by EDUC controlling
      for SEX using the NORC84 SPSS system file, described in Appendix B. Include the
      command necessary to produce the chi-square and Cramer's *V* statistics.

TABLE 5.4 One Page of Actual Output from Multivariate Crosstabulation

	CROSSTABULATION OF		
HAPPY GENERAL HAPPINESS		BY EDUC	HIGHEST YEAR OF SCHOOL COMPLETED

CONTROLLING FOR..
     SEX   RESPONDENT'S SEX   VALUE =   1. MALE

		EDUC			
	COL PCT				ROW TOTAL
HAPPY		1	2	3	
VERY HAPPY	1	33.5	27.1	38.8	185 31.7
PRETTY HAPPY	2	45.9	58.9	53.7	315 53.9
NOT TOO HAPPY	3	20.6	13.9	7.5	84 14.4
	COLUMN TOTAL	170 29.1	280 47.9	134 22.9	584 100.0

CHI-SQUARE	D.F.	SIGNIFICANCE	MIN E.F.	CELLS WITH E.F. <5
16.54304	4	0.0024	19.274	NONE

STATISTIC	VALUE	SIGNIFICANCE
CRAMER'S V	0.11901	

6
COMPARING MEANS

New SPSS[x] Command:

BREAKDOWN

We know from previous chapters that women, the more educated, and persons age 40 and older are more likely to report being very happy. You should be curious about shedding more light on these associations. Many questions are unanswered. For example: Are the more educated happier because they have higher incomes? Are women at all income levels happier than men?

Crosstabulations are difficult to interpret for variables like income that have many categories. The BREAKDOWN command provides output that is simpler to read and is a useful tool when the dependent variable is an ordinal or interval level measure. To clarify this point, we need to explain levels of measurement.

6.1 Levels of Measurement

Nominal level of measurement variables have categories that cannot be ranked from lesser to greater. One's religious affiliation is a nominal variable. Another example of a nominal variable is place of birth. It does not make sense to calculate a mean (average) or median (midpoint of a distribution) for such variables. (Nominal variables are also called *categorical* variables.)

Ordinal level of measurement variables have categories that can be ranked. **Interval** level of measurement variables have categories that can be ranked *and* are of equal size. In our example data set presented in Chapter 2, the HAPPY variable is ordinal and the EDUC variable is interval. HAPPY is an ordinal variable because we can rank the categories "very happy," "somewhat happy," and "not too happy" in an order on the dimension of happiness. The EDUC variable is interval because the categories can be ranked and each interval is of an equal size—that is, the distance between 9 years of education and 11 years of education is the same as the distance between 13 years of education and 15 years of education. Some statistical techniques are designed to be used only with interval variables.

Two-category nominal variables like SEX are called *dichotomous* or *binomial.* They are a special case of nominal variables because, after being coded with numerical values, they can be used in interval level statistical analyses like Pearson correlations (see Chapter 7). [For a discussion of this point, see Roderick P. McDonald's *Factor Analysis and Related Methods* (Hillsdale, N.J.: Lawrence Erlbaum Associates, 1985), pages 9–11, 198–202.] As an example, look at our treatment of the SEX variable in Chapter 7.

Further distinctions can be made between levels of measurement, and the classification of a variable's level of measurement is not always clear-cut (see Blalock, 1979, pages 15–26). At times there are disputes over whether variables are "interval enough" to justify the use of statistics designed for interval measures. Researchers like to use interval measure statistics because they are better than ordinal measure statistics for handling multiple variable analyses and for detecting weak associations between variables. Consequently, there is a tendency to use interval level statistics with ordinal variables. The risk of this practice is that the results may be biased. However, William L. Hays' *Statistics for the Social Sciences,* Second Edition (New York: Holt, Rinehart and Winston, 1973, pages 87–90) observes that at issue here is not really mathematics and statistics, but the good judgment of the researcher in selecting a method for the problem at hand and interpreting the meaning of the results. There is no simple, hard-and-fast rule about which statistical technique to use for a particular set of variables.

6.2 Comparing Means between Groups: BREAKDOWN

The command BREAKDOWN produces an analysis that compares group means on a dependent or criterion variable. This technique, however, can be employed only when the mean is a useful measure for the dependent variable. (Recall that a dependent variable is the one we think is being affected by another variable in the analysis. The independent variable is the one having an effect.)

We can consider, for example, whether there are differences between males and females in happiness. Because we are considering whether the respondent's sex affects the probability of his or her being happy, sex is the independent variable and happiness is the dependent variable. Happiness is an ordinal variable, so we can use BREAKDOWN.

To determine the effect of a person's sex on the probability of happiness, the BREAKDOWN command would be:

BREAKDOWN   HAPPY BY SEX

The word BREAKDOWN must begin in column 1. Again, as with the CROSS-TABS commands, we place the dependent variable, HAPPY, before the BY and the independent variable, SEX, after the BY.

For our example data file, described in Chapter 2, the necessary set of SPSS^x commands for a BREAKDOWN is:

```
DATA LIST   ID 1-2   EDUC 3-4   SEX 5   HAPPY 6
BEGIN DATA
010912
021223
031521
041222
050611
061612
071522
081612
091821
101412
111321
121611
130922
141212
151221
161821
170821
181222
191613
20142
END DATA
BREAKDOWN   HAPPY BY SEX
```

TABLE 6.1 Partial Output Produced by BREAKDOWN   HAPPY   BY   SEX

```
CRITERION VARIABLE      HAPPY
     BROKEN DOWN BY      SEX

  VARIABLE      CODE   MEAN     N

     SEX         1     1.8      8
     SEX         2     1.5     11
```

Table 6.1 is part of the output that would be produced by this BREAK-DOWN. The first line of the sample output presented in the table reads "CRITE-RION VARIABLE HAPPY." The **criterion variable** is the one whose mean scores will be given by the BREAKDOWN output—in our example, it is HAPPY. The second line of output indicates that the criterion variable HAPPY is "broken down by SEX." Thus we see the mean score for HAPPY in each SEX category.

The line reading "VARIABLE   CODE   MEAN   N" provides the column headings. On the following line, the word SEX indicates the independent variable. The 1 under the word CODE indicates that this line is for cases coded 1 on SEX—that is, the male cases. The 1.8 is the mean for these cases on the criterion variable. The 8 indicates the number of cases in this category. The final line provides information for the cases coded 2 on the variable SEX—the females. The mean for the females on the criterion variable HAPPY is 1.5.

Recall that the HAPPY variable is coded 1 for "very happy" and 3 for "not too happy." Therefore, the fact that the mean value for women is lower than for men indicates that, on the average, the women were happier than the men. These findings are based on a sample of only 20 respondents; when the analysis is repeated with the entire SPSS system file NORC84 with 1473 respondents, women again are happier but the difference is not as great.

6.3 Using BREAKDOWN with an SPSS System File

The SPSS^x commands necessary to do the BREAKDOWN of HAPPY by SEX with the NORC84 file (described in Appendix B) are:

```
GET   FILE=NORC84
BREAKDOWN   HAPPY BY SEX
```

In this analysis the direction of causality is certain—we know that one's level of happiness does not affect the likelihood of being male or female. Exactly why women are more likely to respond that they are very happy is one of those thought-provoking questions that lead researchers to call for further study of a subject. Are the health and lifestyle of women more likely than those of men to yield happiness? Are women more reluctant to say they are not happy? Is the objective situation of women better than that of men? Our analysis does not answer these questions. It shows only that, in general, women are more likely than men to tell pollsters they are happy.

In our next BREAKDOWN example, we will consider the question "Does money buy happiness?" Both money and happiness are variables for which a mean score is useful. Our hypothesis, however, is that money affects happiness, so we will break down the mean level of happiness for each income category. In other words, happiness will be our dependent variable. Using our SPSS system file NORC84, the necessary commands are as follows:

```
GET  FILE=NORC84
BREAKDOWN  HAPPY BY INCOME
```

As before, the happiness variable has three categories: the lower the mean score on the variable HAPPY, the happier are the respondents. Table 6.2 contains the overall mean and the mean score for each income group. We can

TABLE 6.2 Partial Output Produced by BREAKDOWN   HAPPY   BY   INCOME

CRITERION VARIABLE HAPPY		
BROKEN DOWN BY INCOME		
VARIABLE	MEAN	N
FOR ENTIRE POPULATION	1.8	1,320
INCOME LESS THAN $5000	2.0	124
INCOME $5000-9999	2.0	170
INCOME $10000-14999	1.9	197
INCOME $15000-19999	1.8	153
INCOME $20000-24999	1.8	190
INCOME $25000-34999	1.7	206
INCOME $35000-49999	1.6	163
INCOME $50000+	1.6	117

TOTAL CASES=1,473

MISSING CASES=153 OR 10.4 PERCENT

see that the higher income categories have lower mean scores on the happiness variable. Since lower scores indicate greater happiness, our findings show that people in higher-income families tend to be happier.

In this analysis we have some uncertainty in deciding the direction of causality. Perhaps happy people are more successful at making money because people like to do business with them; that is, maybe happiness earns money rather than money buying happiness.

6.4 Multivariate Analysis with BREAKDOWN

We can do multivariate analyses using the BREAKDOWN command, as with CROSSTABS. For example, we can examine the association between income and happiness to find out whether the relationship is the same for women as for men. The command to produce this analysis would be:

```
BREAKDOWN   HAPPY BY SEX BY INCOME
```

This command would produce the output presented in Table 6.3 for the NORC84 file. The output is usually easier to read if the control variable is listed before the independent variable. Thus, in our example, SEX is placed in the BREAKDOWN command before INCOME.

Table 6.3 shows that the mean happiness level tends to be lower (indicating greater happiness) as income goes up for both males and females.

Assignment Question 6.9 asks you to answer the first question we posed at the beginning of the chapter about whether the more educated are happier because they have higher income. You can answer this question by doing a breakdown of happiness by education controlling for income. (Remember that EDUC needs to be recoded and that the proper sequence of the command would be BREAKDOWN HAPPY BY INCOME BY EDUC.)

6.5 The STATISTICS Command with BREAKDOWN

If we wanted to test for the statistical significance of the mean differences in happiness by income, we would add the command STATISTICS ALL. The statistical significance is the probability that the differences are because of sampling error.

TABLE 6.3 Output Produced by BREAKDOWN   HAPPY BY SEX BY INCOME

```
CRITERION VARIABLE      HAPPY
    BROKEN DOWN BY      SEX
                        INCOME
```

VARIABLE	MEAN	N
FOR ENTIRE POPULATION	1.8	1,320
SEX MALE	1.8	556
INCOME LESS THAN $5000	2.2	39
INCOME $5000-9999	1.9	60
INCOME $10000-14999	1.9	84
INCOME $15000-19999	1.8	69
INCOME $20000-24999	1.9	67
INCOME $25000-34999	1.8	95
INCOME $35000-49999	1.6	80
INCOME $50000+	1.6	62
SEX FEMALE	1.7	764
INCOME LESS THAN $5000	1.9	85
INCOME $5000-9999	2.0	110
INCOME $10000-14999	1.8	113
INCOME $15000-19999	1.7	84
INCOME $20000-24999	1.7	123
INCOME $25000-34999	1.6	111
INCOME $35000-49999	1.6	83
INCOME $50000+	1.6	55

```
TOTAL CASES=1,473

MISSING CASES=153 OR 10.4 PERCENT
```

The output produced by the STATISTICS command for BREAKDOWN gives the F ratio from which the statistical significance level for the differences in happiness between income categories is calculated. (For a discussion of the logic and calculations of F, see Blalock, 1979:336–346.) Furthermore, the association is broken down into its linear and nonlinear components. The linear component assumes that the effects of a particular difference in INCOME are the same throughout its range—for example, that the effects of the difference between $5,000 and $10,000 are the same as the difference between $20,000 and $25,000.

Note that the statistical significance test is only for the first BREAKDOWN variable. Therefore, the control variable would have to be dropped from the BREAKDOWN command on runs using STATISTICS ALL. Otherwise the statis-

TABLE 6.4 Partial Output of Statistics for BREAKDOWN

		ANALYSIS OF VARIANCE	
SOURCE	D.F.	F	SIG.
BETWEEN GROUPS	7	8.5	.000
LINEARITY	1	56.6	.000
DEVIATION FROM LINEARITY	6	.5	.820

tics would be for the control variable. For example, if we added the STATISTICS ALL command to the command

BREAKDOWN   HAPPY BY SEX BY INCOME

without deleting the control variable SEX, the statistical significance test would be only for the association between HAPPY and SEX. The correct commands to examine the statistical significance of the association between HAPPY and INCOME would be:

BREAKDOWN   HAPPY BY INCOME
STATISTICS ALL

The output produced by the STATISTICS ALL command would include the statistics presented in Table 6.4. The abbreviation SIG. stands for statistical significance, which is the probability that between-groups mean differences of this magnitude would be due to sampling error. A statistical significance of .000 indicates that the probability is less than .001. Table 6.5 at the end of this chapter provides an example of the complete output from the BREAKDOWN command.

If we want to focus on the mean differences between just two groups— an analysis similar to the traditional *t*-test—all we need to do is use a SELECT IF statement to limit the BREAKDOWN to those two groups. Once the analysis is complete, taking the square root of the *F* ratio will give the *t* value. The statistical significance level is the same as for the *F* ratio. Doing multiple *t*-tests, however, is to be avoided because the significance levels for *t*-tests are based on individual trials. Looking at a set of *t* scores increases the probability that one will discover a score that is "significant." (See Blalock, 1978:347–348 for further discussion of this point.)

6.6 Summary

In this chapter we explain how to use BREAKDOWN to analyze the differences between groups in their means on a variable. The variable for which means are calculated is called the criterion variable; usually it is thought of as the dependent variable in the analysis.

Using the STATISTICS command with BREAKDOWN produces a table that indicates the statistical significance of the differences between group means. Also produced in the table are two advanced statistics explained further in Part II: the significance of the linear regression using the group variable as a predictor and the significance of deviations from the linear model.

The analysis in this chapter showed that reported happiness increases with income. This association remains when we control for sex.

6.7 Where to Look in the SPSS[x] User's Guide

• BREAKDOWN is discussed on pages 373–383.

RESEARCH PROJECT WORK FOR CHAPTER 6

For the following work you might want to pool your data file with that of other students in your class so that the group means are based on five or more cases. An alternative would be to recode variables that have too few cases in some categories.

1. Using your research project data file, do breakdowns of SATFAM, SATFRND, and SATJOB by INCOME controlling for SEX.

2. Describe the associations you find in the breakdowns from Problem 1.

3. Discuss what might be causing the associations you find in the breakdowns from Problem 1.

REVIEW QUESTIONS FOR CHAPTER 6

(Answers to Review Questions are given at the back of the book.)

6.1 Write a command that would produce the mean scores on the variable INCOME for each category of the variable SEX.

6.2 Write a command that would produce the mean scores on the variable HEALTH for each category of the variable EDUC and for each category of the variable INCOME.

6.3   Write all the commands necessary to produce the mean scores on the variable HAPPY for each category of the variable EDUC for our example data set given in Chapter 2.

6.4   Write all the commands needed to produce the mean scores on the variable HAPPY for each category of the variable HEALTH for the SPSS system file NORC84, described in Appendix B.

6.5   What is the criterion variable in a BREAKDOWN output?

6.6   In a BREAKDOWN analysis, does the dependent variable appear before or after the word BY in the BREAKDOWN command?

6.7   What command would be used to produce the mean scores on INCOME for each category of EDUC controlling for SEX?

6.8   What commands would produce the statistics that would enable the user to judge whether the differences in income by education were statistically significant?

6.9   What commands would be needed to determine whether the mean income for those with 15 years of education is statistically different from those with 12 years of education?

ASSIGNMENT QUESTIONS FOR CHAPTER 6

(Solutions to the Assignment Questions are given in the *Instructor's Manual*.)

6.1   Write all the commands necessary to produce the mean years of education completed for each of the categories of the variable HAPPY in our example data set from Chapter 2.

6.2   For the SPSS system file NORC84, write all the commands necessary to produce the mean score on the variable POLVIEWS for each category of the variable SEX.

6.3   For the SPSS system file NORC84, write all the commands necessary to produce the mean score on the variable HAPPY for each category of the variable POLVIEWS.

6.4   For the SPSS system file NORC84, write all the commands necessary to produce the mean score on the variable HAPPY for each category of the variable CHILDS.

6.5   For the Happiness Questionnaire in Appendix C, write the BREAKDOWN command necessary to produce the mean score on SATJOB for each category of the variable SEX.

6.6   For the Happiness Questionnaire in Appendix C, write the BREAKDOWN command necessary to produce the mean score on the variable HAPPY for each category of the variable TVHOURS.

6.7   What BREAKDOWN command would you need to produce the mean score on the variable HAPPY for each category of the variable TVHOURS controlling for the variable SEX?

6.8 What commands would be needed to produce statistics indicating the statistical significance of the association between HAPPY and TVHOURS?

6.9 Use the SPSS system file NORC84 to do a breakdown of happiness by education controlling for income.

TABLE 6.5 Complete Output from Commands: BREAKDOWN   HAPPY BY INCOME
STATISTICS ALL

| CRITERION VARIABLE | HAPPY | GENERAL HAPPINESS |
| BROKEN DOWN BY | INCOME | TOTAL FAMILY INCOME |

VARIABLE	VALUE	LABEL	MEAN	STD DEV	CASES
FOR ENTIRE POPULATION			1.7788	.6536	1320
INCOME82	1	LESS THAN $5000	2.0081	.6686	124
INCOME82	2	$5000-$9999	1.9529	.7201	170
INCOME82	3	$10000-$14999	1.8680	.6411	197
INCOME82	4	$15000-$19999	1.7516	.6416	153
INCOME82	5	$20000-$24999	1.7526	.6315	190
INCOME82	6	$25000-$34999	1.7136	.6093	206
INCOME82	7	$35000-$49999	1.5828	.6067	163
INCOME82	8	$50000+	1.5983	.6026	117

TOTAL CASES   = 1473
MISSING CASES = 153 OR 10.4 PCT.

****

*   A N A L Y S I S   O F   V A R I A N C E   *

****

SOURCE	SUM OF SQUARES	D.F.	MEAN SQUARE	F	SIG.
BETWEEN GROUPS	24.4328	7	3.4904	8.4965	.0000
LINEARITY	23.2387	1	23.2387	56.5690	.0000
DEV. FROM LINEARITY	1.1941	6	.1990	.4844	.8203

R = -.2031   R SQUARED = .0412

| WITHIN GROUPS | 538.9733 | 1312 | .4108 | | |

ETA = .2082   ETA SQUARED = .0434

****

7

CORRELATIONS AND SCATTERGRAMS

New SPSS[x] Commands:

PEARSON CORR
SAMPLE
SCATTERGRAM

We have done frequencies, crosstabulations, and breakdowns to determine that the variable HAPPY is associated with SEX, AGE, EDUC, and INCOME. To do these analyses, however, we recoded AGE and EDUC. INCOME also would have been recoded, if the data were not already grouped into large intervals on the SPSS system file NORC84. Whenever we recode data into large intervals, detail is lost and we cannot study the association as precisely as we could before recoding the data. PEARSON CORR and SCATTERGRAM provide two analytical methods that do not require the regrouping of data into a small number of intervals. However, these methods were designed only for interval level variables.

In this chapter we will use PEARSON CORR to re-examine the associations of SEX, AGE, EDUC, and INCOME with HAPPY and with one another. We will use SCATTERGRAM to present the association between INCOME and EDUCATION. We will add to our analysis the variable HEALTH from the SPSS system file NORC84. HEALTH is the response to the question: "Would you say your own health, in general, is excellent, good, fair, or poor?'' The answers were coded: excellent (1), good (2), fair (3), and poor (4). Strictly speaking HEALTH is an ordinal level of measurement variable, because the categories can be ranked but the intervals are not clearly of equal size. A common practice, however, is to assume that the categories on a variable like HEALTH represent roughly equal steps on the measurement and to use the variable as an interval variable. This is done by assigning sequential numbers to the categories as we have done in our coding of the HEALTH variable. Dichotomous (two-category) nominal variables like SEX can also have their categories assigned numerical values and be used with statistical techniques like Pearson's correlation coefficient that are designed for interval level variables.

7.1 When and How to Use PEARSON CORR

The output of the PEARSON CORR command summarizes the strength of an association through the Pearson correlation coefficient, which is in the range from -1.0 to $+1.0$. One advantage of the Pearson correlation coefficient is that it indicates whether the association is positive or negative. A negative coefficient means that, when one variable is higher in value, the other variable tends to be lower in value. A positive coefficient means that, when one variable is higher, the other variable also tends to be higher. For example, we might expect the correlation between education and income to be positive.

The best indicator of the strength of the association between a pair of variables is the Pearson correlation coefficient squared. A correlation of .20 is four times as strong as a correlation of .10, because $(.20)^2 = .04$ and $(.10)^2 = .01$. However, once the coefficient is squared, it no longer indicates whether the association is positive or negative. Thus tables usually present the unsquared coefficient.

PEARSON CORR requires the assumptions that the variables are interval level and linearly associated. For example, if income is low for young adults, peaks in late middle age, and drops off after age 60, the association is not linear and would be underestimated by Pearson's correlation coefficient. Other types of nonlinear associations would not be appropriate material for PEARSON CORR analysis. Two hypothetical examples are given in scattergrams in Figure 7.1.

To run PEARSON CORR, we simply list after the command the variables whose associations we want printed. For example, to look at the association between each of the variables we have considered so far, use the following commands:

PEARSON CORR   HAPPY SEX AGE EDUC INCOME HEALTH

FIGURE 7.1 Nonlinear Associations That Would Be Inappropriate for PEARSON CORR Analysis: (a) Exponential Increase—For Example, Number of Big Macs Sold Each Year, 1960–1985; (b) Logistic Curve—For Example, Resident Population Size of a Housing Development by Months Since Opening

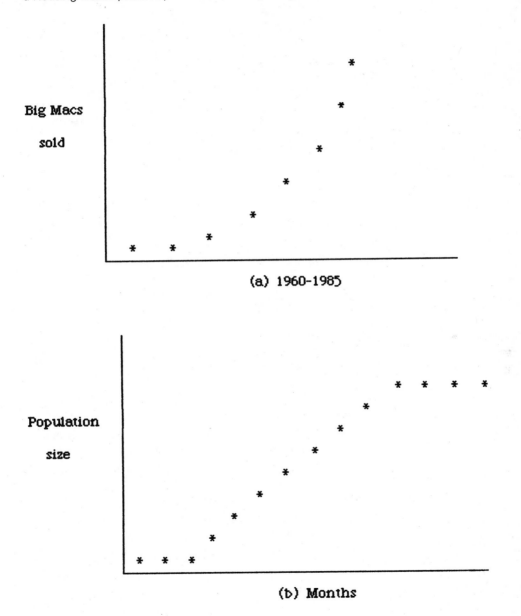

TABLE 7.1 Partial Output Produced by
PEARSON CORR HAPPY SEX AGE EDUC INCOME HEALTH

PEARSON CORRELATION COEFFICIENTS

VARIABLE
PAIR

HAPPY -.203	HAPPY -.092	HAPPY -.107
WITH N(1320)	WITH N(1439)	WITH N(1442)
SEX SIG .014	AGE SIG .000	EDUC SIG .000

HAPPY -.195	HAPPY .209
WITH N(1366)	WITH N(1437)
INCOME SIG .000	HEALTH SIG .000

For users unfamiliar with correlation matrices, the output will be easier to read if OPTION 6 is also used. Without OPTION 6 the variable labels are in the margins instead of next to each correlation. Together the commands would be:

PEARSON CORR   HAPPY SEX AGE EDUC INCOME HEALTH
OPTION   6

Part of the Pearson correlation output from these commands is given in Table 7.1. (An example of complete output is in Table 7.2 at the end of this chapter.) In this output the Pearson correlation coefficient is the number to the right of the top variable (HAPPY) of each pair. In the upper-left part of the table, we see that for HAPPY with SEX the correlation coefficient is −.057. The N(1445) under HAPPY indicates the number of cases used in calculating the correlation. This number is different for each pair because the number of missing cases is not the same for all variables. The SIG .014 shows that a correlation this size would occur because of sampling error only 14 times out of 1000.

The correlation for HAPPY with HEALTH is .209, the highest for any of the pairs. Only the correlation of HAPPY with INCOME is nearly as great. Although the correlation with EDUC is less strong, it is still greater than a random association that might be expected from sampling error. So, the old folklore that to be healthy, wealthy, and wise brings happiness has some empirical support in our NORC84 survey.

FIGURE 7.2 Simplified Output of SCATTERGRAM   INCOME WITH AGE (hypothetical data)

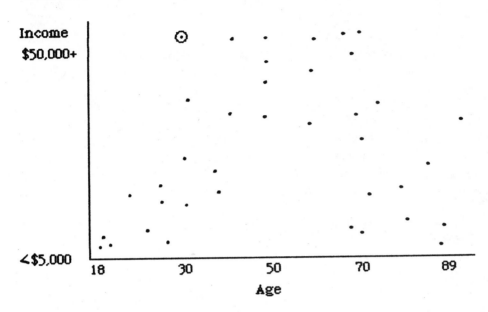

7.2 When and How to Use SCATTERGRAM

The SCATTERGRAM command produces a picture of the association between two variables by plotting a point for each case.* These points lie on a plane in which each axis corresponds to the intervals of one of the variables. To understand SCATTERGRAM, one picture is truly worth a thousand words. Look at Figure 7.2. The circled dot represents the case of someone age 30 earning over $50,000 per year. (We should all do so well!) The dot's distance from the vertical axis corresponds to the age interval 30, and its distance from the horizontal axis corresponds to an income of $50,000+. You can see that the scatter of cases tends to be higher on the vertical income axis for the older cases, which are more to the right on the age axis. At the oldest ages, however, income once more is at lower levels.

As of SPSS[X] Release 2.0, SCATTERGRAM is being replaced by PLOT. See the *SPSS[X] User's Guide*, Chapter 32. If you substitute the command keyword PLOT for SCATTERGRAM and omit the STATISTIC 1 command, the examples we give will run, but without producing the correlation coefficient. As of SPSS[X] Release 2.1, the SCATTERGRAM command still worked besides PLOT.

SCATTERGRAM output is difficult to interpret when either variable has fewer than five intervals. For this reason we did not use the variable HAPPY in a scattergram example. SCATTERGRAM output is also difficult to interpret when there are hundreds of times more cases than there are intervals in the two variables. We can solve the problem of too many cases by taking a sample of our cases before doing the SCATTERGRAM. We do so with the command **SAMPLE** followed by the proportion of the cases we want in the sample. For Table 7.3, which is at the end of this chapter and gives complete output, we sampled .1, or 10 percent, of the males over age 34 to use in a scattergram of income with education.

To run SCATTERGRAM you need only use the command followed first by the name of the variable you want on the vertical axis, then the word WITH, and finally the name of the variable you want on the horizontal axis. Normally dependent variables are placed on the vertical axis and independent variables on the horizontal axis.

The commands to obtain a scattergram of INCOME with AGE like that in Figure 7.2 are:

```
SAMPLE    .1
SCATTERGRAM   INCOME WITH AGE
```

The Pearson correlation coefficient between the two variables can be produced with the scattergram by adding the command STATISTIC 1, which begins in column 1 and follows the SCATTERGRAM command. Note that in SPSS[x] singular and plural forms of the command (STATISTIC versus STATISTICS) can be used interchangeably. This is also true of OPTION (versus OPTIONS).

```
SCATTERGRAM   INCOME WITH AGE
STATISTIC   1
```

In the next chapter we will discuss the analytical technique known as multiple regression. This technique will enable you to look at the combined effects of several independent variables. At the same time, you can control for the effects of the independent variables on one another's association with the dependent variable. Sounds like fun, huh? Please, no groans.

7.3 Summary

In this chapter we explain how to produce scattergrams and Pearson correlation coefficients by using the SPSS[x] commands SCATTERGRAM and PEARSON CORR. Both procedures use interval level data or ordinal data that approximate interval data. Dichotomous (two-category) nominal level variables can be used in Pearson correlation analyses. Both procedures are well suited for handling variables with a large number of values.

An advantage of SCATTERGRAM is that it depicts nonlinear relationships accurately, but its disadvantage is its inability to handle variables that have only a few values. PEARSON CORR does not indicate accurately the association between two variables if the association is nonlinear.

We also introduced the command SAMPLE, which enables you to use a randomly selected portion of your cases when you want to reduce the sample size.

7.4 Where to Look in the SPSS^x User's Guide

- PEARSON CORR is discussed on pages 639–646.
- SCATTERGRAM is discussed on pages 928–934. See also PLOT, which is superseding as of Release 2.0 on pages 603–636.
- SAMPLE is discussed on pages 183–184.

RESEARCH PROJECT WORK FOR CHAPTER 7

1. For your research project data set, do a SCATTERGRAM of the association between TVHOURS and INCOME.

2. For your data set, produce the Pearson correlation coefficients of all the variables with one another.

REVIEW QUESTIONS FOR CHAPTER 7

(Answers to Review Questions are given at the back of the book.)

7.1 Write a command to produce a scattergram with INCOME on the vertical axis and EDUC on the horizontal axis.

7.2 Write a command to produce two scattergrams, one with INCOME on the vertical axis and AGE on the horizontal axis and one with EDUC on the vertical axis and AGE on the horizontal axis. Add an additional command to produce the Pearson correlation coefficient for each scattergram.

7.3 Write a command to produce the Pearson correlation coefficient of HAPPY with HEALTH.

7.4   Write the commands to produce the Pearson correlation coefficients of INCOME, AGE, FAMSIZE, and CARSIZE in the output format discussed in this chapter.

7.5   Would a scattergram with number of cars per family on the vertical axis and family income on the horizontal axis be very revealing?

7.6   What problem would arise if you produced a scattergram of income (coded into 10 categories) with education using a data file with 10,000 cases? How could you solve the problem?

7.7   What types of variables can be used in a PEARSON CORR analysis?

7.8   Infant deaths drop off exponentially as infant weight increases. Why would it be poor methodology to use PEARSON CORR to analyze the association between infant death rates and infant weight without transforming one of the variables? Which variable would you transform and how?

7.9   What is the difference between a Pearson correlation coefficient of −.50 and a Pearson correlation coefficient of +.50?

7.10 If the Pearson correlation coefficient between HEALTH and EDUC were .20 and the Pearson correlation coefficient between HEALTH and INCOME were .30, how would you describe the relative strength of the two associations?

ASSIGNMENT QUESTIONS FOR CHAPTER 7

(Solutions to the Assignment Questions are given in the *Instructor's Manual.*)

7.1   Write the commands necessary to produce a scattergram with INCOME on the vertical axis and AGE on the horizontal axis. Include the command that will add the Pearson correlation coefficient to the scattergram output.

7.2   Write the commands necessary to produce three scattergrams (including Pearson correlation coefficients) with EDUC on the vertical axes and MAEDUC, PAEDUC, and SPEDUC on the horizontal axes.

7.3   Write a command to produce the Pearson correlation coefficient for the association between HEALTH and EDUC.

7.4   Write the commands necessary to produce the Pearson correlation coefficients for all the variables in a data file with one another. Include the command that will produce the format used in this chapter.

7.5   Why would a scattergram of the NORC84 variables HAPPY and HEALTH be inappropriate?

7.6   Would it be correct to use PEARSON CORR to examine the association between the NORC84 variables HAPPY and MARITAL? Why?

7.7   What is the difference in meaning between positive and negative Pearson correlation coefficients?

TABLE 7.2 Complete Output from Command PEARSON CORR   HAPPY SEX AGE EDUC INCOME HEALTH
OPTION 6

P E A R S O N   C O R R E L A T I O N   C O E F F I C I E N T S

VARIABLE PAIR	VARIABLE PAIR	VARIABLE PAIR	VARIABLE PAIR	VARIABLE PAIR
-.0575 HAPPY WITH SEX	.0651 HAPPY WITH AGE	-.0921 HAPPY WITH EDUC	-.1069 HAPPY WITH INCOME	-.2031 HAPPY WITH HEALTH
N(1445)	N(1467)	N(1439)	N(1442)	N(1320)
SIG .014	SIG .006	SIG .000	SIG .000	SIG .000

VARIABLE PAIR	VARIABLE PAIR	VARIABLE PAIR	VARIABLE PAIR	VARIABLE PAIR
.2091 SEX WITH AGE	.2662 SEX WITH EDUC	-.0560 SEX WITH INCOME	-.1065 SEX WITH HEALTH	.0501 AGE WITH EDUC
N(1437)	N(1456)	N(1470)	N(1342)	N(1461)
SIG .000	SIG .000	SIG .016	SIG .000	SIG .028

VARIABLE PAIR	VARIABLE PAIR	VARIABLE PAIR	VARIABLE PAIR	VARIABLE PAIR
-.2862 AGE WITH INCOME	-.0518 AGE WITH HEALTH	-.2855 EDUC WITH INCOME	.4151 EDUC WITH HEALTH	-.3353 INCOME WITH HEALTH
N(1465)	N(1341)	N(1331)	N(1341)	N(1458)
SIG .000	SIG .029	SIG .000	SIG .000	SIG .000

SIG IS 1-TAILED, '.' IS PRINTED IF A COEFFICIENT CANNOT BE COMPUTED.

7.8   If the Pearson correlation coefficient between AGE and HAPPY were .20 and the
      Pearson correlation coefficient between HEALTH and HAPPY were .40, what
      would we know about their relative strength?

7.9   What distortion would probably occur if the association between INCOME and
      AGE were measured with the Pearson correlation coefficient?

7.10 What could be done to make the Pearson correlation coefficient a better measure
      of the associaton between INCOME and AGE?

TABLE 7.3 Complete Output from Commands
SELECT IF   SEX EQ 1   AND   AGE GT 34
SAMPLE   . 1
SCATTERGRAM   INCOME WITH EDUC
STATISTIC   1

DOWN= INCOME   TOTAL FAMILY INCOME   ACROSS= EDUC   HIGHEST YEAR OF SCHOOL COMPLETED
              6   8   10   12   14   16   18   20   22   24

```
     11 |                    |                              |                              |  11
     10 |                    |                              |                              |  10
      9 |                    |                              |                              |   9
      8 |                    |  *      *      *   * *       |  *                           |   8
        |--------------------|------------------------------|------------------------------|
      7 |                    |         *   2  2             |  *                           |   7
      6 |         *          |  *   *      *      *         |  *                           |   6
      5 |             2      |     *                        |                              |   5
        |--------------------|------------------------------|------------------------------|
      4 |                    |  *                           |                              |   4
      3 | *      *      *   *| *      *      *              |                              |   3
      2 |                    |  *                           |                              |   2
      1 |        *   *       |                              |                              |   1
        |--------------------|------------------------------|------------------------------|
          5      7      9     11     13     15     17     19     21     23     25
```

STATISTICS. .
    CORRELATION (R) -   . 64485
    PLOTTED VALUES -   32   EXCLUDED VALUES-   0   MISSING VALUES -   0

PART 2

ADVANCED TECHNIQUES

Very useful analyses can be produced using the statistical procedures discussed in Part 1, and you have to use these procedures to clean your data and become familiar with the distributions of your variables and their bivariate associations. There will come a time, however, when you want to move on to more powerful techniques for analyzing multivariate associations. The procedures we present in Part 2 (multiple regression, analysis of variance, discriminant function analysis, log-linear analysis, and factor analysis) enable you to uncover associations that are difficult or impossible to detect using the techniques discussed in Part 2.

We present the material in Part 2 with the assumption that you now have a basic knowledge of statistics and of SPSS[x]. The examples will present only the statistical procedure commands and will assume that you have already used the GET command to access an SPSS system file.

We present a short discussion of the statistical basis of each procedure, but our primary intent is to introduce the SPSS[x] commands rather than to teach statistics. For a complete explanation of these statistical techniques, you will need to refer to an advanced statistics book. The Russell Sage Foundation publishes a good series of papers on these methods written for the nonmathematician reader: *Quantitative Applications in the Social Sciences.* At the beginning of each chapter we will refer you to the appropriate paper from this series.

The statistical procedures discussed in Part 2 require data sets with at least 100 cases for most analyses. Therefore, to use the research project data that was gathered and used in Part 1, you will need to merge together the data files of several students.

8

EXAMINING COMBINED EFFECTS OF MANY INDEPENDENT VARIABLES: MULTIPLE REGRESSION

New SPSS^X Command:

REGRESSION

We have seen that health, age, education, income, and sex are all associated with the probability of people's reporting they are happy. However, what if we want to examine the effects of each of those variables controlling for the effects of all the other variables in our analysis? A crosstabulation or breakdown would be very difficult to interpret. Multiple regression is a technique that will do what we want and still be easy to interpret.* Multiple regression will show us the effects of each variable controlling for the effects of other variables.

8.1 When to Use REGRESSION

The advantage of multiple regression is that it shows both the combined effects of a set of independent variables and the separate effects of each inde-

---

*For a more complete discussion of the statistics of regression analysis, see Michael S. Lewis-Beck's *Applied Regression: An Introduction* (Beverly Hills, CA: Sage Publications, 1980).

pendent variable controlling for the others. A drawback of multiple regression is that it requires several assumptions about the distribution of each variable and the associations among the variables. Multiple regression applies best to an analysis in which both the dependent variable and the independent variable are normally distributed interval variables (for a discussion of the normal distribution see Blalock, 1979). However, ordinal variables are commonly used as well, and moderate deviations from normality do not bias the results greatly.

Multiple regression also assumes that the effects of the independent variables are linear—that is, that the effect of a unit difference in an independent variable is the same at all points in the range of the variable. (There is further explanation of the nature of this assumption in the Chapter 7 discussion of the Pearson correlation coefficient.)

Another assumption of multiple regression is that the independent variables are not correlated with one another (see Section 8.4).

Multiple regression can be used with categorical variables through a technique known as dummy coding (see Section 8.5).

If the relationship between the independent variable and the dependent variable is nonlinear, the independent variable can be transformed (see Section 8.6).

8.2 How to Use REGRESSION

The command that produces multiple regression analyses in SPSS^x is **REGRESSION.** REGRESSION has three required subcommands. The first subcommand, **VARIABLES =,** is followed by a list of all the variables that will be used. The second required subcommand, **DEPENDENT =,** is followed by each variable that you want to use as a dependent variable. For both subcommands variable names are separated by one or more spaces or commas. A different multiple regression analysis will be produced for each dependent variable. The third subcommand is **METHOD = ENTER.** (Besides ENTER there are five other methods that are a bit more complex.)

To run REGRESSION with HAPPY as the dependent variable and SEX, AGE, EDUC, INCOME, HEALTH, and MARITAL as independent variables, the following commands are needed. MARITAL was recoded into a dichotomous variable (married = 1, unmarried = 0).

```
REGRESSION   VARIABLES=HAPPY SEX AGE EDUC INCOME
                  HEALTH MARITAL/
             DEPENDENT=HAPPY/
             METHOD=ENTER/
```

TABLE 8.1 Partial Output from REGRESSION Command

MULTIPLE R		.33261	F=27.03512		
R SQUARE		.11063	SIGNIF F=.0000		
ADJUSTED R SQUARE		.10654			

——————————————— VARIABLES IN THE EQUATION ———————————————

VARIABLE	B	SE B	BETA	T	SIG T
MARITAL	-.229411	.037532	-.174122	-6.112	.0000
AGE	-.004886	.001057	-.128587	-4.622	.0000
SEX	-.111437	.034736	-.084366	-3.208	.0014
EDUC	-.009457	.006322	-.045987	-1.496	.1349
HEALTH	.152315	.023174	.189434	6.573	.0000
INCOME	-.025004	.009729	-.081975	-2.570	.0103
(CONSTANT)	2.230345	.125061		17.834	.0000

Note that each subcommand is followed by a slash. Part of the output from these commands is presented in Table 8.1. An example of complete output is given in Table 8.2 at the end of this chapter.

8.3 Interpreting REGRESSION Output

In Table 8.1 the multiple R is the correlation between the dependent variable and the entire set of independent variables. The multiple R squared (R^2) is the proportion of variance in the dependent variable associated with variance in the independent variables. This proportion is a good indicator of the explanatory power of the regression model.

The adjusted R^2 is corrected for the number of cases. A small number of cases relative to the number of variables in the multiple regression can bias upwards the estimate of R^2. When your sample size is less than ten cases per variable, you will notice that the adjusted R^2 decreases substantially relative to the unadjusted R^2 if the sample size is reduced.

The beta column indicates the values of the standardized regression coefficient. Beta represents the effect that a standard deviation difference in the independent variable would have on the dependent variable in standard deviation (the standardized scores of the dependent variable). The beta for HEALTH is .189, which means a difference of one standard deviation in HEALTH is predicted to cause a difference of .189 standard deviation in HAPPY. Because the coefficient is positive, a person with a lower score on HEALTH is predicted to have a lower score on HAPPY. Recall that the happiest category and the healthi-est category are coded 1, the least healthy category is coded 4, and the least happy category is coded 3. So the beta for HEALTH indicates that people who report feeling healthy are more likely to report feeling happy. Based on the betas, differences in health have the greatest impact on happiness, and differences in marital status have the second greatest impact.

Because the beta coefficient for MARITAL is negative with married people coded 1 and unmarried coded 0, we can conclude that married people tend to be happier than unmarried people.

Another method of evaluating the importance of an independent variable is to observe the change in the R^2 when it is added to or dropped from the analysis. This can be done by using more than one METHOD=ENTER subcommand with independent variables specified after ENTER. The variables specified on each METHOD=ENTER subcommand will be added to the ones already in the analysis. To produce two regressions, one with MARITAL and one without, the commands would be:

```
REGRESSION   VARIABLES=HAPPY SEX AGE EDUC INCOME
                     HEALTH MARITAL/
             DEPENDENT=HAPPY/
             METHOD=ENTER   SEX AGE EDUC INCOME HEALTH/
             METHOD=ENTER   MARITAL/
```

The T statistic is a measure of the distance of beta from zero in a proba-bility distribution. The SIG T (significance of t) is the probability that such a deviation from zero would be due to sampling error. For MARITAL, the first pre-dictor variable, the SIG T is .0000, which indicates that a beta this large would occur from sampling error less than one time out of 1000.

Residuals are the errors in prediction. They are obtained by subtracting the actual score from the predicted score for each case. If the actual score for a case were 3 and the predicted score were 2.5, the residual would be 0.5.

Doing a scattergram of the standardized residuals by the standardized pre-dicted scores is a convenient test of whether the model violates assumptions about linearity. If the model is good, the residuals will be randomly distributed for each value of the predicted values. At the same time, there should be more predicted values near zero (the mean of a standardized variable) because the dependent variable is assumed to be normally distributed. To obtain this scat-tergram, use the subcommand

```
SCATTERPLOT   (*RES, *PRE) /
```

Like the subcommands given in Section 8.2, SCATTERPLOT must begin after column 1 and is usually aligned with the other subcommands for clarity.

To see a histogram of the residuals, use the subcommand RESIDUAL = HISTOGRAM. (Recall that a histogram is the graphic representation of a frequency distribution by a series of bars.) The histogram of the residuals should reveal that they have a normal distribution.

8.4 Multicollinearity

Before doing a regression analysis, you should do a FREQUENCIES analysis to determine whether the variables are normally distributed. Theoretically, the variables should be normally distributed. In practice, multiple regression is recognized as a robust technique that can include non–normally distributed variables, if their deviations from normality are not extreme.

You also need to know the intercorrelations among the variables, which can be obtained using the PEARSON CORR command. Theoretically, the independent variables should be correlated with the dependent variable, but not with one another. In practice, one often sees intercorrelations as high as .60 among independent variables in a regression analysis. Use only one of a group of highly correlated variables or construct an index.

8.5 Dummy Variables

Nominal variables may be used in REGRESSION by employing a coding technique known as **dummy variables.** The simplest dummy variable would be for a two-category variable like SEX. Simply code one category 0—let this be the males—and code the other category 1—for the females. This variable can be entered in the REGRESSION as an independent variable. A dummy variable should not be used as a dependent variable in regression if one of the categories contains less than 20 percent of the cases, because the assumption of a normally distributed dependent variable would be violated too greatly. Such a violation would tend to produce unreliable estimates of the regression coefficients.

For a nominal variable with more than two categories, a set of dummy variables is used. The number of dummy variables will be one less than the number of categories. For example, the variable RELIG (religious preference) in the NORC84 file has five categories: Protestant, coded 1; Catholic, coded 2; Jewish, coded 3; None, coded 4; and Other, coded 5. To create a set of dummy variables, the following commands could be used:

```
IF   RELIG EQ 1   D1=1
IF   RELIG NE 1   D1=0
IF   RELIG EQ 2   D2=1
IF   RELIG NE 2   D2=0
IF   RELIG EQ 3   D3=1
IF   RELIG NE 3   D3=0
IF   RELIG EQ 4   D4=1
IF   RELIG NE 4   D4=0
```

For each case, except those in the "other" category, one dummy variable would equal 1 and the rest would equal 0. For those in the "other" category, all the dummy variables would equal zero. A Protestant, for example, would have a score of 1 on D1 and a score of 0 on D2, D3, and D4.

D1 through D4 would then be entered as independent variables in the RE-GRESSION. To evaluate the total effects of the RELIG variable on the dependent variable, the dummy variables' collective effects would be used by looking at the R^2 with the set of dummy variables included in the REGRESSION and then the R^2 with the dummy variables dropped from the REGRESSION. The difference in R^2 would be one measure of the impact of the RELIG variable.

Another indicator of the importance of RELIG would be if any of the dummy variables had a statistically significant beta coefficient. The beta coefficient for each dummy variable represents how much greater (or lesser if the sign is negative) cases coded 1 on that variable are predicted to score on the dependent variable (in standardized scores) compared to cases in the category for which all the dummy variables are coded 0. The output in Table 8.2 at the end of this chapter includes RELIG as a dummy variable.

8.6 Nonlinear Effects Corrected through Variable Transformations

When the residual plot reveals nonlinear effects, the researcher can make adjustments by transforming the dependent variable. For example, if the residuals increase in value as the predicted value increases, you can compute the log of the dependent variable and try using that transformed score as the dependent variable to reduce the errors in your predictions.

There are many ways of transforming the predictor variables or the dependent variables to compensate for nonlinear relationships. The SPSS^x COMPUTE functions make it easy to transform variables, thereby facilitating adjustments for nonlinearity. However, the choice of what transformations to make and how to interpret the coefficients is a complex topic beyond the scope of this book.

8.7 Interaction Effects

An interaction effect exists when the effects of one variable are influenced by scores on another variable. For example, if the effects of income on happiness were greater for high-education respondents than for low-education respondents, there would be an interaction between income and education. Look for interaction effects when knowledge of your research subject suggests that they exist or when you find irregularities in your residuals.

One way to adjust for interaction effects is to include in the analysis a variable that is a composite of the two variables. For our example of income interacting with education, we could adjust by computing a new variable (income multiplied by education) and including this interaction term in the regression as an independent variable along with its two components. If the beta coefficient for the interaction term is statistically significant, it indicates that its variables have a combined effect as well as their separate effects.

8.8 Summary

In this chapter we discuss multiple regression. This technique is used to evaluate the effects of a set of independent variables on one dependent variable.

The output from REGRESSION indicates the combined effects of a set of independent variables and also each independent variable's separate effects controlling for the other independent variables. The variables are assumed to be interval or ordinal measures; however, nominal variables can be used with a technique known as dummy variable coding.

Multiple regression assumes that the independent variables are normally distributed and not highly correlated with one another.

8.9 Where to Look in the *SPSS^x User's Guide*

- REGRESSION is discussed on pages 663–686.

RESEARCH PROJECT WORK FOR CHAPTER 8

1. For your research project data set, do a REGRESSION using HAPPY as the dependent variable and INCOME, SEX, EDUC, MARITAL, AGE, HEALTH, and TVHOURS as the independent variables. (If your file has fewer than 100 cases, combine it with those of other students to obtain a minimum of 100 cases.)

2. Interpret the results from Problem 1.

TABLE 8.2 Complete Output Produced by:

```
RECODE  MARITAL  (2,3,4,5=0)
IF  RELIG EQ 1   D1=1
IF  RELIG NE 1   D1=0
IF  RELIG EQ 2   D2=1
IF  RELIG NE 2   D2=0
IF  RELIG EQ 3   D3=1
IF  RELIG NE 3   D3=0
IF  RELIG EQ 4   D4=1
IF  RELIG NE 4   D4=0
REGRESSION  VARIABLES=HAPPY SEX AGE EDUC INCOME HEALTH MARITAL
                      D1 D2 D3 D4/
                      DEPENDENT=HAPPY/
                      METHOD=ENTER/
```

```
              * * * *    M U L T I P L E   R E G R E S S I O N    * * * *

LISTWISE DELETION OF MISSING DATA

EQUATION NUMBER 1    DEPENDENT VARIABLE..    HAPPY      GENERAL HAPPINESS

BEGINNING BLOCK NUMBER  1.  METHOD:   ENTER

VARIABLE(S) ENTERED ON STEP NUMBER   1..  D4
                                     2..  HEALTH   CONDITION OF HEALTH
                                     3..  D3
                                     4..  SEX      RESPONDENT'S SEX
                                     5..  MARITAL  MARITAL STATUS
                                     6..  D2
                                     7..  AGE      AGE OF RESPONDENT
                                     8..  EDUC     HIGHEST YEAR OF SCHOOL COMPLETED
                                     9..  INCOME   TOTAL FAMILY INCOME
                                    10..  D1
```

110

MULTIPLE R	.35324
R SQUARE	.12478
ADJUSTED R SQUARE	.11824
STANDARD ERROR	.61219

ANALYSIS OF VARIANCE

	DF	SUM OF SQUARES	MEAN SQUARE
REGRESSION	10	71.48974	7.14897
RESIDUAL	1338	501.45318	.37478

F = 19.07522   SIGNIF F = .0000

VARIABLES IN THE EQUATION

VARIABLE	B	SE B	BETA	T	SIG T
D4	.133964	.157880	.053604	.849	.3963
HEALTH	.163908	.022675	.203980	7.228	.0000
D3	.034640	.197044	.006580	.176	.8605
SEX	-.097991	.034201	-.074147	-2.865	.0042
MARITAL	-.224775	.036831	-.170641	-6.103	.0000
D2	.137044	.148249	.091480	.924	.3554
AGE	-.005198	.001028	-.138673	-5.058	.0000
EDUC	-.011497	.006088	-.056019	-1.888	.0592
INCOME	-.011288	.004534	-.076652	-2.489	.0129
D1	.004695	.146190	.003449	.032	.9744
(CONSTANT)	2.193919	.191145		11.478	.0000

END BLOCK NUMBER   1   ALL REQUESTED VARIABLES ENTERED.

REVIEW QUESTIONS FOR CHAPTER 8

8.1   What types of variables theoretically can be used in a multiple regression analysis?

8.2   Write the commands necessary to do a multiple regression analysis with HEALTH as the dependent variable and INCOME, EDUC, HAPPY, AGE, and SEX as the independent variables.

8.3   Write the commands necessary to do a multiple regression analysis with HAPPY as the dependent variable and INCOME, HEALTH, and RELIG as the independent variables. (Remember to recode religion into dummy variables.)

8.4   What is the meaning of the multiple R at the top of the table in the REGRESSION output (Table 8.1)? How is it related to the predictive strength of the REGRESSION model?

8.5   What does it mean to have multicollinearity problems? How are multicollinearity problems resolved?

8.6   What would it mean if the SCATTERPLOT of standardized residuals by standardized predicted values was not random?

8.7   Add to the commands required for Review Question 8.2 the subcommand necessary to produce the scatterplot of standardized residuals by standardized predicted values.

ASSIGNMENT QUESTIONS FOR CHAPTER 8

8.1   Write the commands necessary to do a multiple regression analysis with INCOME as the dependent variable and EDUC, AGE, and SEX as the independent variables.

8.2   Write the commands necessary to do a multiple regression with the NORC84 file using HAPPY as a dependent variable and INCOME and MARITAL as independent variables. Remember to recode MARITAL into either a dichotomous variable or a set of dummy variables.

8.3   What is the difference between the R^2 and the adjusted R^2 at the top of the table in the REGRESSION output (Table 8.1)?

8.4   Which more accurately indicates the proportion of variance in the dependent variable explained in a multiple regression analysis, the R or the R^2?

8.5   What would you need to do if two independent variables in a multiple regression were correlated at the .95 level?

8.6   How can a researcher detect if the assumptions of linear effects on the dependent variables are violated?

8.7   What subcommand must be added to the REGRESSION command to plot the standardized residuals by the standardized predicted values?

9

MULTIVARIATE COMPARISON OF MEANS: ANALYSIS OF VARIANCE AND MULTIPLE ANALYSIS OF VARIANCE

New SPSS[x] Command:

MANOVA

We have seen that, in general, the probability of being happy is higher for people who are female, 40 or older, more educated, more affluent, healthy, and married. However, what about interactions among these variables? Are the effects of being older, for example, greater for men than for women? Are the effects of education the same for both sexes? Are the effects of marital status affected by income?

The BREAKDOWN procedure allows multivariate comparisons of means. However, BREAKDOWN does not calculate the statistical significance or the strength of the association for more than one predictor variable at a time. In other words, we cannot learn the statistical significance of one variable controlling for the effects of one or more other variables. Nor is it easy to assess the strength of the interactions among the predictor variables.

Several SPSS[x] programs do analysis of variance of one sort or another.

Rather than study them all, we will examine MANOVA, the one most powerful SPSS[x] program for addressing these questions.

9.1 Doing Many Types of Analysis of Variance: MANOVA

The MANOVA program does many types of analysis of variance. Analysis of variance (ANOVA) is especially appropriate when the dependent variable is an interval measure and the predicting variables are nominal.* It is also useful when the predicting variables are interval but nonlinear in their effects.

MANOVA allows us to study the effects of nominal variables and interval variables together. In such an analysis, the interval level variables are termed **covariates** and the technique is called **covariate analysis.**

Finally, MANOVA allows us to look at differences on a set of dependent variables, rather than just one. For example, if we have several measures of happiness, we can do a composite analysis to determine whether groups differ on them. This last application is the actual multiple analysis of variance from which the program received its name—MANOVA.

Analysis of variance assumes that the dependent variable is interval and that the variances are equal for all groups.

9.2 One Dependent Variable with Two or More Independent Variables

We will begin our study of the MANOVA command with the case of one dependent variable and two or more independent variables. (The case of one dependent variable and one independent variable can be handled more easily with the BREAKDOWN command. See Chapter 6.)

Consider the question of whether differences in happiness by marital status are the same for both males and females. The only statistical procedure command we need is:

MANOVA   HAPPY BY MARITAL(1,5) SEX(1,2)

The (1,5) after MARITAL is required to indicate the low and high categories of MARITAL. The (1,2) after SEX is required to indicate the low and high

---

*For a more complete discussion of the statistics of analysis of variance see Gudmund R. Iversen and Helmut Norpoth's *Analysis of Variance* (Beverly Hills, CA: Sage Publications, 1976).

TABLE 9.1 Partial Output from MANOVA

SOURCE OF VARIATION	MEAN SQUARE	F	SIG. OF F
WITHIN CELLS	.41		
MARITAL	7.66	18.8	.000
SEX	.21	.5	.473
MARITAL BY SEX	.41	1.0	.399

categories of SEX. Missing values should not be included in the range specified on the command. The MANOVA program assumes that there are no empty categories. If MARITAL category 4 were empty, the values would need to be recoded. For example, the cases with a score of 5 could be recoded as 4. (If you are using any value labels, remember to change them as well.)

The output from this command will contain a table entitled "Analysis of Variance," partial contents of which are given in Table 9.1.

The WITHIN CELLS row represents the variance that remains within cells after the cases have been partitioned by the MARITAL and SEX categories. This variance may be thought of as "unexplained." This row does not convey information about an association; hence it has no F ratio.

The MARITAL row represents the association between HAPPY and MARITAL. The F ratio is the mean of the differences on HAPPY between MARITAL categories squared (7.66) divided by the mean within-cells of the differences on HAPPY squared (.41). For MARITAL the F ratio is 18.8, which indicates that, when we control for the effects of SEX, the differences between MARITAL categories are much greater than the differences within the MARITAL categories. The significance level of F is .000, which indicates that a difference this size would occur fewer than 1 time out of 1000 by random sampling error.

The SEX row reveals a mean sum of squares of .21, an F of .5, and a significance level of .473. The last statistic indicates that, controlling for MARITAL, the differences by SEX are so small that the probability is 473 times out of 1000 that such differences could occur because of mere sampling error.

Our purpose in this analysis is to examine the interaction between marital status and sex. In the MARITAL BY SEX row we see that the mean of differences squared by MARITAL and SEX interactions (.41) round to the same as the mean of differences squared within cells (.41). Hence the F is 1, and the significance level of .399 is too high to give us confidence that the MARITAL BY SEX interactions are anything more than sampling error. We would conclude, then, that the effects of marital status are roughly the same for males and females. Similarly, the effects of the variable SEX are the same for all marital statuses.

9.3 One Dependent Variable, Two Group Variables, and One Covariate

At the beginning of this chapter, we raised the question of whether variances in income would affect the MARITAL–HAPPY association. One way to examine this question is to control for income by including it as a covariate; that is, each individual's score will be adjusted for the effects of income. (Depending on the statistical program used and the options specified, the control will be done before, while, or after the group effects are examined. In MANOVA, as we are using it in this chapter, the control for the covariate is done simultaneously with the examination of the group effects. If an association exists between MARITAL and HAPPY only because married couples have more money than unmarried people, then the association between MARITAL and HAPPY will vanish once we control for income by including it as a covariate.

The statistical procedure command necessary to produce this analysis is:

```
MANOVA   HAPPY BY MARITAL(1,5) SEX (1,2) WITH INCOME
```

Note that the covariate is preceded by the word WITH instead of the word BY. Note also that the name of the covariate is not followed by its low and high values.

Part of the output produced by this MANOVA command using the NORC84 file is given in Table 9.2. Essentially the output at the top of Table 9.2 resembles that of the MANOVA without the covariate. Note, however, that the mean sum of squares for MARITAL groups has been reduced from 7.66 to 4.38. This result indicates that roughly one third of the differences by marital status disappear when we control simultaneously for the effects of income. Nonetheless, the remaining mean square has an F of 10.6 with a significance level below .001. Hence the differences by marital status remain significant even after controlling for the effects of INCOME.

The lower portion of the table allows us to evaluate the impact of the covariate INCOME. We are given its standardized regression coefficient, or beta ($-.127$), t value, and significance level, all of which indicate that, for cases with higher incomes, the happiness score is lower. (Recall that lower scores on HAPPY indicate greater happiness.) We can see that the effects of income are significant. Note that the error, or within-cells mean square, has been reduced to .40 from the .41 of the previous example, which did not control for income.

TABLE 9.2 Partial Output from MANOVA Command

ANALYSIS OF VARIANCE

SOURCE OF VARIATION	MEAN SQUARE	F	SIG. OF F
WITHIN CELLS	.40		
REGRESSION	8.85	22.2	.000
CONSTANT	468.59	1174.2	.000
MARITAL	4.38	11.0	.000
SEX	.24	.6	.443
MARITAL BY SEX	.35	.9	.475

REGRESSION ANALYSIS FOR WITHIN CELLS ERROR TERM

DEPENDENT VARIABLE...HAPPY   GENERAL HAPPINESS

COVARIATE	BETA	T-VALUE	SIG. OF T
INCOME	−.127	−4.7	.000

9.4 Multiple Dependent Variables and One or More Group Variables

The distinction between MANOVA and other SPSS^x programs is that MANOVA can handle multiple dependent variable analysis of variance. For example, instead of using only one dependent variable, you can use a set of dependent variables like SATCITY, SATFAM, SATFRND, and HAPPY. One reason for using multiple variables is that a bias creeps into an analysis when there are a large number of tests of group differences. If you do tests of group differences on several dependent variables, you increase the likelihood that a given-sized difference will occur from sampling error—much like you would increase the likelihood of rolling 12 with a pair of dice if you rolled the dice four times instead of once.

The command to test whether there are differences by marital status or sex on this set of dependent variables would be:

MANOVA   SATCITY SATFAM SATFRND HAPPY BY MARITAL (1, 5)   SEX (1, 2)

When there are multiple dependent variables, the output from MANOVA will present first a set of tables for the interaction effects, then a set for the last variable in the command, then a set for the next-to-last variable, and so forth.

TABLE 9.3 Partial Output from MANOVA Multiple Dependent Variable Command

---

EFFECT .. MARITAL BY SEX

MULTIVARIATE TESTS OF SIGNIFICANCE
TEST NAME   VALUE   APPROX. F   SIG. OF F

PILLAIS   .031   2.8   .000

UNIVARIATE F-TESTS
VARIABLE   HYPOTH. MS   ERROR MS   F   SIG. OF F

VARIABLE	HYPOTH. MS	ERROR MS	F	SIG. OF F
SATCITY	1.40	2.04	.7	.601
SATFAM	11.07	1.57	7.0	.000
SATFRND	1.00	1.37	.7	.572
HAPPY	.95	.40	.6	.671

//

EFFECT .. SEX

MULTIVARIATE TESTS OF SIGNIFICANCE
TEST NAME   VALUE   APPROX. F   SIG. OF F

PILLAIS   .013   4.6   .001

UNIVARIATE F-TESTS
VARIABLE   HYPOTH. MS   ERROR MS   F   SIG. OF F

VARIABLE	HYPOTH. MS	ERROR MS	F	SIG. OF F
SATCITY	.00	2.04	.0	.977
SATFAM	26.05	1.57	16.5	.000
SATFRND	7.66	1.37	5.6	.018
HAPPY	.55	.40	1.4	.241

//

EFFECT .. MARITAL
MULTIVARIATE TESTS OF SIGNIFICANCE

TEST NAME   VALUE   APPROX. F   SIG. OF F

PILLAIS   .136   12.6   .000

UNIVARIATE F-TESTS
VARIABLE   HYPOTH. MS   ERROR MS   F   SIG. OF F

VARIABLE	HYPOTH. MS	ERROR MS	F	SIG. OF F
SATCITY	18.36	2.04	9.0	.000
SATFAM	51.38	1.57	32.6	.000
SATFRND	4.54	1.37	3.3	.010
HAPPY	7.66	.40	19.0	.000

Each set of tables covers a page of output. See Table 9.4 at the end of this chapter for an example of complete MANOVA output.

The first statistics on each page are multivariate tests of significance, which are measures of whether groups differ significantly in their scores on the set of dependent variables. The most powerful and robust of these measures is Pillai's trace, which is printed first.

The last statistics on each page are the univariate *F* tests, which indicate whether groups differ on each of the dependent variables considered separately, instead of as a set.

Table 9.3 presents the key statistics produced by our example command. For the interaction effects of MARITAL BY SEX, we can see from the significance level of Pillai's trace that the effects of marital status differ between men and women. The univariate *F* tests reveal that the differences in effects of marital status are concentrated in satisfaction with family life.

Pillai's trace is also statistically significant for the effects of SEX. The univariate *F* tests reveal that the differences are concentrated in satisfaction with family and satisfaction with friends.

For the effects of MARITAL, Pillai's trace is again statistically significant. The univariate *F* tests reveal that the differences are statistically significant on all four dependent measures.

9.5 Summary

The MANOVA program does many types of analysis of variance. Analysis of variance is especially appropriate when the dependent variable is an interval measure and the predicting variables are nominal. It is also useful when the predicting variables are interval but nonlinear in their effects.

MANOVA allows us to study the combined effects of nominal variables and interval variables. In such an analysis, the interval-level variables are termed covariates, and the technique is called covariate analysis.

Finally, MANOVA allows us to look at differences on a set of dependent variables, instead of just one. For example, if we have several measures of happiness, we can do a composite analysis to determine whether groups differ on them. This last application is the actual multiple analysis of variance for which the MANOVA program is named.

Analysis of variance assumes that the dependent variable is interval and that the variances are equal for all groups.

In multiple analysis of variance, we also assume that (1) the dependent variables are multivariately normally distributed and (2) the covariance matrices are equal for all groups.

9.6 Where to Look in the *SPSS*^{x} *User's Guide*

- MANOVA is discussed on pages 477–551.

RESEARCH PROJECT WORK FOR CHAPTER 9

1. For your research project data set, replicate the example MANOVA analyses in this chapter, but replace SATCITY with SATJOB for the last example.

2. For your research project data set, reanalyze the effects of INCOME and EDUC on HAPPY. Choose the form of analysis of variance that you think is most appropriate, and explain the reasons for your choice.

REVIEW QUESTIONS FOR CHAPTER 9

(Answers to Review Questions are given at the back of the book.)

9.1   What are the advantages of using MANOVA instead of BREAKDOWN?

9.2   What assumptions does MANOVA make about the dependent and independent variables?

9.3   What command is needed to do an analysis of variance of EDUC by MARITAL by SEX using the MANOVA procedure?

9.4   Would there be any difficulty with the command in Review Question 9.3 if no cases were coded 4 for the MARITAL variable?

9.5   What command is needed to do an analysis of variance of EDUC by MARITAL by SEX with INCOME as a covariate?

9.6   What command is needed to do an analysis of variance using CONFINAY to CONARMYY in the NORC84 file as a set of dependent variables and RELIG and SEX as predictor variables?

9.7   What does it mean if the significance of F for MARITAL in Review Question 9.3 is .002?

9.8   What would it mean if the significance of F for MARITAL BY SEX in Review Question 9.3 were .000?

9.9   Would marital status be a significant variable in the analysis if the interaction effects of MARITAL BY SEX were significant but the effects of MARITAL were not?

9.10 When there are multiple dependent variables, what statistic indicates whether there are group differences among the predictor groups in their scores on the set of dependent variables?

ASSIGNMENT QUESTIONS FOR CHAPTER 9

(Solutions to the Assignment Questions are given in the *Instructor's Manual*.)

9.1 When is MANOVA preferred over REGRESSION as an analytical technique?

9.2 Would it be appropriate to do an analysis of variance using MANOVA in which MARITAL from the NORC84 file was the dependent variable and the predictor variables were SEX and AGE?

9.3 Write the MANOVA command to do an analysis of variance of INCOME by MARITAL by RELIGION.

9.4 Write the MANOVA command to do an analysis of variance of INCOME by MARITAL by RELIGION using AGE as a covariate.

9.5 Write the MANOVA command to do an analysis of variance using SATCITY to SATHEALT from the NORC84 file as a set of dependent variables and REGION by MARITAL as predictor variables.

9.6 What would it mean if the Pillai's trace in the output from the command in Assignment Question 9.4 were significant at the .005 level for the REGION effect?

9.7 What would it mean if, in output for the REGION effect from Assignment Question 9.5, the univariate F test for SATCITY had a significance of .545?

TABLE 9.4 Complete Output Produced by Command:
MANOVA SATCITY SATFAM SATFRND HAPPY BY MARITAL(1,5) SEX(1,2)

*************************** A N A L Y S I S   O F   V A R I A N C E   ***************************

1431 CASES ACCEPTED.
  0 CASES REJECTED BECAUSE OF OUT-OF-RANGE FACTOR VALUES.
 42 CASES REJECTED BECAUSE OF MISSING DATA.
 10 NON-EMPTY CELLS.

  1 DESIGN WILL BE PROCESSED.

CORRESPONDENCE BETWEEN EFFECTS AND COLUMNS OF BETWEEN-SUBJECTS DESIGN 1

STARTING COLUMN	ENDING COLUMN	EFFECT NAME
1	1	CONSTANT
2	5	MARITAL
6	6	SEX
7	10	MARITAL BY SEX

EFFECT .. MARITAL BY SEX

MULTIVARIATE TESTS OF SIGNIFICANCE (S = 4, M = -1/2, N = 708)

TEST NAME	VALUE	APPROX. F	HYPOTH. DF	ERROR DF	SIG. OF F
PILLAIS	.03105	2.77924	16.00	5684.00	.000
HOTELLINGS	.03175	2.81049	16.00	5666.00	.000
WILKS	.96909	2.79715	16.00	4332.70	.000
ROYS	.02573				

EIGENVALUES AND CANONICAL CORRELATIONS

ROOT NO.	EIGENVALUE	PCT.	CUM. PCT.	CANON. COR.
1	.02641	83.19290	83.19290	.16041
2	.00359	11.32384	94.51674	.05985
3	.00171	5.38369	99.90043	.04131
4	.00003	.09957	100.00000	.00562

122

DIMENSION REDUCTION ANALYSIS

ROOTS	WILKS LAMBDA	F	HYPOTH. DF	ERROR DF	SIG. OF F
1 TO 4	.96909	2.79715	16.00	4332.70	.000
2 TO 4	.99469	.84095	9.00	3453.62	.578
3 TO 4	.99826	.61770	4.00	2840.00	.650
4 TO 4	.99997	.04492	1.00	1421.00	.832

UNIVARIATE F-TESTS WITH (4, 1421) D. F.

VARIABLE	HYPOTH. SS	ERROR SS	HYPOTH. MS	ERROR MS	F	SIG. OF F
SATCITY	5.61702	2902.96685	1.40426	2.04290	.68738	.601
SATFAM	44.28819	2237.42740	11.07205	1.57454	7.03191	.000
SATFRND	3.98933	1941.69981	.99733	1.36643	.72988	.572
HAPPY	.95107	573.50268	.23777	.40359	.58913	.671

EFFECT .. SEX

MULTIVARIATE TESTS OF SIGNIFICANCE (S = 1, M = 1, N = 708)

TEST NAME	VALUE	APPROX. F	HYPOTH. DF	ERROR DF	SIG. OF F
PILLAIS	.01268	4.55155	4.00	1418.00	.001
HOTELLINGS	.01284	4.55155	4.00	1418.00	.001
WILKS	.98732	4.55155	4.00	1418.00	.001
ROYS	.01268				

EIGENVALUES AND CANONICAL CORRELATIONS

ROOT NO.	EIGENVALUE	PCT.	CUM. PCT.	CANON. COR.
1	.01284	100.00000	100.00000	.11259

DIMENSION REDUCTION ANALYSIS

ROOTS	WILKS LAMBDA	F	HYPOTH. DF	ERROR DF	SIG. OF F
1 TO 1	.98732	4.55155	4.00	1418.00	.001

TABLE 9.4 *Continued*

MANOVA SATCITY SATFAM SATFRND HAPPY BY MARITAL(1,5) SEX(1,2)

UNIVARIATE F-TESTS WITH (1, 1421) D. F.

VARIABLE	HYPOTH. SS	ERROR SS	HYPOTH. MS	ERROR MS	F	SIG. OF F
SATCITY	.00165	2902.96685	.00165	2.04290	.00081	.977
SATFAM	26.05844	2237.42740	26.05844	1.57454	16.54983	.000
SATFRND	7.65518	1941.69981	7.65518	1.36643	5.60231	.018
HAPPY	.55615	573.50268	.55615	.40359	1.37801	.241

EFFECT .. MARITAL

MULTIVARIATE TESTS OF SIGNIFICANCE (S = 4, M = -1/2, N = 708)

TEST NAME	VALUE	APPROX. F	HYPOTH. DF	ERROR DF	SIG. OF F
PILLAIS	.13646	12.54725	16.00	5684.00	.000
HOTELLINGS	.15184	13.44275	16.00	5666.00	.000
WILKS	.86603	13.05460	16.00	4332.70	.000
ROYS	.11565				

EIGENVALUES AND CANONICAL CORRELATIONS

ROOT NO.	EIGENVALUE	PCT.	CUM. PCT.	CANON. COR.
1	.13077	86.12266	86.12266	.34007
2	.01534	10.10438	96.22704	.12293
3	.00534	3.51442	99.74146	.07286
4	.00039	.25854	100.00000	.01981

DIMENSION REDUCTION ANALYSIS

ROOTS	WILKS LAMBDA	F	HYPOTH. DF	ERROR DF	SIG. OF F
1 TO 4	.86603	13.05460	16.00	4332.70	.000
2 TO 4	.97928	3.31606	9.00	3453.62	.000
3 TO 4	.99430	2.03161	4.00	2840.00	.087
4 TO 4	.99961	.55785	1.00	1421.00	.455

UNIVARIATE F-TESTS WITH (4, 1421) D. F.

VARIABLE	HYPOTH. SS	ERROR SS	HYPOTH. MS	ERROR MS	F	SIG. OF F
SATCITY	73.43940	2902.96685	18.35985	2.04290	8.98713	.000
SATFAM	205.50113	2237.42740	51.37528	1.57454	32.62867	.000
SATFRND	18.15035	1941.69981	4.53759	1.36643	3.32076	.010
HAPPY	30.65423	573.50268	7.66356	.40359	18.98843	.000

EFFECT .. CONSTANT

MULTIVARIATE TESTS OF SIGNIFICANCE (S = 1, M = 1, N = 708)

TEST NAME	VALUE	APPROX. F	HYPOTH. DF	ERROR DF	SIG. OF F
PILLAIS	.79593	1382.64165	4.00	1418.00	.000
HOTELLINGS	3.90026	1382.64165	4.00	1418.00	.000
WILKS	.20407	1382.64165	4.00	1418.00	.000
ROYS	.79593				

EIGENVALUES AND CANONICAL CORRELATIONS

ROOT NO.	EIGENVALUE	PCT.	CUM. PCT.	CANON. COR.
1	3.90026	100.00000	100.00000	.89215

DIMENSION REDUCTION ANALYSIS

ROOTS	WILKS LAMBDA	F	HYPOTH. DF	ERROR DF	SIG. OF F
1 TO 1	.20407	1382.64165	4.00	1418.00	.000

UNIVARIATE F-TESTS WITH (1, 1421) D. F.

VARIABLE	HYPOTH. SS	ERROR SS	HYPOTH. MS	ERROR MS	F	SIG. OF F
SATCITY	3815.17176	2902.96685	3815.17176	2.04290	1867.52359	.000
SATFAM	2583.02598	2237.42740	2583.02598	1.57454	1640.49118	.000
SATFRND	2365.25846	1941.69981	2365.25846	1.36643	1730.97420	.000
HAPPY	1747.01570	573.50268	1747.01570	.40359	4328.67957	.000

125

10

DISCRIMINANT FUNCTION ANALYSIS

New SPSS^x Command:

DISCRIMINANT

Our regression analysis in Chapter 8 indicated that, when the effects on reported happiness of the variables sex, age, education, income, health, and marital status are considered simultaneously, the most important variable is health, followed by marital status and income. All the variables had statistically significant effects. However, as we discussed, regression requires the assumption that, for each value of the predictor variable, scores on the dependent variable be normally distributed with equal variances. We might be concerned that this assumption is not met adequately by our happiness measure. Or an examination of the residuals might reveal that the assumption is seriously violated. What could we do then?

  The discriminant function analysis produced by the command DISCRIMINANT does not require assumptions about the variance of the dependent variable. In fact, it is designed to work with nominal dependent variables.* DISCRIMINANT is a convenient technique for seeing the associations between a

---

*For a more complete discussion of the statistics of discriminant function analysis see William R. Klecka's *Discriminant Analysis* (Beverly Hills, CA: Sage Publications, 1980).

large set of independent variables and a dependent variable. One of its limitations, however, is that it cannot handle well a dependent variable with a large number of values. Interval variables like income or education must be recoded into a small number of categories, which involves a loss of detailed information. Hence you would want to use REGRESSION with interval dependent variables, unless they deviate sharply from a normal distribution.

The variable HAPPY can be used with DISCRIMINANT because it has only three categories. In this chapter we will replicate, using DISCRIMINANT, the regression analysis we did of happiness in Chapter 8. We will add to the analysis the variable CHILDS, the number of children the respondent has ever had, which we will refer to as parenthood.

10.1 What Discriminant Function Analysis Is and When to Use It

Discriminant function analysis is a technique for deciding into which category of a variable a case is most likely to fall. For example, you might want to know whether a job applicant is more likely to succeed in a particular position or is more likely to quit or be fired. Or you might want to know whether a home-mortgage applicant is a good risk or is more likely to default on the loan. Perhaps the least popular user of discriminant analysis is the dread Internal Revenue Service (IRS). IRS employs the technique to determine the probability that you cheated in filing your income tax return.

The greatest advantage of discriminant function analysis over regression analysis is that the dependent variable can be a nominal measure. Regression analysis can be used for a dichotomous (two-category) nominal dependent variable, if at least 20 percent of the cases are in the smallest category. However, discriminant analysis has the great advantage of being able to classify cases into three or more nominal categories—a task that regression analysis cannot handle. With discriminant analysis, we can judge better whether a person will be a Democrat, Republican, or Independent. We can predict whether one's vacation preference will most likely be Hawaii, Alaska, or Europe.

Discriminant analysis is best served when the independent variables being used to predict the correct classification of cases are interval measures and normally distributed. However, as in regression analyses, nominal independent variables often can be used through dummy variable codings with acceptable results.

10.2 How to Use DISCRIMINANT

Let's consider what occurs in discriminant analysis by replicating our regression analysis of Chapter 8. The dependent variable will still be HAPPY. The discriminant function analysis will predict for each case which of the three happiness scores is most likely. For classification variables we will use sex, age, education, income, marital status, and parenthood.

Our example uses variables from the SPSS system file NORC84. It considers the task of classifying cases into one of the three categories of HAPPY using as predictors the variables SEX, AGE, EDUC, INCOME, and MARITAL. (CHILDS will be added later.)

The SPSS^x commands would be:

```
RECODE   MARITAL  (2 THRU 5 = 0)
DISCRIMINANT   GROUPS=HAPPY(1,3)/
               VARIABLES=SEX AGE EDUC INCOME HEALTH
                         MARITAL/
               PRIORS=SIZE/
STATISTICS 13
```

The **GROUPS =** subcommand indicates the dependent variable for which group membership is being predicted. The numbers in parentheses following the variable name indicate the low and high values of the dependent variable.

The **VARIABLES =** subcommand is followed by a list of the predictor variables.

The **PRIORS = SIZE** subcommand is needed when we want the cases to be classified using prior knowledge of the proportion in each category in the sample. For example, if 15 percent of the cases in the sample are in category 1, then the analysis uses this knowledge in making the predicted classifications.

When group sizes are very unequal, small groups can have a low percentage of correct classifications even though the overall correct classification percentage is high. Using PRIORS=SIZE can worsen this problem by causing the classification of a disproportionately large number of cases into the category that has the highest proportion of the cases.

The **STATISTICS 13** command produces a table showing the accuracy of the DISCRIMINANT analysis in classifying cases.

10.3 The Accuracy of Discriminant Analysis

We use discriminant analysis to predict group membership; therefore, an obvious measure of our success is the percentage of cases that are classified correctly. Table 10.1 shows a portion of the actual output from our commands of the preceding section, a table entitled CLASSIFICATION RESULTS. The simplest summary statistic to look at is the percent of cases correctly classified, which is given at the end of the table. In our example, the percent of cases correctly classified is 57.4%. Let's compare this result to how many cases would be correctly classified by random assignment.

With two groups of equal size, we would expect 50 percent of the classifications to be correct by chance. However, when the groups are not of equal size and when each group is randomly assigned the number of cases equal to its size, the expected percent of correct classifications is found by squaring the proportion in each group and then summing the squares. In our example, this expected percent would be $(.35)^2 + (.53)^2 + (.12)^2 \times 100 = 42\%$. We can evaluate our model by comparing its proportion of errors $(1 - .57 = .43)$ to the proportion of errors that would occur if cases were classified randomly $(1 - .42 = .58)$. Therefore, our model enabled us to reduce the proportion of errors by $[(.58 - .43)/.58] \times 100 = 26\%$. (This amount is the random-error proportion minus the model-error proportion, and then divided by the random-error proportion so that the reduction in error is expressed as a proportion of the original-error proportion.

Returning to the classification results given in Table 10.1, note that each horizontal row represents the actual group membership. The first column head-

TABLE 10.1 Partial Output of DISCRIMINANT

ACTUAL GROUP	NO. OF CASES	PREDICTED GROUP MEMBERSHIP 1	2	3
GROUP 1 VERY HAPPY	456	160 35.1%	292 64.0%	4 0.9%
GROUP 2 PRETTY HAPPY	689	96 13.9%	588 85.3%	5 0.7%
GROUP 3 NOT TOO HAPPY	166	16 9.6%	145 87.3%	5 3.0%

PERCENT OF "GROUPED" CASES CORRECTLY CLASSIFIED: 57.4%

ing is ACTUAL GROUP. Under this heading the 1 identifies the row of group 1's statistics, 2 identifies the row of group 2's statistics, and so on. Proceeding to the NO. OF CASES column, we see that group 1 has 456 cases, group 2 has 689 cases, and group 3 has 166 cases.

The next three columns indicate the predicted group memberships. In this table the correct predictions are given by the diagonal percents from the upper-left number, 35.1%, to the bottom-right number, 3.0%. The number above each percentage is the actual number of cases predicted to have that group membership.

10.4 Classifying Unknown Cases

Thus far we have discussed how to derive a predictive discriminant model from a set of cases for which we know the score on the dependent variable. What if, after we have the predictive discriminant model, we want to use it to predict the group membership of cases for which we do not have that information?

The simplest method is to use the SELECT subcommand to choose the cases used for calculating the discriminant function. The STATISTICS 13 command will produce two sets of classification statistics—one for the SELECT cases and one for the remaining cases. The STATISTICS 14 command will produce each case's predicted group membership and the probability of its being in that group.

Suppose, for example, we want to predict happiness levels for a sample of people for whom we have data for the predictor variables but not for the dependent variable, HAPPY. We first would create a variable that separated the cases with known HAPPY data from those with unknown HAPPY data. Let's assume that the unknown cases are for the year 1985 and that a variable YR is coded 84 for the known cases and 85 for the unknown cases. If we add the SELECT subcommand to the DISCRIMINANT command, our example will read:

```
RECODE   MARITAL (2 THRU 5 = 0)
DISCRIMINANT   GROUPS=HAPPY (1,3)/
               VARIABLES=SEX AGE EDUC INCOME HEALTH
                         MARITAL/
               PRIORS=SIZE/
               SELECT=YR(84)/
STATISTICS 13,14
```

10.5 Evaluating the Importance of Variables: The Discriminant Function Coefficients

To determine the contribution of a particular variable to the accuracy of the discriminant analysis classifications, you can repeat the analysis but drop or add the variable in question from the VARIABLES= subcommand. The change in the percent of cases classified correctly when the variable is dropped or added represents the variable's contribution:

Contribution = % correct with variable − % correct without variable

Another method of assessing the importance of a particular variable is to look at its discriminant function coefficient. Discriminant analysis produces discriminant function coefficients for each predicting variable. For each case the score on a variable is multiplied by that variable's discriminant function coefficient. For each case this multiplication is done for all its variable scores and the products are summed. This sum is the case's **discriminant function score.** The discriminant function coefficients are calculated to maximize the differences between the groups in discriminant function scores. In other words, the ratio of between-groups variance to within-groups variance is maximized.

The set of standardized discriminant function coefficients for the predicting variables is produced as part of the DISCRIMINANT output. The standardized coefficients for our example are given in Table 10.2.

The term *standardized* indicates that each variable score is standardized before it is multiplied by the coefficient. In standardizing a variable score, the mean for that variable is subtracted from the score, and then the difference is divided by the standard deviation of the variable. For AGE the mean is 34 and

TABLE 10.2 Partial Output of DISCRIMINANT

STANDARDIZED CANONICAL DISCRIMINANT FUNCTION COEFFICIENTS

	FUNCTION 1	FUNCTION 2
SEX	0.27	0.06
AGE	0.40	−0.67
EDUC	0.15	0.63
INCOME	0.26	0.13
HEALTH	−0.59	0.32
MARITAL	0.54	0.04

the standard deviation is 8. Thus, for a case with a score of 40 on AGE, the standardized score would be $(40 - 34)/8 = .75$. Algebraically the formula is:

$$\frac{X - \bar{X}}{S_X}$$ where X equals a case score on a variable

$\bar{X}$ is the mean for the variable

S_X is the standard deviation for the variable

Standardized variables have a mean of 0 and a standard deviation of 1.

Standardized coefficients are used to remove the effects of differing means and differing standard deviations in the predicting variables. Otherwise, variables with smaller standard deviations would tend to have larger coefficients, making it difficult to assess the relative importance of the predicting variables.

As we show in section 10.6 below, the coefficients for the first function are the most important. As in our regression analysis example in Chapter 8, the variable with the biggest effect on happiness is health, followed by marital status and age. The signs of the coefficients in discriminant analysis have no special meaning. Because the dependent variable is treated as a nominal measure, we cannot think in terms of positive or negative associations.

As in regression analysis, correct assessment of each predictor variable's importance depends on having all the relevant variables in the equation.

The DISCRIMINANT program does not produce an estimate of the statistical significance of each predictor variable. To approximate the contribution of a particular variable to the statistical significance of a discriminant analysis, you will need to drop the variable in question, repeat the analysis, and then compare the statistical significance of the analyses with and without the variable. The variable's contribution is the reduction in the statistical significance, which is the likelihood that the group differences are the result of sampling probability error. (The statistical significance of an analysis is given by the Wilks' lambda, discussed in the next section.)

10.6 Evaluating the Importance of Functions: Eigenvalue, Canonical Correlation, and Wilks' Lambda

Discriminant analysis maximizes the between-groups differences on discriminant scores and minimizes the within-groups differences. Hence, one measure of how well a discriminant analysis worked is to compare the between-groups variance to the within-groups variance. The **eigenvalue,** which in DISCRIMI-

TABLE 10.3 Partial Output of DISCRIMINANT

CANONICAL DISCRIMINANT FUNCTIONS

		CANONICAL
FUNCTION	EIGENVALUE	CORRELATION
1	0.12	0.33
2	0.01	0.11

AFTER	WILKS'	
FUNCTION	LAMBDA	SIGNIFICANCE
0	0.88	0.0000
1	0.99	0.0039

NANT output is the between-groups variance divided by the within-groups variance, is one statistic for evaluating the worth of a discriminant analysis. An eigenvalue of 0 means that the discriminant analysis had no discriminating value, whereas an eigenvalue above 0.40 is considered excellent. (The discriminant analysis eigenvalue has no upper limit.) The eigenvalues for our example are given in the second column of Table 10.3.

The canonical correlation squared is the ratio of the between-groups variance in scores on the function to the total variance in scores. It is a good measure of how well the function discriminates between groups on a scale that ranges from 0.0 to 1.0.

Wilks' lambda (also called the U statistic) is the within-groups sum of squares divided by the total sum of squares. This ratio can vary from 0.0 to 1.0. The *lower* Wilks' lambda is, the better the discriminating power of the model. The Wilks' lambdas for our example are given in Table 10.3. In the AFTER FUNCTION column, the 0 indicates what the Wilks' lambda in that row is for when all the functions are in the analysis. The lambda of 0.88 indicates that differences between groups account for 12 percent of the variance in the predicting variables. The lambda for AFTER FUNCTION 1 indicates what percent of the variance is accounted for by group differences after the effects of function 1 are removed. The lambda of 0.99 indicates that the proportion of accounted for variance remaining after the effects of function 1 are removed is .01. We can see, therefore, that the effects of function 1 are much greater than the effects of function 2.

Produced with Wilks' lambda is its statistical significance. Table 10.3 shows that, when none of the functions have been dropped from the analysis, the statistical significance is 0.0000 and, when the first function is dropped from the analysis, the statistical significance is 0.0039.

10.7 Pooled Within-Groups Correlations with Functions

A statistic for examining a variable's association with a discriminant function is the Pearson correlation coefficient between a variable and that function. The DISCRIMINANT output produces this statistic for each of the variables (see Table 10.4).

The first function accounted for 12 percent of the "explained" variance (its canonical correlation squared) in the predictor variables, compared to 1 percent for the second function. Therefore, the correlations with the first function are more important than the correlations with the second function.

Variables that correlate below 0.20 with a function have only a weak association with it, and their effects tend to be unstable. The standardized discriminant function coefficients are better than the correlations for assessing a variable's impact on the discriminant function scores of cases and their predicted classification.

We can also judge the impact of an individual variable by adding or dropping it from the analysis and observing changes in the percent of cases classified correctly, the eigenvalues, the canonical correlations, and the Wilks' lambda. Table 10.6 at the end of this chapter gives the complete output from DISCRIMINANT when CHILDS is added to the analysis. (The sample changes slightly because there were 11 cases with missing values on CHILDS who were not dropped from the analysis.) When CHILDS is included in the analysis, the percentage of correctly classified cases actually drops, as does the canonical correlation coefficient. CHILDS' standardized discriminant coefficient for function 1 is the lowest for any of the predictor variables (−0.09). All the evidence suggests that parenthood is not having an impact on happiness.

TABLE 10.4 Partial Output for DISCRIMINANT

STRUCTURE MATRIX:
POOLED WITHIN-GROUPS CORRELATIONS BETWEEN DISCRIMINATING VARIABLES
    AND CANONICAL DISCRIMINANT FUNCTIONS
(VARIABLES ORDERED BY SIZE OF CORRELATION WITHIN FUNCTION)

	FUNC 1	FUNC 2
MARITAL	0.62	0.07
INCOME	0.59	0.35
HEALTH	−0.58	−0.11
SEX	0.16	0.00
AGE	0.19	−0.76
EDUC	0.32	0.76

10.8 Multicollinearity Problems

Two or more of the predictor variables may be highly correlated with each other. This condition is termed **multicollinearity** and results in unstable coefficients. One way to deal with multicollinearity is to combine the highly correlated variables into a composite variable. A second way to eliminate multicollinearity is to drop one of the two highly correlated variables.

Before doing a discriminant analysis, produce a Pearson's correlation coefficient matrix and examine the correlations among the predictor variables. If any of the correlations between two *predictor* variables is above 0.70, consider carefully the possibility of dropping one of the variables from the analysis or combining the variables.

If the group membership variable has only two categories, the higher the correlation between a *predictor* variable and the *dependent* variable the better. Just be sure you do not have a tautological relationship; that is, be sure you are not using one measure of an attribute to predict another measure of the same attribute. For example, it would not be reasonable to use years of education to predict whether or not a person is a college graduate. If the group membership variable has more than two nominal categories that cannot be ranked, its Pearson correlation coefficients with other variables are useless, even though the program will calculate them (see the discussion in Chapter 6 of levels of measurement).

10.9 Group Centroids

The **group centroid** is the point corresponding to the mean score of the group on each function. In Table 10.6, the mean score for the very happy cases on function 1 is 0.42, and their mean score on function 2 is −0.09. In classifying cases, the predicted group membership is the one whose centroid is closest to the case's discriminant function scores. For two functions, the group centroids can be plotted on a plane with each function serving as an axis. A case will be classified into the group that has the centroid closest to the case's own point when plotted on the grid formed by the two functions.

10.10 The Number of Functions

When there are more than two groups in a discriminant analysis, more than one discriminant function can be calculated. If the number of groups is K, then $K - 1$ discriminant functions can be computed. Thus with three groups, two discriminant functions can be calculated. With four groups, three discriminant functions can be calculated, and so on.

The first function has the maximum ratio of between-groups variance to within-groups sums of squares. The second function will be uncorrelated with the first function and will maximize the remaining between-groups variance to within-groups sums of squares, subject to the constraint that the functions are uncorrelated.

The output from the multigroup discriminant analysis will include an analysis of variance for each function. We may decide to use in the analysis only those functions that have a substantial between-groups *F* ratio. To limit the number of functions used in the analysis, use the **FUNCTIONS** subcommand as illustrated (indented at least one space if it begins a line):

```
FUNCTIONS=1
```

Note that the number of functions to be used is specified after the equals sign. In our example it is 1.

10.11 Summary

In a discriminant analysis we are concerned with predicting correctly to which of two or more groups each case belongs.

Information in the DISCRIMINANT output lets us know

- the percent of cases we predict correctly,
- how much better our model is than random assignment (this relationship must be calculated), and
- how much of the variance in the predicting variables is accounted for by each function, and whether this amount is statistically significant.

DISCRIMINANT does not directly provide a statistic showing how much each predictor variable contributes to our ability to classify correctly and whether this contribution is statistically significant. We can, however, approximate the contribution of an individual variable by repeating the analysis without the variable and noting the change in the percent of cases classified correctly and the change in the statistical significance of the analysis.

RESEARCH PROJECT WORK FOR CHAPTER 10

1. For your research project data set, do a discriminant function analysis of HAPPY using AGE, EDUC, HEALTH, INCOME, MARITAL, and SEX as predictor variables.

2. Discuss the possibility of spuriousness (when a variable appears to cause something but does not) for each of the predictor variables in Problem 1. That is, might

they be affected by HAPPY instead of, or in addition to, affecting HAPPY? Might both HAPPY and the predictor variable be affected by a third variable and hence be associated without being causally related?

REVIEW QUESTIONS FOR CHAPTER 10

(Answers to Review Questions are given at the back of the book.)

10.1 Write the SPSS^x command necessary to produce a discriminant analysis with CLASS as the group (dependent) variable and SEX, RACE, AGE, INCOME, EDUC, DEFENSE, and SPEND as predictor variables.

10.2 Using the SPSS system file NORC84, write all the SPSS^x commands necessary to access the file and produce the following discriminant analysis. Create the group variable FAMWORK, a combination of family status (CHILDS) and work status (WRKSTAT). Code FAMWORK 1 for nonworking women without children, 2 for nonworking women with children, 3 for working women without children, 4 for working women with children. Do the analysis for women only. Use as predictor variables: RACE, EDUC, INCOME, AGE, MAWORK, CLASS.

10.3 How can you evaluate whether a discriminant analysis was effective?

10.4 How can you determine the number of cases that would be misclassified by random assignment?

10.5 How can you determine whether a discriminant analysis is statistically significant?

10.6 How can you determine how much an individual function adds to your ability to classify cases correctly?

10.7 How do you determine the statistical significance of a particular function?

10.8 How do you determine the contribution of a particular variable to the correct classification of cases?

10.9 How do you determine the statistical significance of a particular variable?

10.10 Once you have the final discriminant function (or functions) to use for classifying new cases, how do you use it (or them) to classify new cases?

ASSIGNMENT QUESTIONS FOR CHAPTER 10

(Solutions to the Assignment Questions are provided in the *Instructor's Manual.*)

10.1 Write the SPSS^x commands necessary to access the file NORC84 and to do a discriminant analysis using UNEMP as the group variable and SEX, AGE, MARITAL, RACE, CHILDS, HEALTH, and HAPPY as the predictor variables.

10.2 What subcommand would you need to add following the VARIABLES= subcommand if the probability of being unemployed was not equal to the probability of being employed? (Let the probability of being unemployed equal .1 and the probability of being employed equal .9.)

10.3 If you ran two discriminant analyses, one with SEX and the other without SEX, in order to determine the importance of SEX in predicting unemployment correctly, how would you interpret the following results:

Percent unemployed classified correctly with SEX: 15%

Percent unemployed classified correctly without SEX: 12%

Statistical significance with SEX = .003

Statistical significance without SEX = .060

10.4 How much did the variable SEX affect the statistical significance of the discriminant analysis in Assignment Question 10.3? In other words, how much did the variable SEX reduce the likelihood that the predictions were due to sampling probability error?

10.5 How would you evaluate how much the discriminant functions improved your ability to predict whether a person would be unemployed in Assignment Question 10.3?

10.6 Looking at Table 10.5, how would you evaluate the decision to include all these variables in a discriminant analysis of being employed versus being unemployed? (Assume that they have all been coded as internal or dichotomous variables, and focus your evaluation on the correlation coefficients.)

TABLE 10.5 Pearson Correlation Coefficient Matrix for Assignment Question 10.6

	TRAINING	AGE	SEX	MARITAL	EDUC	DIPLOMA	RACE
TRAINING	1.00						
AGE	− .31	1.00					
SEX	.20	.05	1.00				
MARITAL	.70	.85	.20	1.00			
EDUC	.75	.25	.25	− .20	1.00		
DIPLOMA	.80	.15	.30	− .35	.90	1.00	
RACE	− .15	− .15	.15	− .15	.30	.10	1.00
EMPLOY	.40	.55	− .10	.60	.40	.55	− .30

TABLE 10.6 Complete Output from Commands:

```
RECODE MARITAL (2 THRU 5=0)
DISCRIMINANT  GROUPS=HAPPY(1,3)/
              VARIABLES=SEX AGE EDUC INCOME HEALTH MARITAL CHILDS/
              PRIORS=SIZE/
STATISTICS  13
```

D I S C R I M I N A N T   A N A L Y S I S

ON GROUPS DEFINED BY HAPPY   GENERAL HAPPINESS

1473 (UNWEIGHTED) CASES WERE PROCESSED.
 173 OF THESE WERE EXCLUDED FROM THE ANALYSIS.
     18 HAD MISSING OR OUT-OF-RANGE GROUP CODES.
    145 HAD AT LEAST ONE MISSING DISCRIMINATING VARIABLE.
     10 HAD BOTH.
1300 (UNWEIGHTED) CASES WILL BE USED IN THE ANALYSIS.

NUMBER OF CASES BY GROUP

	NUMBER OF CASES		
HAPPY	UNWEIGHTED	WEIGHTED	LABEL
1	451	451.0	VERY HAPPY
2	685	685.0	PRETTY HAPPY
3	164	164.0	NOT TOO HAPPY
TOTAL	1300	1300.0	

ON GROUPS DEFINED BY HAPPY   GENERAL HAPPINESS

ANALYSIS NUMBER   1

140

DIRECT METHOD: ALL VARIABLES PASSING THE TOLERANCE TEST ARE ENTERED.

MINIMUM TOLERANCE LEVEL.............. 0.00100

CANONICAL DISCRIMINANT FUNCTIONS

MAXIMUM NUMBER OF FUNCTIONS............... 2
MINIMUM CUMULATIVE PERCENT OF VARIANCE..... 100.00
MINIMUM SIGNIFICANCE OF WILKS' LAMBDA........ 1.0000

PRIOR PROBABILITIES

GROUP	PRIOR	LABEL
1	0.34692	VERY HAPPY
2	0.52692	PRETTY HAPPY
3	0.12615	NOT TOO HAPPY
TOTAL	1.00000	

CANONICAL DISCRIMINANT FUNCTIONS

FUNCTION	EIGEN-VALUE	PERCENT OF VARIANCE	CUMULATIVE PERCENT	CANONICAL CORRELATION	: AFTER : FUNCTION	WILKS' LAMBDA	CHI-SQUARED	D.F.	SIGNIFICANCE
					: 0	0.8733569	175.22	14	0.0
1*	0.12520	87.68	87.68	0.3335760	: 1	0.9827055	22.575	6	0.0010
2*	0.01760	12.32	100.00	0.1315086	:				

* MARKS THE 2 CANONICAL DISCRIMINANT FUNCTIONS REMAINING IN THE ANALYSIS.

STANDARDIZED CANONICAL DISCRIMINANT FUNCTION COEFFICIENTS

	FUNC 1	FUNC 2
SEX	0.27448	0.04831
AGE	0.43428	-0.44218
EDUC	0.13995	0.42995
INCOME	0.22672	0.12290
HEALTH	-0.59839	0.31491
MARITAL	0.57623	0.13901
CHILDS	-0.09066	-0.53120

141

TABLE 10.5 *Continued*

STRUCTURE MATRIX:

POOLED WITHIN-GROUPS CORRELATIONS BETWEEN DISCRIMINATING VARIABLES
   AND CANONICAL DISCRIMINANT FUNCTIONS
(VARIABLES ORDERED BY SIZE OF CORRELATION WITHIN FUNCTION)

	FUNC 1	FUNC 2
MARITAL	0.62334*	0.06193
HEALTH	-0.58351*	-0.07599
INCOME	0.57782*	0.30161
SEX	0.16060*	-0.04068
CHILDS	0.07290	-0.74606*
AGE	0.18091	-0.68500*
EDUC	0.31873	0.65358*

CANONICAL DISCRIMINANT FUNCTIONS EVALUATED AT GROUP MEANS (GROUP CENTROIDS)

GROUP	FUNC 1	FUNC 2
1	0.41776	-0.09231
2	-0.11326	0.11816
3	-0.67576	-0.23966

CLASSIFICATION RESULTS -

ACTUAL GROUP	NO. OF CASES	PREDICTED GROUP MEMBERSHIP		
		1	2	3
GROUP 1 VERY HAPPY	451	158 35.0%	288 63.9%	5 1.1%
GROUP 2 PRETTY HAPPY	685	103 15.0%	569 83.1%	13 1.9%
GROUP 3 NOT TOO HAPPY	164	18 11.0%	139 84.8%	7 4.3%
UNGROUPED CASES	18	4 22.2%	14 77.8%	0 0.0%

PERCENT OF "GROUPED" CASES CORRECTLY CLASSIFIED: 56.46%

CLASSIFICATION PROCESSING SUMMARY

   1473   CASES WERE PROCESSED.
      0   CASES WERE EXCLUDED FOR MISSING OR OUT-OF-RANGE GROUP CODES.
    155   CASES HAD AT LEAST ONE MISSING DISCRIMINATING VARIABLE.
   1318   CASES WERE USED FOR PRINTED OUTPUT.

143

11

LOG-LINEAR MODELS

New SPSS^x Command:

HILOGLINEAR

We have seen that happiness is affected by income, age, and sex. We have questioned whether the effects of these variables are the same for all groups. For example, perhaps income is more important for men than for women in affecting happiness. Perhaps income is more important at some ages than at others. Maybe the effects of age are not the same for men as for women. Answers to these questions may be found in crosstabulation tables, but the tables are so complex and have so many cells that it is a tedious task to evaluate all the possible interactions among the variables.

The log-linear analyses that can be done with the SPSS^x command HILOGLINEAR swiftly untangle the information in a crosstabulation table. The output reveals which associations are most important and whether or not they are statistically significant. With a little additional work, we can state very precisely how interactions among certain variables affect the likelihood that a subject will be in a particular category on another variable.

11.1 When to Use **HILOGLINEAR**

The program produced by the HILOGLINEAR command is a way of summarizing and highlighting the associations in a complex crosstabulation table. Log-linear models such as HILOGLINEAR are called for when (1) your analysis involves three or more variables and (2) the variables are nominal, highly skewed in their distribution, or nonlinear in their effects.*

Often nominal variables are dummy coded and treated as interval variables in regression or analysis of variance. The more skewed the variable is to one category, the more this practice leads to biased coefficients. For example, if over 80% of the labor force is employed, married, and nonmigrant, dummy coding any of these variables in a study of worker satisfaction in the United States could distort the results.

The greatest disadvantage of log-linear models is that they need a large number of cases. A rough rule of thumb is that your sample size should be at least five times the number of cells in the table.

One way researchers reduce the number of cells in the analysis (and hence the number of cases they need) is by collapsing categories of ordinal or interval variables that are being used in a log-linear model. For example, instead of having the exact age of each respondent, one can code age into ten-year intervals. In recoding the categories some precision is lost, and we assume that the effects of the variable do not differ significantly within these categories. Collapsing of categories is a practice to be adopted only from necessity.

11.2 How to Use **HILOGLINEAR**

As with other advanced techniques, begin a HILOGLINEAR analysis by checking the frequency distribution of all the variables you intend to use to ensure they are coded correctly and to familiarize yourself with their distribution. Because we have already done this initial work with the NORC84 data file in earlier chapters, we can move on to an actual log-linear analysis.

Let's see what more can be learned about happiness using the log-linear analysis produced by the HILOGLINEAR command. (Other log-linear techniques are available with SPSS^x; however, HILOGLINEAR is the simplest to

---

*For a more complete discussion of log-linear analysis see David Knoke and Peter J. Burke's *Log-Linear Models* (Beverly Hills, CA: Sage Publications, 1980) and H. T. Reynolds' *Analysis of Nominal Data* (Beverly Hills, CA: Sage Publications, 1977).

use, requires less computer time, and uses less CPU memory space.) To use HILOGLINEAR, you must assume that the log-linear effects are hierarchical. This means that if a variable is in the model as a third-order effect, it must be in the model as a second-order effect. (A second-order effect involves the interaction of two variables, a third-order effect involves the interaction of three variables, and so on.) In most analyses this assumption is not bothersome, because the researcher would not conceptualize a variable as having important higher-order effects unless the lower-order effects were also important.

We have reason to believe that happiness is affected by a person's sex and age. Perhaps the effects of age will be different for males than for females. Further along in the analysis, we will be adding more variables (and thus more cells), so we will recode age into ten-year intervals to ensure that we have enough cases. (98 and 99 are missing value codes. Therefore, we cannot use the keyword HI in our RECODE command.) Likewise, we can consider the interactions of INCOME with the other variables, but we need to recode it into a smaller number of categories. Our RECODE statements will be

```
RECODE    AGE  (18 THRU 29=1) (30 THRU 39=2) (40 THRU 49=3)
               (50 THRU 59=4) (60 THRU 69=5) (70 THRU 97=6)
RECODE    INCOME  (1,2=1) (3,4=2) (5,6=3)
               (7,8=4)
```

This recoding of variables leaves us with 120 cells in our crosstabulation table. We find this number by multiplying together the number of categories in each variable (HAPPY $*$ SEX $*$ AGE $*$ INCOME = 3 $*$ 2 $*$ 6 $*$ 4 = 120). Our NORC84 sample size of 1473 is far more than 5 $*$ 120 = 600. (Recall that the sample size should be at least five times the number of cells.)

The simplest approach to using the HILOGLINEAR command in SPSS^x is with the subcommand **PRINT ALL.** This subcommand produces a table that shows the chi-square and probabilities of each order effect. Recall that a chi-square statistic is based on the difference between what you would expect to find in each cell, if there were no associations, versus what was actually found.

The first-order effects test the assumption that each category of a variable has the same number of cases. This assumption is rarely true, and, because it tells us nothing about associations among the variables, we are not very interested in this statistic.

The two-way, or second-order, effects test the assumption that the variables are independent. The likelihood ratio chi-square for this model can be treated as a total error term that can be partitioned into parts associated with each variable. These effects are the bivariate associations controlling for the effects of the other variables.

The three-way and higher-order effects are interaction effects. These effects are usually small and difficult to interpret. Essentially, an interaction effect means that a variable has one effect for one group but a different effect for another group. For example, if the effects of age on the likelihood of being happy were different for men than for women, this effect would be third-order.

The HILOGLINEAR command and accompanying PRINT=ALL subcommand needed for our analysis of the effects on happiness of age controlling for sex and income are:

```
HILOGLINEAR   SEX (1,2)  AGE (1,6)  INCOME (1,4)
              HAPPY (1,3)/
              PRINT ALL
```

Note that the PRINT subcommand is preceded by a slash indicating the variable specifications have ended. The printout is easier to read if the dependent variable is listed last. When placed in the context of the SPSS^x commands needed to recode AGE and INCOME, our set of commands is:

```
RECODE   AGE   (18 THRU 29=1) (30 THRU 39=2) (40 THRU 49=3)
               (50 THRU 59=4) (60 THRU 69=5) (70 THRU 97=6)
RECODE   INCOME  (1,2=1) (3,4=2) (5,6=3)
                 (7,8=4)
HILOGLINEAR   SEX (1,2)  AGE (1,6)  INCOME (1,4)
              HAPPY (1,3)/
              PRINT ALL
```

11.3 Interpreting HILOGLINEAR Output

The output from the preceding set of commands will include the information given in Table 11.1. (An example of the complete output is given in Table 11.4 at the end of this chapter.) In the first row of the table, the 1 indicates that this row contains the information on the first-order effects. This information tests the hypothesis that the cases are equally distributed throughout the cells. We are not interested in testing this hypothesis, because we do not expect to have the same number of males as females or the same number of older people as younger people in our sample.

In the second row, the 2 indicates that these effects are second-order. These effects are of interest because we want to know whether the variables SEX, AGE, and INCOME are associated with HAPPY. The 41 in the DF column

TABLE 11.1 Partial Output from HILOGLINEAR

TESTS THAT K-WAY EFFECTS ARE ZERO.

K	DF	L.R. CHISQ	PROB
1	11	593.2	.000
2	41	263.4	.000
3	62	84.5	.019
4	29	29.9	.579

indicates that there are 41 degrees of freedom when all the second-order effects are considered. The next number to the right, 263.4 in the L.R. CHISQ column, is the likelihood ratio chi-square for the second-order effects. If there were no associations among the variables, this measure would be 0.0. The next number to the right, .000 in the PROB column, is the probability that the chi-square for this row differs from 0.0 because of sampling error. We can see that it is unlikely—less than 1 time out of 1000—that the associations we find in this row are due to sampling error.

The row beginning with a 3 in the K column pertains to third-order effects. The probability of .019 tells us that the third-order effects are **statistically significant,** meaning that they are unlikely to be caused by sampling error.

The final row regards the fourth-order effects. These effects have a sampling error probability, .579. Fourth-order effects are difficult to verbalize and interpret. For example, significant fourth-order effects might indicate that the effects of income on happiness for older males are different from the effects of income for older females or that the effects of age on happiness are different for wealthy males than for poor males. It is helpful to know that there are significant fourth-order effects in our analysis, but we are still faced with the task of ransacking a crosstabulation table to locate them precisely.

The next table of special interest in the output is entitled TESTS OF PARTIAL ASSOCIATIONS (see Table 11.2). This table gives the partial chi-square and the probabilities for all the associations except the highest-order association. (Information for the highest-order association was given in the preceding table.)

Examine Table 11.2 carefully. The left column, entitled EFFECT NAME, designates each association examined in the analysis. The top row, SEX*AGE* INCOME, shows the association between sex, age, and income. In that row, we can see the following statistics: there are 15 degrees of freedom in this association, the partial chi-square is 21.4, and the probability that an association this large could occur by sampling error is .125. The third-order effect that is

TABLE 11.2 Partial Output from HILOGLINEAR

TESTS OF PARTIAL ASSOCIATIONS.

EFFECT NAME	DF	PARTIAL CHISQ	PROB
SEX*AGE*INCOME	15	21.4	.125
SEX*AGE*HAPPY	10	5.7	.839
SEX*INCOME*HAPPY	6	8.9	.176
AGE*INCOME*HAPPY	30	47.6	.022
SEX*AGE	5	5.0	.413
SEX*INCOME	3	19.8	.000
AGE*INCOME	15	149.0	.000
SEX*HAPPY	2	8.8	.012
AGE*HAPPY	10	33.2	.000
INCOME*HAPPY	6	76.8	.000
SEX	1	32.6	.000
AGE	5	190.6	.000
INCOME	3	25.9	.000
HAPPY	2	344.0	.000

most statistically significant is AGE*INCOME*HAPPY, which has a probability of .022 of resulting from sampling error. This suggests that the effects of income differ by age, or the effects of age differ by income, or both.

With the exception of the association between age and sex, all the second-order effects are significant, below the .05 level.

The chi-squares for the single variables are all significant; however, this result merely means that there were not an equal number of cases in each of the cells. It tells us nothing about associations between the variables.

We return to our original question of whether the effects of age on happiness differ for men and women. The SEX*AGE*HAPPY row shows that the differences are so small that 839 times out of 1000 they could result from sampling error.

Are the effects of income on happiness different for men than for women? The SEX*INCOME*HAPPY row indicates that there are most likely some differences, but they are so small that 176 times out of 1000 such differences would occur from sampling error.

The output from HILOGLINEAR includes an initial portion entitled OBSERVED, EXPECTED FREQUENCIES AND RESIDUALS (see Table 11.3). We can use this table to describe each association more precisely. For example, we can compare the odds of a male over age 70 with $10,000 to $19,000 income reporting being very happy with the odds of a male under age 30 with the same income being very happy. (Recall that very happy respondents were coded 1 on

HAPPY.) To make this comparison, we examine the OBS. COUNT (observed count) column of the table. In Table 11.3 the numbers for the 4 middle-age categories are omitted for brevity.

We can see that 12 out of 55, or 22 percent, of the under-30 males report being very happy. (55 is the total of 12 + 32 + 11.) For the males over age 70, 6 out of 15, or 40 percent, report being very happy. Thus, in this income range the likelihood that a male over age 70 will be very happy is almost twice as great as the likelihood for a male under age 30.

The HILOGLINEAR output gives a staggering amount of information. A sensible approach is to look at the summary statistics on the associations to see which are most important. Then dig into the table of observed counts to see the details of the association.

One also has the option of printing out coefficients and significance levels for each cell. Unfortunately, the present form of HILOGLINEAR output for these statistics is not easy to interpret. As Reynolds notes, researchers will probably use log-linear models to detect the presence or absence of a model. Afterwards, "it may be easier to measure the strength of association with other statistics." (H. T. Reynolds, 1977, p. 65.) For example, doing a crosstabulation of HAPPY by AGE controlling for SEX and INCOME would allow us to see easily the percentage of men who were very happy compared to the percentage of women who were very happy in each income group. (See Chapter 5 for a discussion of crosstabulations.)

TABLE 11.3 Partial Output of HILOGLINEAR

OBSERVED, EXPECTED FREQUENCIES AND RESIDUALS

FACTOR	CODE	OBS. COUNT
SEX	1	
AGE	1	
INCOME	2	
HAPPY	1	12
HAPPY	2	32
HAPPY	3	11
AGE	6	
INCOME	2	
HAPPY	1	6
HAPPY	2	7
HAPPY	3	2

11.4 Summary

Log-linear models are a way of summarizing and highlighting the associations in a complex crosstabulation table. Log-linear models such as HILOGLINEAR are called for when your analysis involves three or more variables, all of which are either nominal, highly skewed in their distribution, or nonlinear in their effects.

The greatest disadvantage of log-linear models is that they require a large number of cases. A rough rule of thumb is that your sample size should be at least five times the number of cells in the table.

11.5 Where to Look in the *SPSS*ˣ *User's Guide*

*   HILOGLINEAR is discussed on pages 553–566.

RESEARCH PROJECT WORK FOR CHAPTER 11

For your research project data file, replicate the example analysis of this chapter. Describe any differences between the outcome of your analysis and the outcome of our example, and discuss the possible causes of these differences.

REVIEW QUESTIONS FOR CHAPTER 11

(Answers to Review Questions are given at the back of the book.)

11.1 What assumptions are made for regression analysis that are not required for log-linear models?

11.2 What advantages are there to doing a log-linear analysis instead of a cross-tabulation?

11.3 How many cases would normally be required to do a log-linear analysis of health (four categories) by marital (five categories) by religion (five categories)?

11.4 Write the SPSSˣ commands that would produce a hierarchical log-linear analysis of the variables HEALTH, MARITAL, and RELIGION. Treat HEALTH as the dependent variable. Include the subcommand necessary to produce a printout of associations.

11.5 What would the first-order effects in the analysis of Review Question 11.4 indicate?

11.6 What would the second-order effects from Review Question 11.4 indicate?

11.7 What would the third-order effects from Review Question 11.4 indicate?

11.8 The chi-square and probability of the highest-order effects are omitted from the HILOGLINEAR output for TESTS OF PARTIAL ASSOCIATIONS. How can these statistics be found?

11.9 How would you interpret a probability of .023 for the partial chi-square of the effect HEALTH*MARITAL?

11.10 If the output from HILOGLINEAR indicates that a particular association is significant, what is the simplest way to determine the strength of the association?

ASSIGNMENT QUESTIONS FOR CHAPTER 11

(Solutions to the Assignment Questions are provided in the *Instructor's Manual.*)

11.1 What assumptions are made in analysis of variance that are not required in log-linear analysis?

11.2 Write the HILOGLINEAR command and subcommands needed to analyze SEX by RELIGION by MARITAL by SATFAM in the NORC84 file making SATFAM the dependent variable.

11.3 If the following table resulted from the commands in Assignment Question 11.2, what would these statistics mean?

TESTS THAT K-WAY AND HIGHER ORDER EFFECTS ARE ZERO.

K	DF	L.R. CHISQ	PROB
4	14	5.4	.452
3	26	8.2	.220
2	37	40.7	.043
1	45	607.7	.000

11.4 What would the following portion of output from Assignment Question 11.2 indicate?

TESTS OF PARTIAL ASSOCIATIONS.

EFFECT NAME	DF	PARTIAL CHISQ	PROB
SEX*RELIG*SATJOB	24	13.654	.354
SEX*MARITAL*RELIG	16	34.234	.463
SEX*MARITAL*SATJOB	70	73.004	.453
SEX*MARITAL	5	5.929	.312
SEX*RELIG	2	2.141	.343
SEX*SATJOB	24	13.654	.050
MARITAL*RELIG	16	34.234	.463

MARITAL*SATJOB	70	73.004	.003
SATJOB*RELIG	5	5.929	.312
SEX	10	2.141	.343
MARITAL	1	33.433	.000
RELIG	5	129.233	.000
SATJOB	2	404.293	.000

11.5 What would the following portion of output from Assignment Question 11.2 indicate?

OBSERVED, EXPECTED FREQUENCIES AND RESIDUALS.

FACTOR	CODE	OBS. COUNT & PCT.
SEX	1	
MARITAL	1	
RELIGION	1	
SATJOB	1	11.00
SATJOB	2	25.00
SATJOB	3	33.00
SATJOB	4	24.00
SATJOB	5	23.00
SATJOB	6	33.00
SATJOB	7	23.00
SEX	2	
MARITAL	1	
RELIGION	1	
SATJOB	1	22.00
SATJOB	2	50.00
SATJOB	3	66.00
SATJOB	4	48.00
SATJOB	5	46.00
SATJOB	6	66.00
SATJOB	7	46.00

TABLE 11.4 More Complete Output From Commands:

```
HILOGLINEAR   SEX(1,2)   AGE(1,6)   INCOME(1,4)   HAPPY(1,3) /
              PRINT ALL

*********************   H I E R A R C H I C A L   L O G   L I N E A R   *********************

DATA INFORMATION
    1319 UNWEIGHTED CASES ACCEPTED.
       0 CASES REJECTED BECAUSE OF OUT-OF-RANGE FACTOR VALUES.
     154 CASES REJECTED BECAUSE OF MISSING DATA.
    1319 WEIGHTED CASES WILL BE USED IN THE ANALYSIS.

FACTOR INFORMATION
    FACTOR    LEVEL    LABEL
    SEX         2      RESPONDENT'S SEX
    AGE         6      AGE OF RESPONDENT
    INCOME      4      TOTAL FAMILY INCOME
    HAPPY       3      GENERAL HAPPINESS

DESIGN 1 HAS GENERATING CLASS

    SEX*AGE*INCOME*HAPPY

THE ITERATIVE PROPORTIONAL FIT ALGORITHM CONVERGED AT ITERATION 1.
THE MAXIMUM DIFFERENCE BETWEEN OBSERVED AND FITTED MARGINAL TOTALS IS     .000
AND THE CONVERGENCE CRITERION IS    .250
```

TABLE 11.4 *Continued*

OBSERVED, EXPECTED FREQUENCIES AND RESIDUALS.

FACTOR	CODE	OBS. COUNT & PCT.		EXP. COUNT & PCT.		RESIDUAL	STD. RESID.
SEX	MALE						
AGE	1						
INCOME	1						
HAPPY	1	10.00	(.76)	10.00	(.76)	.000	.000
HAPPY	2	20.00	(1.52)	20.00	(1.52)	.000	.000
HAPPY	3	8.00	(.61)	8.00	(.61)	.000	.000
INCOME	2						
HAPPY	1	12.00	(.91)	12.00	(.91)	.000	.000
HAPPY	2	32.00	(2.43)	32.00	(2.43)	.000	.000
HAPPY	3	11.00	(.83)	11.00	(.83)	.000	.000
INCOME	3						
HAPPY	1	13.00	(.99)	13.00	(.99)	.000	.000
HAPPY	2	25.00	(1.90)	25.00	(1.90)	.000	.000
HAPPY	3	1.00	(.08)	1.00	(.08)	.000	.000
INCOME	4						
HAPPY	1	9.00	(.68)	9.00	(.68)	.000	.000
HAPPY	2	13.00	(.99)	13.00	(.99)	.000	.000
HAPPY	3	3.00	(.23)	3.00	(.23)	.000	.000
AGE	2						
INCOME	1						
HAPPY	1	1.00	(.08)	1.00	(.08)	.000	.000
HAPPY	2	12.00	(.91)	12.00	(.91)	.000	.000
HAPPY	3	2.00	(.15)	2.00	(.15)	.000	.000
INCOME	2						
HAPPY	1	8.00	(.61)	8.00	(.61)	.000	.000
HAPPY	2	19.00	(1.44)	19.00	(1.44)	.000	.000
HAPPY	3	4.00	(.30)	4.00	(.30)	.000	.000
INCOME	3						
HAPPY	1	9.00	(.68)	9.00	(.68)	.000	.000

. . .

GOODNESS-OF-FIT TEST STATISTICS

LIKELIHOOD RATIO CHI SQUARE =   .00000   DF = 0   P = 1.000
PEARSON CHI SQUARE   =   .00000   DF = 0   P = 1.000

TESTS THAT K-WAY AND HIGHER ORDER EFFECTS ARE ZERO.

K	DF	L.R. CHISQ	PROB	PEARSON CHISQ	PROB	ITERATION
4	29	29.866	.4207	26.858	.5794	NA
3	91	114.382	.0493	114.080	.0512	NA
2	132	377.831	.0000	385.269	.0000	NA
1	143	970.997	.0000	1101.051	.0000	0

TESTS THAT K-WAY EFFECTS ARE ZERO.

K	DF	L.R. CHISQ	PROB	PEARSON CHISQ	PROB	ITERATION
1	11	593.166	.0000	715.782	.0000	0
2	41	263.449	.0000	271.190	.0000	0
3	62	84.516	.0303	87.221	.0191	0
4	29	29.866	.4207	26.858	.5794	0

TESTS OF PARTIAL ASSOCIATIONS.

EFFECT NAME	DF	PARTIAL CHISQ	PROB	ITER
SEX*AGE*INCOME	15	21.390	.1248	4
SEX*AGE*HAPPY	10	5.711	.8389	3
SEX*INCOME*HAPPY	6	8.949	.1764	4
AGE*INCOME*HAPPY	30	47.643	.0215	5
SEX*AGE	5	5.025	.4128	5
SEX*INCOME	3	19.757	.0002	5
AGE*INCOME	15	149.014	.0000	4
INCOME*HAPPY	2	8.780	.0124	5
SEX	10	33.179	.0003	4
AGE	6	76.839	.0000	3
INCOME	1	32.618	.0000	2
HAPPY	5	190.649	.0000	2
	3	25.886	.0000	2
	2	343.995	.0000	2

12

FACTOR ANALYSIS

New SPSS^x Command:

FACTOR

Looking at the variables in the NORC84 file, we can see many that may affect happiness that are not yet in our analysis, including SIBS, CHILDS, HELPFUL, FAIR, CONEDUC, CONPRESS, CONLEGIS, SATFAM, SATFRND, SATJOB. On closer inspection, some of these variables together appear to be measuring a more general variable. For example, HELPFUL, FAIR, CONEDUC, CONPRESS, and CONLEGIS may all measure trust in others. SATFAM, SATFRND, and SATJOB may all be indicators of satisfaction with one's social position. SIBS, CHILDS, and MARITAL (which is already in our analysis) may be measures of the extensiveness of one's family network.

Working with a large number of variables is tedious. If the variables are really just different measures of another more general variable, we can facilitate and simplify our work by constructing a measure of the general variable and using that measure in our analysis. **Factor analysis** is a way of measuring a general variable, or **factor,** underlying a large set of variables. This method

159

also helps in dealing with the problem of multicollinearity, discussed in earlier chapters.*

12.1 What Factor Analysis Is and When to Use It

Often a researcher has several variables that appear to be related to one another because they are different ways of measuring one general variable or factor.

Factor analysis is a technique for condensing many variables into a few underlying constructs. For example, we might have a 100-item test that we think measures three distinct abilities: verbal, mathematical, and analytical. Using factor analysis we could try to obtain a "factor score" for each of these abilities. Our analysis would reveal whether there were less or more than three distinct factors. Our analysis would also reveal which variables were most closely associated with each factor and would weigh those variables most heavily in calculating the factor scores.

Factor analysis is not necessary when one already knows (1) which variables measure each factor and (2) the variables' relative importance—for example, one may have predetermined that all the variables will be weighted equally.

Before doing a factor analysis, you should examine a correlation matrix of the variables. Because you are assuming that underlying factors account for the variance in all the variables, it is questionable to include any variable whose correlations with the other variables are all below 0.4 in absolute value.

Factor analysis is sometimes used when the researcher has a large set of variables and suspects that they could be summarized more concisely by a few underlying factors but is not certain what these factors would be. This use of factor analysis would be termed *exploratory*.

12.2 How to Use FACTOR

To do a factor analysis for the variables mentioned at the beginning of this chapter as possible influences on happiness, we would use the following commands:

---

*For a more complete discussion of factor analysis see Jae-On Kim and Charles W. Mueller's *Introduction to Factor Analysis: What It Is and How to Do It* (Beverly Hills, CA: Sage Publications, 1978).

FACTOR   VARIABLES=SIBS MARITAL CHILDS HELPFUL FAIR
                    CONEDUC CONPRESS CONLEGIS SATFAM
                    SATFRND SATJOB

By default, FACTOR in SPSS^x uses a technique called *principal components* to extract factors. Several other extraction techniques are available; however, principal components is the most frequently used. (See the *SPSS^x User's Guide*, pages 718–719, for a list of the other SPSS^x extraction techniques available and the subcommands used to initiate them.)

First the principal-components method calculates a factor that will explain the maximum variance in all the variables. Then a second factor is calculated that explains the maximum amount of the remaining variance. However, the second factor has the restriction that it cannot be correlated with the first factor. Another way of stating that two factors are not correlated with each other is to say they are **orthogonal.**

The process can be continued until all the variance in the variables has been explained. Normally this point is reached when the number of factors equals the number of variables. Such a solution is not helpful, however, because we are striving for greater simplicity. Having as many factors as there are variables does not simplify anything! Most researchers use the eigenvalue statistic, discussed in the next section, to decide how many factors to use in their analysis.

12.3 Output from FACTOR

The first part of the factor analysis output will be a table entitled INITIAL STATISTICS. Part of this output is given in Table 12.1. (Table 12.7 presents complete output.) The far left column gives the names of all variables used in the factor analysis. To the right of the names is a column of COMMUNALITY statistics. The **communality** statistic for each variable is the proportion of variance in the variable explained by all the factors. The communality of a variable can range from 0.0, indicating absolutely no association, to 1.0, indicating a perfect association. When a principal-components extraction is done, the communality of each variable in the initial statistics will be 1.0, which results from the initial analysis having as many factors as there are variables.

The third column gives the factor numbers. All the statistics to the right of the factor number apply to that factor number—not to the variable named on the far left. Accordingly, the column of eigenvalue statistics pertains to the factors, not the variables. For example, the eigenvalue 1.96 in the first row indicates the amount of variance underlying all the variables associated with factor 1. The sum of the eigenvalues equals the number of variables; hence, an eigen-

TABLE 12.1 Partial Output of FACTOR

INITIAL STATISTICS:

VARIABLE	COMMUNALITY	*	FACTOR	EIGENVALUE	PCT OF VAR
		*			
SIBS	1.0	*	1	1.96	17.8
MARITAL	1.0	*	2	1.45	13.2
CHILDS	1.0	*	3	1.35	12.3
HELPFUL	1.0	*	4	1.04	9.5
FAIR	1.0	*	5	.91	8.3
CONEDUC	1.0	*	6	.87	7.9
CONPRESS	1.0	*	7	.84	7.6
CONLEGIS	1.0	*	8	.79	7.1
SATFAM	1.0	*	9	.69	6.2
SATFRND	1.0	*	10	.67	6.1
SATJOB	1.0	*	11	.45	4.1

TABLE 12.2 Partial Output of FACTOR

FACTOR MATRIX:

	FACTOR 1	FACTOR 2	FACTOR 3	FACTOR 4
SIBS	.10	.39	.61	.21
MARITAL	.40	-.47	-.09	.16
CHILDS	-.17	.56	.40	.39
HELPFUL	.36	.31	.28	-.44
FAIR	-.42	-.20	-.13	.59
CONEDUC	.30	.46	-.45	.03
CONPRESS	.09	.37	-.47	.16
CONLEGIS	.38	.44	-.46	.08
SATFAM	.71	-.28	.04	.39
SATFRND	.69	-.03	.24	.23
SATJOB	.46	-.14	.08	-.21

value of 1.96 in an analysis of 11 variables shows that the proportion of the variance explained by factor 1 is 1.96 divided by 11, or 17.8 percent, as indicated in the PCT OF VAR (percent of variance) column on the right.

Following the initial statistics is a table entitled FACTOR MATRIX that gives more information about the first extraction (see Table 12.2). In the factor matrix are the loadings of each variable on each factor. The **factor loading** is the correlation of a variable with a factor. For example, the factor loading of SIBS on factor 1 is .10. The factor loadings of SIBS on factor 2, factor 3, and factor 4 are

TABLE 12.3 Partial Output of FACTOR

FINAL STATISTICS:

VARIABLE	COMMUNALITY	*	FACTOR	EIGENVALUE	PCT OF VAR
		*			
SIBS	.58	*	1	1.96	17.8
MARITAL	.42	*	2	1.45	13.2
CHILDS	.65	*	3	1.35	12.3
HELPFUL	.49	*	4	1.04	9.5
FAIR	.58	*			
CONEDUC	.52	*			
CONPRESS	.39	*			
CONLEGIS	.55	*			
SATFAM	.73	*			
SATFRND	.59	*			
SATJOB	.28	*			

.39, .61, and .21, respectively. A factor loading of .10 means that $(.10)^2$ or 1 percent of the variance in SIBS is accounted for by factor 1.

The next portion of FACTOR output is a table entitled FINAL STATISTICS (see Table 12.3). Note that the communalities no longer equal 1. The final statistics are based only on factors with an eigenvalue greater than 1. In our example, only the first four factors had an eigenvalue greater than 1 (see Table 12.1). Although the communalities no longer equal 1, meaning that not all the variance in the variables is accounted for, we have simplified our data from 11 variables to 4 factors.

For example, with SIBS we have accounted for $(.58)^2$ or 34 percent of its variance using the first four factors.

12.4 Rotating Factors

Rotating factors is a method of simplifying factors so that each variable tends to load highly on only one factor. Remember that the first factor was calculated to maximize the total amount of variance it could explain. In using this procedure, the factor may have distorted somewhat in order to accommodate some of the variance of variables that are not really part of the factor. Rotating the factors helps correct this distortion.

An important decision we have to make is whether to do an **orthogonal rotation,** which means that the factors will remain uncorrelated, or an **oblique rotation,** which means that the factors will be allowed to correlate with one another. The choice is up to the researcher. If we thought the factors were truly

TABLE 12.4 Partial Output for FACTOR: Orthogonal Rotation

ROTATED FACTOR MATRIX:

	FACTOR 1	FACTOR 2	FACTOR 3	FACTOR 4
SIBS	.09	−.11	.73	.16
MARITAL	.57	−.07	−.29	−.07
CHILDS	−.14	.08	.78	−.13
HELPFUL	.01	.04	.17	.68
FAIR	−.02	−.07	.06	−.76
CONEDUC	.02	.71	−.01	.12
CONPRESS	−.06	.61	−.01	−.12
CONLEGIS	.11	.72	.00	.11
SATFAM	.85	.09	.01	.00
SATFRND	.69	.07	.23	.23
SATJOB	.34	−.03	−.14	.39

distinct and unassociated with one another, we would do an orthogonal rotation. For example, we might be doing a profile of consumers in which one factor is rustic preferences and a second factor is luxury designer preferences. If we decide that these two factors are not associated with each other, we can do an orthogonal rotation.

As another example, we might be doing a profile of diet preferences that has a sweet food factor and a fatty food factor. If we decide these two factors are associated, we will want to do an oblique rotation.

A varimax orthogonal rotation is produced by default, so no additional commands are needed. In a **varimax rotation,** the calculations are done to maximize the tendency of each variable to load highly on only one factor. Other orthogonal rotation techniques are available; however, the varimax is the most frequently used. (See the *SPSS* *User's Guide,* Section 37.15, for a list of other rotation techniques available.)

The final portion of output from the FACTOR command would be the ROTATED FACTOR MATRIX presented in Table 12.4. In this factor matrix after the rotation, the variables tend to be more extreme in their loadings. Interpretation of the results is simplified because each factor is more clearly identified by a subset of variables that load high on it but low on other factors. Note, for example, that MARITAL loads .57 on factor 1 and −.07 on factor 2. Before the rotation, its loading was .40 on factor 1 and −.47 on factor 2 (see Table 12.2).

An orthogonal rotation does not change the communalities of the variables. Just as much variance is explained after the rotation as before. Likewise, an orthogonal rotation does not change the eigenvalues of the factors. Each factor explains the same proportion of the variance as it did before the rotation.

Furthermore, after an orthogonal rotation, the correlation between the factors remains 0.0, as it was before the rotation.

Now let's do an oblique rotation of the same data. An oblique rotation allows for some correlation between factors. To do an oblique rotation, we must add the subcommand **ROTATION = OBLIQUE** preceded by a slash. The SPSS[x] commands for our example will now be:

```
FACTOR   VARIABLES=SIBS MARITAL CHILDS HELPFUL FAIR
              CONEDUC CONPRESS CONLEGIS SATFAM
              SATFRND SATJOB/
         ROTATION=OBLIQUE
```

The default method of oblique rotation employed by SPSS[x] is called **oblimin.** When an oblique rotation is done, the output differs somewhat from an orthogonal rotation. Instead of a factor matrix, an oblique rotation produces both a *factor pattern* matrix and a *factor structure* matrix.

The **factor pattern matrix** contains the regression coefficients of each variable for each factor produced when the variable is regressed on the factors (see Chapter 8 for a discussion of regression). These regression coefficients are not the same as the correlations of the variables with the factors, because a regression coefficient is affected by intercorrelations among the factors. On the other hand, a correlation between a variable and a factor is not affected by intercorrelations among the variables. This distinction is not necessary prior to rotation or after an orthogonal rotation, because there are zero correlations among all the factors until we do an oblique rotation.

As an example of a factor pattern matrix coefficient, look at the first variable, SIBS, in the left-hand column of Table 12.5. To the right of this variable, in the FACTOR 1 column, is the coefficient .12, which is the regression coefficient, or factor loading, of SIBS on factor 1. The loadings of SIBS on factor 2, factor 3, and factor 4, respectively, are .74, .13, and −.12. These loadings indicate the relative importance of the factors in accounting for variance in SIBS.

Looking at the factors, we can see that factor 1 has high pattern matrix coefficients for satisfaction with family (.87) and friends (.70) and a moderately high coefficient for marital status (.57). We might label this the good relationships factor. Factor 2 has high loadings on SIBS (.74) and CHILDS (.78) and might be labeled the relative factor. Factor 3 has high loadings for CONEDUC (−.71), CONPRESS (−.61), and CONLEGIS (−.72) and might be labeled the confidence in public institutions factor. Factor 4 has high coefficients for HELPFUL (−.68) and FAIR (.77) and could be labeled the trust factor. We will discuss in 12.6 how these factors can be used as variables in further analyses.

The second half of Table 12.5 is the **factor structure matrix.** The coefficients in this matrix are the correlation of each variable with each factor. The

TABLE 12.5 Partial Output for FACTOR: Oblique Rotation

PATTERN MATRIX:

	FACTOR 1	FACTOR 2	FACTOR 3	FACTOR 4
SIBS	.12	.74	.13	-.12
MARITAL	.57	-.25	.07	.12
CHILDS	-.08	.78	-.07	.16
HELPFUL	-.06	.14	-.02	-.68
FAIR	.07	.09	.05	.77
CONEDUC	.01	-.02	-.71	-.10
CONPRESS	-.05	-.02	-.61	.13
CONLEGIS	.11	-.01	-.72	-.08
SATFAM	.87	.06	-.08	.09
SATFRND	.70	.26	-.05	-.15
SATJOB	.29	-.14	.04	-.37

STRUCTURE MATRIX:

	FACTOR 1	FACTOR 2	FACTOR 3	FACTOR 4
SIBS	.06	.73	.10	-.20
MARITAL	.57	-.33	.08	.02
CHILDS	-.20	.78	-.09	.11
HELPFUL	.07	.20	-.06	-.68
FAIR	-.10	.02	.08	.75
CONEDUC	.03	.01	-.71	-.14
CONPRESS	-.06	-.01	-.61	.10
CONLEGIS	.12	.01	-.73	-.14
SATFAM	.85	-.04	-.08	-.10
SATFRND	.70	.19	-.08	-.32
SATJOB	.38	-.14	.02	-.42

correlation of SIBS with factor 1 is .06. SIBS' correlations with factor 2, factor 3, and factor 4 are .73, .10, and −.20, respectively. These correlation coefficients differ from the regression coefficients in the factor pattern matrix because they do not adjust for correlations among the factors.

12.5 Factor Correlation Matrix

The factor correlation matrix printed only after an oblique rotation shows the correlation of the factors with one another (see Table 12.6). Prior to rotation, the factors are orthogonal; that is, their correlation with one another is 0.0. Low correlations indicate that the factors are distinct.

TABLE 12.6 Partial Output of FACTOR

```
FACTOR CORRELATION MATRIX:

                FACTOR 1     FACTOR 2     FACTOR 3     FACTOR 4

FACTOR 1          1.00
FACTOR 2          -.11         1.00
FACTOR 3                       -.03         1.00
FACTOR 4          -.21         -.08          .05         1.00
```

12.6 Factor Score Coefficients

We are now faced with the task of calculating the score for each case on each factor. (Remember, the factor pattern coefficients and the factor structure co-efficients concerned the association between *variables* and factors, not *cases* and factors.) To calculate the factor score of each case for each factor, we use yet another type of coefficient—**factor score coefficients.**

The score on a particular variable is multiplied by the factor score coefficient of that variable for that factor. We do this multiplication for each score of the case on each variable and then sum the products.

The factor scores for each case can be saved. Each set of factor scores can then be treated as a new variable. For example, suppose we extracted four factors and wanted to save the factor scores for all four. We would decide on a variable name and then use the subcommand SAVE. (Although we have seen SAVE as a command in earlier chapters, in this context it is a subcommand that must begin after column 1.) For our example, let's use the name FACTVAR. The SAVE subcommand would be:

```
SAVE   (ALL FACTVAR)
```

The first factor's scores would be saved under the variable name FACT-VAR1, the second factor's scores under the name FACTVAR2, and so on. Be careful to allow space for the digits at the end of the variable name; you must not exceed the 8-character limit.

Once the variables based on factor scores are saved, we can do other analyses that include these factors as variables. For example, to use FACTVAR1 (our good relationships factor), FACTVAR2 (our relatives factor), FACTVAR3 (our trust-in-others factor), and FACTVAR4 (our confidence in public institutions factor), the complete commands to calculate the factors and do a regression with HAPPY as the dependent variable are:

```
FACTOR   VARIABLES=SIBS MARITAL CHILDS HELPFUL FAIR
                    CONEDUC CONPRESS CONLEGIS SATFAM
                    SATFRND SATJOB/
         ROTATION=OBLIQUE/
         SAVE  (ALL FACTVAR)/
REGRESSION   VARIABLES=HAPPY FACTVAR1 FACTVAR2 FACTVAR3
             FACTVAR4/
             DEPENDENT=HAPPY/
             METHOD=ENTER/
```

If we wanted, we could include other variables from our file as independent variables in the regression along with the four factors.

Factor analysis has many variations. The SPSS^x program contains seven extraction techniques, four rotation techniques, and three possible calculations of factor scores. We have presented the most commonly used approaches. The *SPSS^x User's Guide*, Chapter 34, gives the commands for the other methods but without much discussion of the various assumptions and advantages of each method. To understand better the various methods of factor analysis, you will need to study articles by statisticians on the subject.

12.7 Summary

A factor is a composite variable underlying the variance in a set of variables.

A factor loading is a measure of the association between a variable and the factor of which it is a component. Factor loadings range from -1.0 to 1.0. Zero would indicate no association; 1 would indicate a perfect association. The sign of the loading indicates whether the association is positive or negative.

The eigenvalue is a measure of variance in the set of variables in the factor analysis. The total eigenvalue is equal to the number of variables in the analysis.

The communality of a variable is the proportion of its variance accounted for by the variables in the analysis. The communality is 0.0 for no association and 1.0 for a perfect association. The communality of all the variables will be 1.0 when the number of factors equals the number of variables.

A factor score is the value of the factor for a particular case.

In an orthogonal rotation, the correlation between the factors in the analysis is kept at 0.0. In an oblique rotation, some correlation is permitted among the factors in the analysis.

12.8 Where to Look in the *SPSS*^x *User's Guide*

- FACTOR is discussed on pages 715–730.

RESEARCH PROJECT WORK FOR CHAPTER 12

Do an exploratory factor analysis on your research data set, including all the variables except ID. Before you execute the analysis, hypothesize which variables you think will cluster together. If your hypotheses prove incorrect, discuss why the findings were different from what you expected.

REVIEW QUESTIONS FOR CHAPTER 12

(Answers to Review Questions are given at the back of the book.)

12.1 What is a factor?

12.2 What is a factor loading?

12.3 What is the eigenvalue in factor analysis?

12.4 What is the communality of a variable in factor analysis?

12.5 What is a factor score?

12.6 How is an orthogonal rotation different from an oblique rotation?

12.7 What is the factor extraction technique used by default in FACTOR?

12.8 What is the default rotation done by FACTOR if no technique is specified?

12.9 What type of oblique rotation is done by FACTOR if the ROTATION=OBLIQUE sub-command is given without specifying a technique?

12.10 What command would be needed to produce a factor analysis with an orthogonal rotation of the 13 variables CONFINA through CONARMY in the SPSS system file NORC84, described in Appendix B?

ASSIGNMENT QUESTIONS FOR CHAPTER 12

(Solutions to the Assignment Questions are provided in the *Instructor's Manual*.)

12.1 What does the following output indicate about the factors produced by the command in Review Question 12.10?

INITIAL STATISTICS:

VARIABLE	COMMUNALITY	*	FACTOR	EIGENVALUE	PCT OF VAR
		*			
CONFINAN	1.0	*	1	3.93	30.2
CONBUS	1.0	*	2	1.32	10.2
CONCLER	1.0	*	3	1.18	9.1
CONEDUC	1.0	*	4	.99	7.6
CONFED	1.0	*	5	.84	6.4
CONLABOR	1.0	*	6	.78	6.0
CONPRESS	1.0	*	7	.74	5.7
CONMEDI	1.0	*	8	.69	5.3
CONTV	1.0	*	9	.61	4.7
CONJUDG	1.0	*	10	.53	4.1
CONSCI	1.0	*	11	.52	4.0
CONLEGIS	1.0	*	12	.47	3.6
CONARMY	1.0	*	13	.42	3.2

12.2   What does the following output indicate about the factors produced by the command in Review Question 12.10?

FACTOR MATRIX:

	FACTOR 1	FACTOR 2	FACTOR 3
CONFINAN	.63	−.03	.35
CONBUS	.50	−.21	.26
CONCLER	.43	−.21	.43
CONEDUC	.51	.00	.14
CONFED	.61	−.02	−.36
CONLABOR	.48	.44	−.20
CONPRESS	.44	.55	.01
CONMEDI	.58	−.36	.19
CONTV	.45	.59	.23
CONJUDG	.60	−.21	−.52
CONSCI	.57	−.46	−.15
CONLEGIS	.69	.09	−.40
CONARMY	.61	.06	.26

12.3 What does the following output indicate about the factors produced by the command in Review Question 12.10?

FINAL STATISTICS:

VARIABLE	COMMUNALITY	*	FACTOR	EIGENVALUE	PCT OF VAR
		*			
CONFINAN	.51	*	1	3.93	30.2
CONBUS	.36	*	2	1.32	10.2
CONCLER	.41	*	3	1.18	9.1
CONEDUC	.28	*			
CONFED	.50	*			
CONLABOR	.46	*			
CONPRESS	.49	*			
CONMEDI	.50	*			
CONTV	.60	*			
CONJUDG	.67	*			
CONSCI	.55	*			
CONLEGIS	.64	*			
CONARMY	.44	*			

12.4 What does the following output indicate about the factors produced by the command in Review Question 12.10?

PATTERN MATRIX:

	FACTOR 1	FACTOR 2	FACTOR 3
CONFINAN	.66	.19	.01
CONBUS	.59	-.03	-.05
CONCLER	.69	-.04	.14
CONEDUC	.40	.17	-.12
CONFED	.05	.13	-.64
CONLABOR	-.07	.56	-.31
CONPRESS	.03	.67	-.08
CONMEDI	.62	-.16	-.19
CONTV	.21	.74	.13
CONJUDG	-.02	-.07	-.84
CONSCI	.37	-.29	-.54
CONLEGIS	.01	.26	-.70
CONARMY	.54	.27	-.04

STRUCTURE MATRIX:

	FACTOR 1	FACTOR 2	FACTOR 3
CONFINAN	.69	.32	−.28
CONBUS	.60	.09	−.27
CONCLER	.63	.07	−.11
CONEDUC	.48	.27	−.30
CONFED	.32	.28	−.69
CONLABOR	.16	.61	−.41
CONPRESS	.20	.69	−.23
CONMEDI	.67	.00	−.40
CONTV	.31	.75	−.10
CONJUDG	.28	.09	−.82
CONSCI	.52	.10	−.62
CONLEGIS	.33	.41	−.76
CONARMY	.61	.39	−.30

12.5 What does the following output indicate about the factors produced by the command in Review Question 12.10?

FACTOR CORRELATION MATRIX

	FACTOR 1	FACTOR 2	FACTOR 3
FACTOR 1	1.00		
FACTOR 2	.05	1.00	
FACTOR 3	−.25	−.04	1.00

TABLE 12.7 Output from command FACTOR   VARIABLES=SIBS MARITAL CHILDS HELPFUL FAIR CONEDUC
CONPRESS CONLEGIS SATFAM SATFRND SATJOB

F A C T O R   A N A L Y S I S

ANALYSIS NUMBER   1 LISTWISE DELETION OF CASES WITH MISSING VALUES

EXTRACTION   1 FOR ANALYSIS   1, PRINCIPAL-COMPONENTS ANALYSIS (PC)

INITIAL STATISTICS:

VARIABLE	COMMUNALITY	*	FACTOR	EIGENVALUE	PCT OF VAR	CUM PCT
SIBS	1.00000	*	1	1.95585	17.8	17.8
MARITAL	1.00000	*	2	1.45114	13.2	31.0
CHILDS	1.00000	*	3	1.34922	12.3	43.2
HELPFUL	1.00000	*	4	1.04273	9.5	52.7
FAIR	1.00000	*	5	.90798	8.3	61.0
CONEDUC	1.00000	*	6	.86666	7.9	68.9
CONPRESS	1.00000	*	7	.83887	7.6	76.5
CONLEGIS	1.00000	*	8	.78533	7.1	83.6
SATFAM	1.00000	*	9	.68567	6.2	89.8
SATFRND	1.00000	*	10	.66593	6.1	95.9
SATJOB	1.00000	*	11	.45063	4.1	100.0

173

TABLE 12.7 *Continued*

PC EXTRACTED 4 FACTORS.

FACTOR MATRIX:

	FACTOR 1	FACTOR 2	FACTOR 3	FACTOR 4
SIBS	-.09865	.39077	.61273	.21206
MARITAL	.40494	-.47021	-.09139	.16334
CHILDS	-.17429	.55635	.39972	.39172
HELPFUL	.36477	.30535	.27723	-.43740
FAIR	-.42376	.19651	-.13437	.58766
CONEDUC	.30087	.46381	-.45940	.03038
CONPRESS	.08544	.36557	-.47187	.15722
CONLEGIS	.37523	.43709	-.45704	.08653
SATFAM	.71220	-.27698	.04482	.38575
SATFRND	.69290	-.02952	.24450	.22986
SATJOB	.46172	-.13624	.07983	-.21497

FINAL STATISTICS:

VARIABLE	COMMUNALITY	*	FACTOR	EIGENVALUE	PCT OF VAR	CUM PCT
SIBS	.58284	*	1	1.95585	17.8	17.8
MARITAL	.42010	*	2	1.45114	13.2	31.0
CHILDS	.65312	*	3	1.34922	12.3	43.2
HELPFUL	.49446	*	4	1.04273	9.5	52.7
FAIR	.58159	*				
CONEDUC	.51761	*				
CONPRESS	.38832	*				
CONLEGIS	.54822	*				
SATFAM	.73475	*				
SATFRND	.59360	*				
SATJOB	.28433	*				

VARIMAX ROTATION 1 FOR EXTRACTION 1 IN ANALYSIS 1 - KAISER NORMALIZATION.

VARIMAX CONVERGED IN 5 ITERATIONS.

ROTATED FACTOR MATRIX:

	FACTOR 1	FACTOR 2	FACTOR 3	FACTOR 4
SIBS	.08699	-.11460	.73203	.16207
MARITAL	.57077	-.07452	-.28956	-.07022
CHILDS	-.14380	.07987	.78025	-.13144
HELPFUL	.01388	.04133	.17165	.68051
FAIR	-.02261	-.06624	.05576	-.75735
CONEDUC	.01825	.70901	-.00547	.12065
CONPRESS	-.06203	.60903	-.01446	-.11553
CONLEGIS	.11303	.72362	.00221	.10863
SATFAM	.85279	.08614	.00888	.00293
SATFRND	.69485	.07004	.22527	.23478
SATJOB	.33990	-.02968	-.13654	.38636

13

ANALYZING CENSUS DATA TAPES WITH SPSS[X]

New SPSS[X] Command:

FILE TYPE

The U.S. Bureau of the Census does not ask any attitudinal questions in its decennial census nor in its current population surveys. Therefore, we cannot extend our analysis of reported happiness to the data gathered by the Bureau of the Census. On the other hand, SPSS[X] is well equipped to cope with some of the difficulties posed by census data files. You may very likely want to use one of these files someday.

An introduction to the many variables in the census data files is beyond the scope of this book, but we will describe the two basic types of files and the requirements for working with them. These files are the PUMS files (Public-Use Microdata Sample) and the STF files (Summary Tape File).

Also beyond the scope of this book, and simply impossible, is a description of the operating system commands or hardware limitations of the numerous types of computer installations around the country. In this chapter we describe the necessary SPSS[X] commands.

13.1 Individual Level Census Data: PUMS Files

The distinguishing characteristic of the PUMS files is that the basic case units are individuals. With over 200 million individuals in the United States, even computer technology does not enable the typical user to work with every individual, so the Bureau of the Census releases samples (on tape) from its decennial census for the public to use. For the 1980 census, the codebook for these tapes is: *Census of Population and Housing: 1980 Public-Use Microdata Samples Technical Documentation* (Washington, D.C.: U.S. Government Printing Office, 1982).

Other useful documentation available about census data includes:

- *1980 Census of Population and Housing Users' Guide* (available from the U.S. Government Printing Office)
- *Telephone Contacts for Data Users* (available from the Bureau of the Census)
- *Data User News* (available from the Bureau of the Census)
- *Directory of Data Files* (available from the Bureau of the Census)

The smallest of these documents, and often the most useful, is the *Telephone Contacts for Data Users,* a free four-page brochure.

State data centers with regional branches provide the census data tapes at nominal cost and are also a convenient source of expertise on how to use them. If you are having trouble locating a state data center or an office of the Bureau of the Census to help you, call the Bureau's Data User Services at (301) 763-4100.

The major difficulty with the PUMS files is that household information is on one record, followed by one or more records containing the information on the persons living in the household—one record for each individual. If you simply want to use household information, there is no problem. Simply give a SELECT IF command that specifies 'H' (in single quotes) for the variable RECTYPE. This alphanumeric variable, in the same location for both types of records, is coded P for individuals and H for households. Likewise, if you want to use individual information, use a SELECT IF command that specifies 'P' for the record type variable.

More likely you will want to use information from both the household and the individual records so that each individual is connected with the attributes of his or her household. In this case, you will be dealing with what is called a *nested hierarchical file* and will need to use the command **FILE TYPE**. For example, to do an analysis using the variable FAMINCOM from the household records and linking it with the variables SEX, MARITAL, and AGE from the individual records for each household, we would use the following set of SPSS^X commands:

```
FILE TYPE   NESTED   FILE=PUMS80   RECORD=RECTYPE 1  (A)
RECORD TYPE 'H'
DATA LIST   FAMINCOM 112-116
RECORD TYPE 'P'
DATA LIST   SEX 7   MARITAL 11   AGE 33-34
END FILE TYPE
```

Note that several other commands and subcommands must accompany the FILE TYPE command. First is the subcommand **NESTED,** which indicates that we want the data from the first record type "spread" to the records of the second record type. In our example, the data from each record of type H will be spread to each P record that follows it, until the next H record is encountered.

The next subcommand in the FILE TYPE command is **FILE = PUMS80,** which specifies the name we gave to the file in our operating system commands (which are not shown here). On the same line is the subcommand **RECORD = RECTYPE 1 (A),** which indicates that the record type will be identified by the variable RECTYPE, which is in column 1. [The (A) indicates that this variable is alphanumeric.]

RECORD TYPE 'H' indicates that the first record type is identified by having the value H for the variable and location specified by the RECORD= subcommand on the first line. So, if the value in column 1 for the variable RECTYPE is H, then the DATA LIST command following RECORD TYPE 'H' applies.

DATA LIST FAMINCOM 112-116 applies to the type H records, because this command follows the RECORD TYPE 'H' command. Likewise RECORD TYPE 'P' indicates that the DATA LIST following it applies to records with the value P in column 1.

END FILE TYPE indicates that the set of commands specifying the file type has been concluded.

After the more complicated set of commands surrounding the DATA LIST phase of your data definition process, you can proceed as usual with other SPSS^X commands.

The Bureau of the Census Current Population Survey data tapes are also hierarchical nested files and require a FILE TYPE set of commands to combine household and individual data.

In the STF data files, however, the units of analysis are geographic units and the data are aggregate statistics. These files present a different set of challenges, which we discuss in the next section.

13.2 Aggregate Data by Geographic Area: STF Files

The STF files consist of tables of data organized by geographic units. Each case is a geographic area, but the areas might be anything from a neighborhood block group to a state. The geographic level is specified by the value of SUMRYLV, a variable whose location varies depending on which type of STF file you are using. You'll need to check your codebook to locate SUMRYLV and to learn the values that correspond to each level. You do not have to treat these files as nested for most analyses, because the same variables are used for each geographic level.

A simple DATA LIST command will suffice to define your data. Often, however, you will want to print out the information for just some of the levels. You can do so by using a SELECT IF command with the SUMRYLV variable after the DATA LIST command. There is also a variable RECOIND for some of the STF files that indicates whether the aggregated statistics are for the total population or a particular ethnic/racial group within it. Using a SELECT IF command with RECOIND enables you to select out the total population or just those subgroups of the total that you wish to examine.

A tricky aspect of STF files is that each cell in a table must be thought of as a variable. If you have the population by age in five-year intervals, each of those five-year intervals must be given a variable name. (The SPSS^x convention of defining a set of variables with the same prefix by using the keyword **TO** is most useful. With it we can define 18 variables by using the words AGE1 TO AGE18 on the DATA LIST command followed by the columns these adjacent variables span.) For example:

```
DATA LIST AGE1 TO AGE18 20-109
```

To produce a table when each cell has its own variable name, use a LIST command that specifies each variable name. Use the VARIABLE LABELS command to identify the cell to which each variable label corresponds. If you make AREANAME (a variable containing the first name of each geographic unit) the first variable named on the LIST command, the output will indicate which area the table is for.

Another problem in working with the STF file is that a 0 sometimes indicates that the information is being suppressed, whereas other times a 0 is a legitimate value. (The Bureau of the Census suppresses some information when there are so few cases that confidentiality would be jeopardized.) To solve this problem, certain variables indicate whether the information for another variable is being suppressed or not. For example, the first **suppression variable** on one of the STF files is coded 1 when the total population count is being suppressed because fewer than 30 persons live in the area. For this file you would need to use an IF command to change values of the total population variable from 0 to a missing value when the suppressor variable has a value of 1.

There are four STF files (STF1, STF2, STF3, and STF4), and for each file there is a document from a series entitled *Census of Population and Housing 1980: Summary Tape File Technical Documentation Series.* These documents contain information on codings, the structure of the file, and its geographic coverage.

Another useful resource for the STF files is the *Geographic Identification Code Scheme* (GICS). This set of tables gives the codes and names of the political and geographic areas used for the 1980 census. This information facilitates selecting out from a tape just the data for areas that interest you.

13.3 Summary

The PUMS files (Public-Use Microdata Samples) have households and individuals as the basic case units.

The major difficulty with the PUMS files is that household information is on one record, followed by one or more records containing the information on the persons living in the household—one record for each individual. If you want to use information from both the household and the individual records such that each individual is connected with the attributes of his or her household, you need to use the FILE TYPE command.

The STF files (Summary Tape Files) consist of tables of data organized by geographic units. Each case is a geographic area, but the areas might be anything from a block group to an SMSA. The geographic level is specified by the value of SUMRYLV, a variable whose location varies depending on which type of STF file you are using.

For STF files each cell in a table must be thought of as a variable.

Another problem in working with the STF files is that a 0 may indicate either suppressed information or a legitimate value. To solve this problem, certain variables indicate whether the information for another variable is being suppressed.

13.4 Where to Look in the *SPSS^x* User's Guide

The *SPSS^x User's Guide* does not discuss using census data tapes. A sophisticated discussion can be found in *SPSS^x Processing of U.S. Census Data* (Chicago, Illinois: SPSS Inc., 1984).

- The FILE TYPE command is discussed on pages 191–209.

REVIEW QUESTIONS FOR CHAPTER 13

13.1 What is the basic difference between PUMS files and STF files?

13.2 Could you use a PUMS file if you wanted to determine the correlation among individuals between family income and educational attainment?

13.3 Could you use an STF file if you wanted to determine the correlation among individuals between family income and educational attainment?

13.4 When is it necessary to use a FILE TYPE command with a PUMS file?

13.5 In using an STF file, if you wanted to produce tables for the county geographic level only, what would you do?

13.6 In using an STF file, if you wanted to produce tables for the total population and for the Spanish-origin populations only, what would you do?

13.7 Suppose that using an STF file you want to produce for SMSAs the table of number of households in each household-value category. Why would you need a variable name for each category in the distribution of household values?

13.8 Why are the 0 values in an STF file problematic?

ASSIGNMENT QUESTIONS FOR CHAPTER 13

13.1 For the PUMS80 file used in the example in Section 13.1, what SPSS^x commands would be necessary to produce a FREQUENCIES run of the variable MARITAL for individuals only?

13.2 For the PUMS80 file, what SPSS^x commands would be necessary to produce a FREQUENCIES run of the variable FAMINCOM for households only?

13.3 For the PUMS80 file, what SPSS^x commands would be necessary to produce a CROSSTABS of FAMINCOM by MARITAL?

13.4 Assuming that the following commands are correct and that no information has been suppressed, what additional SPSS^x commands would be needed to produce a table showing the name and total population size (POPSIZE) for each county?

(The VALUE LABEL information in the following commands shows how SUMRYLV and RECOIND are coded.)

```
DATA LIST   FILE=STF   RECORDS=6
 /1 SUMRYLV 10-11   RECOIND 16-17 (A)   POPSIZE 107-108
     AREANAME 145-174 (A)
VALUE LABELS   SUMRYLV  8 'SMSA'  17 'COUNTY'  24 'CENSUS
               TRACT'
VALUE LABELS   RECOIND  0 'TOTAL'  1 'WHITE'  2 'BLACK'
               3 'HISPANIC'
```

13.5 What SPSS^x commands would you need to add to produce a table of the total population, the black population, and the area name for SMSAs?

14

DOING SPSS WITH A PERSONAL COMPUTER

There are nuisances involved with using a mainframe computer that is part of a complex installation: You need to master the operating system. Turnaround time can be slow when usage is heavy. The system can be down due to part failures or maintenance needs. You or your department may be charged for services. Or you may have to submit several jobs with annoying interruptions before you are able to debug all the errors in your program. One solution to these problems is SPSS/PC+, a version of SPSS designed for the IBM and IBM-compatible microcomputers.*

14.1 Is SPSS/PC+ Right for You?

Even aside from the problems with learning to use and relying on a mainframe system, SPSS/PC+ has some nifty advantages over SPSS^X. A HELP command enables you to ask for help with commands, subcommands, and options while you are entering the program. A REVIEW command activates an editor program that enables you to change your latest output using the top part of the screen,

---

*References to the user manual in this chapter are to *SPSS/PC+ for the IBM PC/XT/AT* by Marija J. Novusis (Chicago: SPSS Inc., 1986).

while at the bottom of the screen you can make changes in the set of commands that produced the output.

If you want to do part of your work on a microcomputer and part of your work on a mainframe, and be able to ship data and command files back and forth, SPSS/PC+ provides for this purpose a communication package called *Kermit,* developed at Columbia University.

An important consideration, however, before you rush out and purchase SPSS/PC+ is the computer hardware requirements. Our discussion in this paragraph presumes you have a basic knowledge of microcomputer hardware. If you don't, take the information here to whoever advises you on these matters. You need not understand the following terminology to operate SPSS/PC+, but you must be sure that your micro system will support SPSS/PC+ before you purchase it. Use of SPSS/PC+ requires a rather beefy microcomputer system. You will need a RAM (random access memory) of at least 380K and a hard disk with at least 10 megabytes of storage space. To ensure adequate RAM when using the more demanding procedures, a RAM of 640K (the maximum manageable by DOS) is recommended, as is a math coprocessor to provide greater speed.

Another drawback is that the SPSS/PC+ software is extensive and expensive. In 1986 the basic package of 11 diskettes costs $795. The Advanced Statistics and Tables enhancements cost an additional $295 each. The Advanced Statistics enhancement has the following procedures: FACTOR, DISCRIMINANT, MANOVA, CLUSTER, QUICK CLUSTER, and HILOGLINEAR. The Tables package enables you to customize tables, a feature also available in mainframe SPSS^x by using the TABLES command. The home or office user with a 256K machine without a hard disk will have to spend two to three thousand dollars on upgrading the system and on the software. There are volume discounts and, for academic institutions, site-licensing contracts that reduce the software costs.

A nice feature is that the number of cases for most procedures is not limited. You are, however, limited to using 200 variables when operating SPSS/PC+. Large data files such as NORC84 that have more than 200 variables would have to be split into smaller files to run with SPSS/PC+.

Despite these requirements and limitations, the typical user of SPSS^x will want to use SPSS/PC+ because of the HELP and REVIEW features and, perhaps most of all, because of the psychological boost of feeling in control of the entire process.

14.2 Installing SPSS/PC+

SPSS/PC+ requires installing programs onto your hard disk. Though this task may sound tricky, there are directions provided in the SPSS/PC+ user manual Appendix G, and you are prompted with on-screen instructions as well while the installation program runs.

Beware the following pitfalls, however. If you install the program following the instructions in Appendix G of the manual, at the end of the installation you are advised to run a test job. But, before this test job will run, you need to give the command CD \SPSS to open the directory that you have created for the SPSS/PC+ programs. Then enter SPSSPC BASETEST.INC to run the test job. Otherwise the system will act as though the SPSS/PC+ files are not in your hard disk's memory. You will need to give this same CD \SPSS command each time you boot the system, if you want to use the SPSS/PC+ programs after booting the system. (If you are familiar with DOS, an alternative is to add to your AUTOEXEC.BAT file a PATH command that points to the SPSS directory.)

There also needs to be a CONFIG.SYS file (which can be created with standard editor programs such as EDLIN or WORDSTAR) with the lines

```
FILES=20
BUFFERS=8
```

Without this file you will receive an enigmatic "file cannot be opened" error message.

If you have created CONFIG.SYS and still receive the "file cannot be opened" error, you may need to limit the size of the workspace used by SPSS/PC+. Do this at the time you call up the program by adding /S=128K to the SPSSPC command on the same line.

```
SPSSPC /S=128K  BASETEST. INC
```

The workspace limit can be varied to fit your system's restrictions. If you do not limit the workspace sufficiently, again the error message is "file cannot be opened."

14.3 Entering Commands and Data Interactively

After you boot the system and enter the CD \SPSS command, you will be given the DOS prompt C>. You then enter the command SPSSPC, which loads the SPSS/PC+ program. A logo appears on the screen, and you are asked to insert the security-key diskette in drive A. (Without the electronic code on this diskette, the SPSS/PC+ programs will not operate. You can copy the files on this and the other diskettes to have backup copies, but the electronic code will not be copied by DISKCOPY or by the programs sold to copy protected programs.)

At this point, the prompt on the screen will be SPSS/PC:, which indicates that the system is ready for you to submit SPSS/PC+ commands. **These commands must either end with a period or be followed by the entry of a blank line.** Otherwise SPSS/PC+ treats the next line as a continuation of the command. Unlike SPSS^x, when using SPSS/PC+ you do not have to begin your commands in column 1 nor do you have to begin continuation lines after column 1. The SPSS^x conventions of beginning commands in column 1 and beginning continuations after column 1 will work with SPSS/PC+, however, and we recommend following these conventions in case you transport a set of commands to a mainframe computer to be executed with SPSS^x. (You would still have to remove the period at the end of each command before the commands will run on SPSS^x.) When a line does not end in a period, the prompt changes from SPSS/PC: to a single colon (:). An entire session that replicates our first example from Chapter 2 would go as follows. (Note that there are no prompts from BEGIN DATA until after END DATA and no periods closing the data lines. The prompts are produced here in boldface for emphasis.)

C> CD /SPSS

C> **SPSS/PC**

SPSS/PC: DATA LIST /ID 1-2 EDUC 3-4 SEX 5 HAPPY 6.

SPSS/PC: BEGIN DATA.
010912
021223
031521
041222
050611
061612
071522
081612
091821
101412
111321
121611
130922

```
141212
151221
161821
170821
181222
191613
201421
END DATA.
SPSS/PC: LIST.
```

After the LIST command is entered, that program will be executed, and the output will appear on the screen. The output can be edited and printed using REVIEW.

14.4 Submitting Commands and Data from a File: INCLUDE and GET

A file containing commands, data, or both can be submitted as a **batch** to be executed all together with the command **INCLUDE.** Follow the command with the name of the file you want submitted enclosed in single quotes. Thus, to submit a file named NORC84, the complete INCLUDE command would be

```
INCLUDE   'NORC84'.
```

If, for the first example in this chapter, the DATA LIST and data were stored in a file named NORC84, our total set of commands for a LIST procedure would be

```
C>  CD  /SPSS

C>  SPSS/PC

SPSS/PC:  INCLUDE    'NORC84'.
SPSS/PC:  LIST.
```

To create files of commands or data, use an editing program like REVIEW, discussed in Section 14.6.

As in SPSS[X], when using SPSS/PC+ you have the option of saving SPSS system files that include the DATA LIST, MISSING VALUES, VARIABLE LABELS, and VALUE LABELS information, as well as the data. Such files are created with the SAVE command and accessed with the GET command, as we discussed in

Chapter 2. To create an SPSS system file named NEWFILE, we would add at the end of our example the command

SAVE   OUTFILE='NEWFILE'.

The advantage of creating SPSS system files is that they run faster than the non-system files, which are submitted with the INCLUDE command. To access an SPSS system file in your PC system, use the GET command. Thus, to access the file NEWFILE just created, the command would be

GET   FILE='NEWFILE'.

SPSS/PC+ also has the capability of reading SPSS system files from an SPSS mainframe system or another SPSS/PC+ system. The files are read with the **IMPORT** command. (See the SPSS/PC+ user manual, pages C76–C78.)

SPSS/PC+ can read files from most editor, spreadsheet, and database programs that use DOS as an operating system. These files are submitted using the INCLUDE command. (See the SPSS/PC+ user manual, pages G–22 to G–24 for an explanation of possibly required alterations to the data files to make them compatible with SPSS/PC+.)

14.5 On-line Assistance: HELP and DISPLAY

The HELP command is the nicest feature of SPSS/PC+ for the beginner who is unfamiliar with SPSS commands. Giving the command HELP ALL will produce a list of general topics for which on-line descriptions are available (see Table 14.1). From this list of topics, select the one you want to know more about and give the HELP command specifying that topic. For example, if you want to know more about the transformations available, give the command

HELP   TRANSFORMATIONS.

The output from this command is given in Table 14.2.

You can also use the HELP command to obtain a description of any SPSS/PC+ command. For example, to obtain information about CROSSTABS, you would enter the command

HELP   CROSSTABS.

TABLE 14.1 Output from HELP Command

HELP TOPICS

The following general topics will provide more information on specific topics, commands, and subcommands for which help is available. Use HELP topicname for more information.

PROCEDURES	Procedures available within SPSS/PC+
TRANSFORMATIONS	Transformations available within SPSS/PC+
CASE SELECTION	Case selection commands
DATA DEFINITION	Data definition commands
SYNTAX RULES	General rules
COMMAND ORDER	Precedence of commands
FILES	File usage
DISPLAY	Command to display dictionary information
SET	Command to set execution parameters
SHOW	Command to display execution parameters
EXECUTE	Command to execute another program
INCLUDE	Command to include SPSS/PC+ command files
MATRIX	Reading and writing special matrices
NEWS	Recent changes to SPSS/PC+
SPSS MANAGER	Installing and Removing Procedures
JOIN	Command to match and add files

SPSS/PC:

TABLE 14.2 Output from HELP TRANSFORMATIONS Command

TRANSFORMATIONS

SPSS/PC+ transformations create new variables and modify existing variables. The following transformations are available:

COMPUTE	Compute a variable as an arithmetic transformation of existing variables and constants.
IF	Conditionally compute a variable as an arithmetic transformation of existing variables and constants.
RECODE	Change or collapse the values of an existing variable into a new set of values.
COUNT	Compute a variable which counts the occurrences of specified values across a list of variables for each case.

Transformation commands can occur prior to procedures and between procedures. Use HELP commandname for more information. Use HELP MISSING TRANSFORMATIONS for information on the effects of missing values.

SPSS/PC:

The output would include a description of the subcommands of CROSSTABS, for which you can use HELP to acquire more information.

Another on-line assistance command is DISPLAY, which produces a list of variable names and variable labels.

If you use the DISPLAY command with the name of one or more variables, it will produce the value labels and missing value codes for the variables. The DISPLAY command is like having an on-line codebook and will save you a great deal of time when you are working with an unfamiliar data file.

14.6 On-line Editing of Commands and Output: REVIEW

As we mentioned above, REVIEW is an editor program that enables you to change your output and the set of commands that produced the output. REVIEW is easy to use because the program contains a HELP display. First enter the command REVIEW. When you enter REVIEW, the output is a split screen with the command log from your last job at the bottom of the screen and the output at the top. Pressing the F1 key brings up the HELP display (see Table 14.3). In this display, an up-arrow means to hold down the shift key, the symbol ^ indicates that you need to hold down the Ctrl key, and an a indicates that you need to hold down the Alt key. Once you have given a command from this display, if more information is needed, you will be given a prompt at the bottom of your screen. If you press the F1 key when a prompt is on the screen, you will see a fuller description of exactly what information is needed.

If you want to edit the listing of output, give the command

```
REVIEW   LISTING.
```

If you want to edit the log of commands, give the command

```
REVIEW   LOG.
```

If you want to edit another file, place the name of that file after the command REVIEW. For example, to edit the NORC84 file, you would enter the line

```
REVIEW   'NORC84'.
```

TABLE 14.3 Output from REVIEW Then F1 Commands (from *SPSS/PC+™ for the IBM PC/XT/AT,* Marija J. Norušis, SPSS Inc., Chicago)

```
╔══════════════════════════════════════════════════════════════╗
║                                                              ║
║          ┌──Setting and Information Commands──┐              ║
║          │More REVIEW Help     F1              │             ║
║          │SPSS/PC+ Help       ↑F1   ^F1  SPSS/PC+ Variables  │
║          │Switch Window        F2   ^F2  Change Window Size  │
║          ├────File Commands──────┐                           ║
║       │Write File to Disk ↑F9   F9  Write Block to Disk │    ║
║       │Exit from REVIEW  aF10   F10 Exit and Run Block  │    ║
║       │Insert File        F3   ↑F3  Edit Different File │    ║
║       │Delete Disk File  ^F9   aF1  Directory of Files  │    ║
║       ├──────Editing Commands──────┐                         ║
║    │Insert Line After    F4   ↑F4  Insert Line Before │      ║
║    │Delete Current Char Del   Del  Join Line If at End │     ║
║    │Delete Prev Char     ←    ^F4  Delete Line        │      ║
║    │Split Line -InsMode  ←┘   aF4  Undelete Line      │      ║
║    │Change Forward       F5   ↑F5  Change Reverse     │      ║
║    │Mark/Unmark Block    F7   ^F8  Delete Block       │      ║
║    │Copy Block           F8   ↑F8  Move Block         │      ║
║    ├────────Motion Commands────────┐                         ║
║  │Top of Page         Home  End  Bottom of Page │           ║
║  │Top of File        ^Home ^End  Bottom of File │            ║
║  │Find SPSS/PC+ Page  ^F6  ^PgDn Put Line at Top│            ║
║  │Start of Line       ^←   ^→    End of Line    │            ║
║  │Start of Next Line  ←┘   ^PgUp Top of Memory  │            ║
║  │Search Down          F6  ↑F6   Search Up      │            ║
║  └──Enter Command or Press Space Bar──┘                      ║
║                                                              ║
╚══════════════════════════════════════════════════════════════╝
```

14.7 Downloading from and Uploading to a Mainframe Computer: KERMIT, IMPORT, and EXPORT

With SPSS/PC+ comes a program called *Kermit* that can be used to ship files back and forth between a mainframe computer with SPSS[x] and a microcomputer with SPSS/PC+. Kermit must be present in both the mainframe and the microcomputer systems; it is distributed free of charge to licensed SPSS[x] installations by SPSS Inc. You will want to use Kermit because SPSS[x] portable files contain special characters that are not communicated correctly by other programs.

To use Kermit, following the DOS prompt **C>** enter the command

KERMIT

This command produces the prompt **Kermit-MS>** and the message that you can receive help about what command to enter next by entering a question mark (?). At any point when entering Kermit commands, you can enter a ? and the program will describe your options. To communicate with a mainframe (or another PC computer system), you enter the command **CONNECT.** You will then be connected to the mainframe system, and you can log on in your system's normal manner. The next step is to give the command to run Kermit on your mainframe system. You will receive a **Kermit-__>** prompt (where the last two characters before the > will depend on which system you are using). Use the command **SEND** followed by the file name to send a file. Use the command **RECEIVE** followed by the file name to receive a file. Use the command **CTRL]C** to go from the mainframe to the PC and the command **CONNECT** to go from the PC to the mainframe.

You must first send the file from one system and then move to the other system to receive it. If you take more than 5 seconds, the first part of the transmission will appear garbled, but don't worry—it will be retransmitted. At both the mainframe and the PC, use the command **EXIT** to leave Kermit. An example of using Kermit is provided in the SPSS/PC+ manual on pages F-4 to F-5.

Kermit must be used when you want to transmit SPSS system files. Other microcomputer communication programs such as PC-TALK III and CROSSTALK cannot transfer SPSS/PC+ system files or portable system files. These communication programs can, however, transfer the non–SPSS system files read and written by SPSS/PC+, such as data files, listings of output, or sets of commands.

To access an SPSS file from your PC, use the command IMPORT FILE= followed by the name of the file enclosed by apostrophes. To send an SPSS file from your PC, use the command EXPORT FILE= followed by the name of the file enclosed by apostrophes.

14.8 Differences between SPSS/PC+ and SPSS^x

We mentioned earlier that SPSS/PC+ commands must end with a period or be followed by a blank line, that commands need not begin in column 1 and continuations need not begin after column 1, and that SPSS/PC+ cannot handle more than 200 variables. SPSS/PC+ also differs from SPSS^x in the names of some commands. The following list shows the SPSS^x command and the corresponding SPSS/PC+ command:

SPSS^x Command	Corresponding SPSS/PC+ Command
PEARSON CORR	CORRELATION
CONDESCRIPTIVE	DESCRIPTIVES
BREAKDOWN	MEANS
N OF CASES	N
MATCH FILES and ADD FILES	JOIN
COMMENT	*

There have also been some changes made in the OPTIONS and STATISTICS of most commands, so you should use the HELP command discussed in Section 14.5 before using any SPSS/PC+ command for the first time, even if you are familiar with a comparable command in SPSS^x.

Note that SPSS/PC+ uses OPTIONS and STATISTICS as subcommands, whereas in SPSS^x they are usually commands, on their own line, following a statistical procedure command. Thus, in SPSS/PC+, OPTIONS and STATISTICS will be placed *before* the period or blank line that ends the command.

14.9 Summary

SPSS/PC+ is an interactive program designed for IBM and IBM-compatible microcomputers. The program can handle up to 200 variables and, for most commands, a practically unlimited number of cases. SPSS/PC+ is expensive and has substantial hardware requirements for a microcomputer program. Your system needs at least 380K and a hard disk; 640K and a coprocessor are desirable.

The advantages of SPSS/PC+ include:

- The HELP and DISPLAY commands, which provide on-line assistance in using commands and an on-line codebook of your data set.
- The REVIEW command, which is an editor program with which you can make changes in your current listing of output at the top of the screen and in your current log of commands at the bottom part.
- The facility for entering commands as a batch as well as interactively.
- The accompanying Kermit program, developed by Columbia University, that can transmit SPSS system files back and forth between SPSS/PC+ microcomputer systems and SPSS^x mainframe systems.

Differences in syntax between SPSS/PC+ and SPSS^x include:

- SPSS/PC+ can begin commands after column 1 and continuations of commands in column 1.
- The end of a command is signaled with a period or a blank line.
- In SPSS/PC+, STATISTICS and OPTIONS are subcommands rather than commands following statistical procedure commands.
- In SPSS/PC+, certain commands have been renamed:
  BREAKDOWN is replaced by MEANS
  COMMENT is replaced by *
  CONDESCRIPTIVE is replaced by DESCRIPTIVES
  MATCH FILES and ADD FILES are replaced by JOIN
  N OF CASES is replaced by N
  PEARSON CORR is replaced by CORRELATION

14.10 Where to Look in the *SPSS^x User's Guide*

A brief discussion of translating between SPSS^x and SPSS/PC+ appears on pages 957–960. There is no explanation, however, of how to use SPSS/PC+ or its earlier version SPSS/PC.

SPSS/PC+ comes with a 400-page manual entitled *SPSS/PC+ for the IBM PC/XT/AT*. A manual also comes with each of the SPSS/PC+ enhancements—SPSS/PC+ Tables and SPSS/PC+ Advanced Statistics.

RESEARCH PROJECT WORK FOR CHAPTER 14

Using SPSS/PC+ instead of SPSS^x, replicate all the research project work for Chapters 3 through 6.

REVIEW QUESTIONS FOR CHAPTER 14

14.1 If your microcomputer system has two floppy disks and 256K of RAM, what hardware changes—if any—would you need to make in order to run SPSS/PC+?

14.2 Starting from the DOS prompt, what two commands are needed to load SPSS/PC+?

14.3 What does it mean when SPSS/PC+ gives the prompt : instead of SPSS/PC:?

14.4 Suppose you have in your microcomputer system an SPSS system file named DATAFILE and now you want to bring it on line for some statistical analyses. What command would you use?

14.5 What command would you give to learn what variables are in the SPSS system file named DATAFILE once you had it on line?

14.6 If one of the variables in DATAFILE was named EDUC, and you wanted to know what its value labels and missing values were, what command would you give?

14.7 Suppose you have a set of data transformation commands and statistical procedure commands stored in a file named COMMANDS. What command would enable you to enter these commands as a batch instead of reentering them individually?

14.8 Suppose, after examining your output from a set of commands, you want to recode some of the variables and then resubmit the job. What command can you use?

14.9 If you want to do a REGRESSION but have forgotten what subcommands are needed, what command can you give to obtain the information?

14.10 What SPSS^x commands have different names in SPSS/PC+?

ASSIGNMENT QUESTIONS FOR CHAPTER 14

14.1 From the NORC84 SPSS system file, create a smaller file containing the following variables (which are also on your research project questionnaire): HAPPY, HEALTH, SATFAM, SATFRND, SATJOB, EDUC, MARITAL, CHILDS, INCOME, TVHOURS, SEX, and AGE. Using Kermit, download this smaller file to your SPSS/PC+ system.

14.2 Compare the central tendencies and distributions of the NORC84 sample created in Assignment Question 14.1 with your research project sample on the variable HAPPY. Compare the same two samples in terms of the effects of the other variables on the variable HAPPY. Explain your choice of statistical procedures for this comparison.

APPENDIX A
SPECIAL TOPICS

A.1 COUNT

The **COUNT** command allows you to create a new variable by counting the number of times a given value occurs for a set of variables. For example, we could count the number of times a respondent gave the most positive response to the first five questions of the Happiness Questionnaire in Appendix C. We create the new variable SAT#MAX as follows:

COUNT   SAT#MAX=HAPPY HEALTH SATFAM SATFRND SATJOB (1)

More than one value can be used in the COUNT command. We could, therefore, count the number of times a respondent gave one of the two most positive responses on the same questions:

COUNT   SAT#POS=HAPPY HEALTH SATFAM SATFRND SATJOB (1,2)

More than one variable can be created with one COUNT command. Separate the new variables with a slash. For example, we could have created the two variables SAT#MAX and SAT#POS with one command:

COUNT   SAT#MAX=HAPPY HEALTH SATFAM SATFRND SATJOB (1) /

        SAT#POS=HAPPY HEALTH SATFAM SATFRND SATJOB (1,2)

If all the data are missing for the variables being used in the COUNT command, the new variable will have a value of 0. If you want to eliminate cases with all missing data, use a SELECT IF command before the COUNT command.

The keywords LO, HI, and THRU can be used with the COUNT within the parentheses to specify the values to be counted.

A.2 DO IF

DO IF instructs SPSS[x] to carry out the operations that follow up to **END IF.** The advantage is that processing time is not wasted on cases that do not meet the initial condition. For example, suppose you want to analyze the traits of immigrants to the United States who are coded 2 on the variable NATIVE. The following commands would recode the variable YRIMMIG for immigrants only; it would not apply to nonimmigrants. These commands also create a new variable, CLASS, that is coded 1 for cases that are coded over 25000 on the variable INCOME. Other cases will have a value of 0. (These variables are from a census public use sample, not NORC84.)

```
DO IF   NATIVE EQ 2
RECODE   YRIMMIG (LO TO 1959=1) (1960 TO 1969=2)
                 (1970 TO 1979=3) (1980 TO HI=4)
COMPUTE   YEARS=YRIMMIG-1986
IF   INCOME GT 25000   CLASS=1
IF   INCOME LE 25000   CLASS=0
END IF
```

Without the DO IF-END IF sequence, the transformations done in the one RECODE command would require four IF commands. In addition to processing time, the DO IF-END IF commands can save the programmer considerable time by doing transformations with fewer commands. When many transformations are involved, this succinctness is a great advantage.

Two commands that can be used within the DO IF-END IF commands are ELSE IF and ELSE. **ELSE IF** refers to another subset of the file not specified by the DO IF specifications. **ELSE** refers to all the remaining cases not specified on the DO IF command or on any ELSE IF commands. You can use only one ELSE command, and it must follow the last ELSE IF command within the DO IF-END IF sequence. The following commands elaborate this section's first example using ELSE IF and ELSE.

```
DO IF   NATIVE EQ 2
RECODE   YRIMMIG (LO TO 1959=1) (1960 TO 1969=2)
                 (1970 TO 1979=3) (1980 TO HI=4)
COMPUTE   YEARS=YRIMMIG-1986
IF   INCOME GT 25000   CLASS=1
```

```
IF   INCOME LE 25000    CLASS=0
ELSE IF   NATIVE EQ 1
RECODE   BIRTHPL (LO TO 15=1) (16 TO 29=2)
                 (30 TO 40=3) (41 TO HI=4)
ELSE
LIST ID
END IF
```

In the elaborated example, the birthplace (BIRTHPL) of cases coded 1 on NATIVE is recoded, and the ID values of cases that are not coded 1 or 2 on NATIVE are listed.

A.3 FREE and LIST Format Statements

In FREE format the user does not need to place the data for each variable in specific columns. All that is necessary is that the data be entered in the correct sequence with one or more blanks between the entries. For example, say we want to enter the income and education of a set of persons and the first person had income of $35,000 and 16 years of education, the second had $9,000 income and 9 years of education, and the third had $130,000 income and 20 years of education. The data entries would be:

```
35000 16
9000 9
130000 20
```

The Subcommand FREE or LIST is added to the DATA LIST command before the variable names.

Using string variables in a FREE or LIST format statement requires that you place an A and the maximum number of columns for the variable in parentheses after the variable name. For example, to access a variable NAME—a string variable—and a variable INCOME—not a string variable—with a **FREE** format, the following command could be used:

```
DATA LIST  FREE/ NAME (A23)   INCOME
```

The greatest advantage of the FREE format is that you do not have to pay attention to column position when entering data. The greatest disadvantage is that you may not notice when you omit the data for a variable.

LIST format is similar to FREE format, except each record begins a new case. Therefore, one cannot use LIST format with multirecord files. However, if data are omitted for one variable, only one case would have data out of sequence, whereas with the FREE format all the subsequent cases would have data out of sequence. To use the LIST format for our example, the DATA LIST command would read:

```
DATA LIST   LIST/ NAME  (A23)    INCOME
```

A.4 Multiple Record Files

If the data are spread over more than one record, we need a RECORDS subcommand in the DATA LIST command to indicate how many records each case has. The following example shows the placement of the RECORDS subcommand in the DATA LIST command:

```
DATA LIST   RECORDS=2/1 ID 1-4   SEX 6
                       /2 MARITAL 5
```

Beginning in column one is the task command DATA LIST. This command is followed by RECORDS=2, which tells the program that each case will have two records. The 1 after the slash indicates that the first variable being referred to will be on the first record. ID indicates the name of the first variable we will use. We are assigning the variable name through this command and could name it whatever we want. The 1-4 indicates that the data for this variable are stored in columns 1, 2, 3, and 4. SEX indicates that we will use another variable named SEX. The 6 indicates that the data for SEX are in column 6.

The next line, which begins with /2, is a continuation of the DATA LIST command. *In SPSS^x all continued commands must begin after column 1.* We indented the line quite a bit to make it more apparent that this line is a continuation of the one above.

Suppose the next variable, marital status, is located in column 5 of the second record. /2 indicates that the next variable will be on the second record. MARITAL indicates our name for the third variable. The 5 indicates that the data for this variable are found in column 5 of the second record. A bit complex? Yes, it is. You may want to read this paragraph a few times to be sure you understand it completely.

A.5 String Variables

String variables may contain nonnumeric characters. To indicate that a variable is a string variable, on the DATA LIST command place an A in parentheses after the column numbers for the variable. For example, if we had a string variable called NAME on columns 1–20 of a single record file, the following DATA LIST command would allow us to access NAME:

```
DATA LIST   NAME  1-20  (A)
```

A string variable cannot be used if multiplication, division, or other arithmetic operations will be performed. A string variable can be used as the variable in BREAKDOWN for which other variable means are calculated. For example, one could use BREAKDOWN INCOME BY SECTION, where INCOME is not a string variable but SECTION is.

When using FREE or LIST formats, the A in parentheses is followed by the maximum number of columns the variable uses (see Section A.3).

A.6 The Keyword TO

The keyword TO enables you to refer easily to a large number of adjoining variables on your DATA LIST command. For example, suppose you have a data file corresponding to that of the Happiness Questionnaire in Appendix C, in which ID is the first variable, HAPPY is the second, and, after several other variables, AGE is the last. If you want to refer to the variables from HAPPY through AGE on a FREQUENCIES command, you can give the command FREQUENCIES VARIABLES=HAPPY TO AGE instead of specifying each variable separately.

New variables created through IF and COMPUTE commands are added to the end of the variable list in the order that they are created. So, in the preceding example, if you create a new variable called CLASS before the FREQUENCIES command, it will not be included in the specification HAPPY TO AGE. You will have to specify HAPPY TO CLASS to include it.

APPENDIX B
THE SPSS SYSTEM FILE
NORC84

Codebook for the SPSS System File NORC84

The SPSS system file NORC84 contains data from the 1984 General Social Survey. The General Social Survey is an annual survey conducted by the National Opinion Research Center. A probability sample of 1473 persons was taken in 1984 using multistage cluster sampling. Following is a list of the variable names in alphabetical order and then a list of the variables by column number. On the same line as the variable name is a more descriptive variable label, the question number of the variable, and the column number(s) of the variable in the file. Use the question number to look up more complete information in the questionnaire that follows the lists. In the questionnaire the column numbers of the variable are given in parentheses under the variable name, and the question number appears to the right at the beginning of the question.

Alphabetical Listing of Variables

Variable Name	Variable Label	Question Number	Column Number
ABDEFECT	Abortion if birth defect likely	62	68
ABHLTH	Abortion if mother's health in danger	63	69
ABNOMORE	Abortion if no more children wanted	64	70
ABPOOR	Abortion if family is poor	65	71
ABRAPE	Abortion if pregnancy from rape	66	72
ABSINGLE	Abortion if unmarried	67	73

Variable Name	Variable Label	Question Number	Column Number
AGE	Age of respondent	1	1–2
ANOMIA1	Conditions getting worse	57	63
ANOMIA2	Not fair to bring child into world	58	64
ANOMIA3	Officials neglect average man	59	65
ATTEND	Frequency of religious attendance	17	23
CAPPUN	Feelings about capital punishment	27	33
CHILDS	Number of children	9	15
CLASS	Social class identification	18	24
COMMUN	Feelings about Communism	30	36
CONFINAN	Confidence in banks	42	48
CONBUS	Confidence in major companies	43	49
CONCLER	Confidence in organized religion	44	50
CONEDUC	Confidence in educational institutions	45	51
CONFED	Confidence in presidency	46	52
CONLABOR	Confidence in organized labor	47	53
CONPRESS	Confidence in press	48	54
CONMEDI	Confidence in medicine	49	55
CONTV	Confidence in television	50	56
CONJUDG	Confidence in Supreme Court	51	57
CONSCI	Confidence in scientific community	52	58
CONLEGI	Confidence in congress	53	59
CONARMY	Confidence in military	54	60
DEGREE	Highest school degree of respondent	10	16
DRUNK	Sometimes drink too much	55	61
EDUC	Years of education of respondent	4	7–8
FAIR	Fairness of people	36	42
FINALTER	Changes in financial situation	60	66
GETAHEAD	Get ahead by hard work	61	67
GOVAID	Ever received government aid	20	26
GRASS	Favor legalizing marijuana	29	35
GUNLAW	Favor gun permits	28	34
HAPPY	Is respondent happy	31	37

Variable Name	Variable Label	Question Number	Column Number
HEALTH	Respondent's health	32	38
HELPFUL	Helpfulness of people	35	41
INCOME	Family income	3	5–6
MARITAL	Current marital status	8	14
MAWORK	Was your mother employed	13	19
NATEDUC	Nation spending enough on education	21	27
NATFARE	Nation spending enough on welfare	22	28
PARTYID	Political party identification	33	39
POLVIEWS	Political ideology	34	40
PRESTIGE	Prestige of occupation	6	11–12
RACE	Race of respondent	12	18
REGION	Region of interview	14	20
RELIG	Religious preference	16	22
SATCITY	Satisfaction with city	37	43
SATFAM	Satisfaction with family	38	44
SATFRND	Satisfaction with friendships	39	45
SATJOB	Satisfaction with job	40	46
SATHEALT	Satisfaction with health	41	47
SEX	Sex of respondent	11	17
SIBS	Number of siblings	2	3–4
SMOKE	Do you smoke	56	62
SPKATH	Allow speakers against churches	24	30
SPKCOM	Allow Communists to speak	25	31
SPKHOMO	Allow homosexuals to speak	26	32
SRCBELT	Size of residential city	15	21
TAX	Paying fair federal income tax	23	29
TVHOURS	Average daily TV watching	5	9–10
UNEMP	Ever unemployed in past ten years	19	25
WRKSTAT	Employment status currently	7	13

Variables by Column Number

AGE 1-2	SIBS 3-4	INCOME 5-6	EDUC 7-8
TVHOURS 9-10	PRESTIGE 11-12	WRKSTAT 13	MARITAL 14
CHILDS 15	DEGREE 16	SEX 17	RACE 18
MAWORK 19	REGION 20	SRCBELT 21	RELIG 22
ATTEND 23	CLASS 24	UNEMP 25	GOVAID 26
NATEDUC 27	NATFARE 28	TAX 29	SPKATH 30
SPKCOM 31	SPKHOMO 32	CAPPUN 33	GUNLAW 34
GRASS 35	COMMUN 36	HAPPY 37	HEALTH 38
PARTYID 39	POLVIEWS 40	HELPFUL 41	FAIR 42
SATCITY 43	SATFAM 44	SATFRND 45	SATJOB 46
SATHEALT 47	CONFINAN 48	CONBUS 49	CONCLER 50
CONEDUC 51	CONFED 52	CONLABOR 53	CONPRESS 54
CONMEDI 55	CONTV 56	CONJUDG 57	CONSCI 58
CONLEGI 59	CONARMY 60	DRUNK 61	SMOKE 62
ANOMIA1 63	ANOMIA2 64	ANOMIA3 65	FINALTER 66
GETAHEAD 67	ABDEFECT 68	ABNOMORE 69	ABHLTH 70
ABPOOR 71	ABRAPE 72	ABSINGLE 73	

Questions by Column Number*

AGE
(1–2)

1. Age (determined by asking date of birth)
   18–90. Actual age
   98. Don't know (DK)   99. No answer (NA)

SIBS
(3–4)

2. How many brothers and sisters did you have? Please count those born alive but no longer living, as well as those alive now. Also include stepbrothers and stepsisters and children adopted by your parents.
   0–20. Actual number
   98. DK   99. NA

———

*Reprinted with permission of the National Opinion Research Company.

INCOME
(5–6)

3. Into which of the following groups did your total FAMILY income, from ALL sources, fall last year—before taxes, that is?
   1. Under $5,000
   2. $5,000 to $9,999
   3. $10,000 to $14,999
   4. $15,000 to $19,999
   5. $20,000 to $24,999
   6. $25,000 to $34,999
   7. $35,000 to $49,999
   8. $50,000+
   9. Refused
  98. DK 99. NA

EDUC
(7–8)

4. Number of years of formal education.
  0–20. Actual number
  98. DK 99. NA

TVHOURS
(9–10)

5. On the average day, about how many hours do you personally watch television?
  0–18. Actual number
  98. DK 99. NA

PRESTIGE
(11–12)

6. Hodge/Siegel/Rossi prestige scale score for respondent's occupation.
  0. No score due to no job
  12–89. Prestige scale score for job

WRKSTAT
(13)

7. Last week were you working full-time, working part-time, going to school, keeping house, or what?
   1. Working full-time
   2. Working part-time
   3. With a job, but not at work because of temporary illness, vacation, strike
   4. Unemployed
   5. Retired
   6. In school
   7. Keeping house
   8. Other

MARITAL   8. Are you currently married, widowed, divorced, separated,
(14)   or have you never been married?
                  1. Married
                  2. Widowed
                  3. Divorced
                  4. Separated
                  5. Never married

CHILDS   9. How many children have you ever had? Please count all
(15)   that were born alive at any time (including any you had
                  from a previous marriage).
                  0–7. Actual number
                  8. Eight or more   9. NA

DEGREE   10. Highest degree.
(16)   0. Less than high school
                  1. High school
                  2. Associate/junior college
                  3. Bachelor's
                  4. Graduate
                  8. DK   9. NA

SEX   11. Sex (coded by interviewer).
(17)   1. Male
                  2. Female

RACE   12. What race do you consider yourself?
(18)   1. White
                  2. Black
                  3. Other

MAWORK   13. Did your mother ever work for pay for as long as a year,
(19)   after she was married?
                  0. Did not live with mother
                  1. Yes
                  2. No
                  8. DK   9. NA

REGION   14. Region of interview.
(20)   1. New England
                  2. Middle Atlantic
                  3. East North Central
                  4. West North Central
                  5. South Atlantic
                  6. East South Central

                    7. West South Central
                    8. Mountain
                    9. Pacific

SRCBELT   15. Size/type of residence location.
(21)   1. Central city of one of 12 largest Standard Metropolitan
                   Statistical Areas (SMSAs)
                2. Central city of remainder of the 100 largest SMSAs
                3. Suburbs of one of 12 largest SMSAs
                4. Suburbs of the remainder of the 100 largest SMSAs
                5. Other urban (counties having towns of 10,000 or more)
                6. Other rural (counties having no towns of 10,000 or
                   more)

RELIG   16. What is your religious preference? Is it Protestant, Catho-
(22)   lic, Jewish, some other religion, or no religion?
                1. Protestant
                2. Catholic
                3. Jewish
                4. None
                5. Other
                9. NA

ATTEND   17. How often do you attend religious services?
(23)   0. Never
                1. Less than once a year
                2. About once or twice a year
                3. Several times a year
                4. About once a month
                5. 2–3 times a month
                6. Nearly every week
                7. Every week
                8. Several times a week
                9. DK/NA

CLASS   18. If you were asked to use one of four names for your social
(24)   class, which would you say you belong in: the lower class,
               the working class, the middle class, or the upper class?
                1. Lower class
                2. Working class
                3. Middle class
                4. Upper class
                8. DK   9. NA

UNEMP
(25)

19. At any time during the last ten years, have you been unemployed and looking for work for as long as a month?
    1. Yes
    2. No
    8. DK   9. NA

GOVAID
(26)

20. Did you ever—because of sickness, unemployment, or
any other reason—receive anything like welfare, unemployment insurance, or other aid from governmental
agencies?
    1. Yes
    2. No
    8. DK   9. NA

We are faced with many problems in this country, none of
which can be solved easily or inexpensively. I'm going to
name some of these problems, and for each one I'd like you
to tell me whether you think we're spending too much money
on it, too little money, or about the right amount. Are we
spending too much, too little, or about the right amount on
[21, 22, 23] . . .

NATEDUC
(27)

21. Improving the nation's educational system?
    1. Too little
    2. About right
    3. Too much
    8. DK   9. NA

NATFARE
(28)

22. Welfare?
    (Same answers as NATEDUC, #21)

TAX
(29)

23. Do you consider the amount of federal income tax that
you have to pay to be too high, about right, or too low?
    1. Too high
    2. About right
    3. Too low
    8. DK   9. NA

SPKATH
(30)

24. If somebody who is against all churches and religion
wanted to make a speech in your city/town/community
against churches and religion, should he be allowed to
speak or not?
    1. Yes, allowed to speak
    2. Not allowed
    8. DK   9. NA

SPKCOM
(31)

25. Suppose a man who admits he is a Communist wanted to make a speech in your community. Should he be allowed to speak or not?
(Same answers as SPKATH, #24)

SPKHOMO
(32)

26. Suppose a man who admits he is a homosexual wanted to make a speech in your community. Should he be allowed to speak or not?
(Same answers as SPKATH, #24)

CAPPUN
(33)

27. Do you favor or oppose the death penalty for persons convicted of murder?
1. Favor
2. Oppose
8. DK   9. NA

GUNLAW
(34)

28. Would you favor or oppose a law that would require a person to obtain a police permit before he or she could buy a gun?
(Same answers as CAPPUN, #27)

GRASS
(35)

29. Do you think the use of marijuana should be made legal or not?
1. Should
2. Should not
8. DK   9. NA

COMMUN
(36)

30. Thinking about all the different kinds of government in the world today, which of these statements comes closest to how you feel about Communism as a form of government?
1. It's the worst kind of all
2. It's bad, but no worse than some others
3. It's all right for some countries
4. It's a good form of government
8. DK   9. NA

HAPPY
(37)

31. Taken all together, how would you say things are these days—would you say that you are very happy, pretty happy, or not too happy?
1. Very happy
2. Pretty happy
3. Not too happy
8. DK   9. NA

HEALTH
(38)

32. Would you say your own health, in general, is excellent, good, fair, or poor?
1. Excellent
2. Good
3. Fair
4. Poor
8. DK   9. NA

PARTYID
(39)

33. Generally speaking, do you usually think of yourself as a Republican, Democrat, Independent, or what?
0. Strong Democrat
1. Not very strong Democrat
2. Independent, close to Democrat
3. Independent (neither, no response)
4. Independent, close to Republican
5. Not very strong Republican
6. Strong Republican
7. Other party, refused to say
8. DK   9. NA

POLVIEWS
(40)

34. I'm going to show you a seven-point scale on which the *political* views that people might hold are arranged from extremely liberal—point 1—to extremely conservative—point 7. Where would you place yourself on this scale?
1. Extremely liberal
2. Liberal
3. Slightly liberal
4. Moderate, middle of the road
5. Slightly conservative
6. Conservative
7. Extremely conservative
8. DK   9. NA

HELPFUL
(41)

35. Would you say that most of the time people try to be helpful or that they are mostly just looking out for themselves?
1. Try to be helpful
2. Just look out for themselves
3. Depends (volunteered)
8. DK   9. NA

FAIR
(42)

36. Do you think most people would try to take advantage of you if they got a chance, or would they try to be fair?
1. Would take advantage of you
2. Would try to be fair

　　　　　　　　3. Depends (volunteered)
　　　　　　　　8. DK　9. NA

SATCITY　　　37. Tell me the number that shows how much satisfaction
(43)　　　　　　　you get from the city or place you live in.
　　　　　　　　1. A very great deal
　　　　　　　　2. A great deal
　　　　　　　　3. Quite a bit
　　　　　　　　4. A fair amount
　　　　　　　　5. Some
　　　　　　　　6. A little
　　　　　　　　7. None
　　　　　　　　8. DK　9. NA

SATFAM　　　38. Tell me the number that shows how much satisfaction
(44)　　　　　　　you get from your family life.
　　　　　　　　(Same answers as SATCITY, #37)

SATFRND　　39. Tell me the number that shows how much satisfaction
(45)　　　　　　　you get from your friendships.
　　　　　　　　(Same answers as SATCITY, 37)

SATJOB　　　40. On the whole, how satisfied are you with the work you
(46)　　　　　　　do—would you say you are very satisfied, moderately
　　　　　　　　satisfied, a little dissatisfied, or very dissatisfied?
　　　　　　　　0. Not applicable due to no job
　　　　　　　　1. Very satisfied
　　　　　　　　2. Moderately satisfied
　　　　　　　　3. A little dissatisfied
　　　　　　　　4. Very dissatisfied
　　　　　　　　8. DK　9. NA

SATHEALT　　41. Tell me the number that shows how much satisfaction
(47)　　　　　　　you get from your health and physical condition.
　　　　　　　　(Same answers as SATCITY, #37)

　　　　　　　　I am going to name some institutions in this country. As
　　　　　　　　far as the *people running* these institutions are con-
　　　　　　　　cerned, would you say that you have a great deal of confi-
　　　　　　　　dence, only some confidence, or hardly any confidence at
　　　　　　　　all in them?

CONFINAN　　42. Banks and financial institutions
(48)　　　　　　　1. A great deal
　　　　　　　　2. Only some

3. Hardly any
8. DK   9. NA

CONBUS   43. Major companies
(49)   (Same answers as CONFINAN, #42)

CONCLER   44. Organized religion
(50)   (Same answers as CONFINAN, #42)

CONEDUC   45. Education
(51)   (Same answers as CONFINAN, #42)

CONFED   46. Executive branch of the federal government
(52)   (Same answers as CONFINAN, #42)

CONLABOR   47. Organized labor
(53)   (Same answers as CONFINAN, #42)

CONPRESS   48. Press
(54)   (Same answers as CONFINAN, #42)

CONMEDI   49. Medicine
(55)   (Same answers as CONFINAN, #42)

CONTV   50. TV
(56)   (Same answers as CONFINAN, #42)

CONJUDG   51. U.S. Supreme Court
(57)   (Same answers as CONFINAN, #42)

CONSCI   52. Scientific community
(58)   (Same answers as CONFINAN, #42)

CONLEGI   53. Congress
(59)   (Same answers as CONFINAN, #42)

CONARMY   54. Military
(60)   (Same answers as CONFINAN, #42)

DRUNK   55. Do you sometimes drink more than you think you should?
(61)   0. Total abstainer
                    1. Yes
                    2. No
                    8. DK   9. NA

SMOKE   56. Do you smoke?
(62)   1. Yes
                    2. No
                    9. NA

ANOMIA1
(63)

57. In spite of what some people say, the lot/situation/condition of the average man is getting worse, not better. Do you more or less agree with that, or more or less disagree?
1. Agree
2. Disagree
8. DK   9. NA

ANOMIA2
(64)

58. It's hardly fair to bring a child into the world with the way things look for the future.
(Same answers as ANOMIA1, #57)

ANOMIA3
(65)

59. Most public officials (people in public office) are not really interested in the problems of the average man.
(Same answers as ANOMIA1, #57)

FINALTER
(66)

60. During the last few years, has your financial situation been getting better or getting worse, or has it stayed the same?
1. Getting better
2. Getting worse
3. Stayed the same
8. DK   9. NA

GETAHEAD
(67)

61. Some people say that people get ahead by their own hard work; others say that lucky breaks or help from other people are more important. Which do you think is most important?
1. Hard work most important
2. Hard work, luck equally important
3. Luck most important
8. DK   9. NA

Please tell me whether or not *you* think it should be possible for a pregnant woman to obtain a *legal* abortion . . .

ABDEFECT
(68)

62. If there is a strong chance of serious defect in the baby.
1. Yes
2. No
8. DK   9. NA

ABNOMORE
(69)

63. If she is married and does not want any more children.
(Same answers as ABDEFECT, #62)

ABHLTH
(70)

64. If the woman's health is seriously endangered by the pregnancy.
(Same answers as ABDEFECT, #62)

ABPOOR   65. If the family has a very low income and cannot afford any
(71)   more children.
                 (Same answers as ABDEFECT, #62)

ABRAPE   66. If she became pregnant as a result of rape.
(72)   (Same answers as ABDEFECT, #62)

ABSINGLE   67. If she is not married and does not want to marry the man.
(73)   (Same answers as ABDEFECT, #62)

APPENDIX C
A COURSE RESEARCH
PROJECT

Completing a research project on your own is much more challenging than using the data we provide in Chapter 2 or in the SPSS system file NORC84. In this appendix we outline a class research project. The subject of this research is happiness, and the questions on this survey come from the SPSS system file NORC84. This similarity will allow you to compare your results with those of a representative national sample.

Following is a questionnaire you can photocopy and use in an interview. The questionnaire is designed for the interviewer to record in the boxes on the right numbers that correspond to the respondent's answers. The numbers under the boxes designate the columns in which these data are to be stored when the information is placed in a computer file.

Let us suppose that you are going to administer this questionnaire to 20 people. The obvious question is which 20? One choice would be to go to a store and hand out questionnaires to people leaving the store.

Another choice would be to go to a random selection of households and interview the individuals in these households.

Or you could randomly dial telephone numbers and interview individuals over the phone.

Each of these sampling methods is reasonably good, although there are always problems with biases that might make your sample different from the general population. The store may attract people from one social class or ethnic group more than others. You may be biased in which shoppers you approach to question and which ones you let pass by. Households with many members are more likely to have someone home when you knock on the door or call on the phone; hence you may undersample single people. Households with ferocious guard dogs are judiciously skipped by prudent interviewers. People without phones will not be netted in a telephone survey.

The fact that it is nearly impossible to obtain a perfect random sample does not mean that research is impossible. Our burden as researchers is to do work that is as free from bias as we can make it, and yet humbly admit that some small distortion still creeps in. An analogy is radio reception from a distant station: Occasionally there may be static distortion, but normally you can distinguish the music and lyrics. Accepted survey practices are accepted because experience has shown that they provide reasonably accurate data about the population being sampled.

You need to consider the purpose of your research. Are there special reasons why, given that purpose, a particular sampling method is desirable or undesirable? For example, if you wanted to study homeless people, a phone survey or a household survey of a middle-class neighborhood would not be efficient or appropriate. If you wanted to survey wealthy people, passing out questionnaires at a fast-food outlet would not be the best approach. There is no substitute for careful thinking. Consider first who is in the population you want to sample, and second what would be the most efficient means of obtaining a sample of these people that is approximately random.

Once you have gathered your data, the next step is to code it. All but one of the questions in the Happiness Questionnaire are precoded; that is, all possible responses for each question have already been given a number, and columns have been designated for the responses for each variable. Precoding saves time; however, it does require painstaking forethought and pretesting of the questionnaire. Precoding usually restricts you to multiple-choice questions. The choices may help the respondents answer as they consider the alternatives, but the set of answers may not allow some respondents to express their position precisely.

The last question on the questionnaire was deliberately left open-ended to provide the option of dealing with less structured data. If you want to have a quick and easy coding experience stop at question 12.

Question 13—"What do you think you could do to be happier five years from now than you are today?" will result in a plethora of answers. Come coding time you will have to decide whether you are going to categorize these responses into numbered groups for quantitative analysis or simply keep the verbal responses as material to quote when illustrating your findings in the coded questions. Open-ended questions can be eye openers for the researcher in illustrating factors that he or she may have overlooked or in pointing out that assumptions are unfounded.

Follow your instructor's guidelines for administering the Happiness Questionnaire to a sample of people.

The DATA LIST command for questions 1 through 12 of the questionnaire will be:

```
DATA LIST   ID 1-4   HAPPY 5   HEALTH 6   SATFAM 7
            SATFRND 8   SATJOB 9
            EDUC 10-11   MARITAL 12   CHILDS 13
            INCOME 14   TVHOURS 15-16   SEX 17   AGE 18
```

Happiness Questionnaire

(Interviewer: Record the answer to each question in the boxes at right.)

ID

Columns 1–4

As a class exercise we are doing a study of what affects happiness. Will you please answer thirteen questions for us?

1. Taken all together, would you say that you are very happy, pretty happy, or not too happy?
   1. Very happy
   2. Pretty happy
   3. Not too happy
   8. Don't know (DK)
   9. No answer (NA)

   HAPPY

   Column 5

2. Would you say your own health, in general, is excellent, good, fair, or poor?
   1. Excellent
   2. Good
   3. Fair
   4. Poor
   8. DK
   9. NA

   HEALTH

   Column 6

3. Tell me the number that shows how much satisfaction you get from your family life.
   1. A very great deal
   2. A great deal
   3. Quite a bit
   4. A fair amount
   5. Some
   6. A little
   7. None
   8. DK
   9. NA

   SATFAM

   Column 7

4. Tell me the number that shows how much satisfaction you get from your friendships. (Use the same choices as for Question 3)

SATFRND

Column 8

5. On the whole, how satisfied are you with the work you do? Would you say you are very satisfied, moderately satisfied, a little dissatisfied, or very dissatisfied.
   0. Not applicable due to no job
   1. Very satisfied
   2. Moderately satisfied
   3. A little dissatisfied
   4. Very dissatisfied
   8. DK
   9. NA

SATJOB

Column 9

6. How many years of formal education have you completed? (Enter number of years.)
   98. DK
   99. NA

EDUC

Columns 10–11

7. Are you currently married, widowed, divorced, or separated, or have you never been married?
   1. Married
   2. Widowed
   3. Divorced
   4. Separated
   5. Never married

MARITAL

Column 12

8. How many children have you ever had? Please count all that were born alive at any time (including any you had from a previous marriage).
   0–7. Actual number
   8. Eight or more
   9. NA

CHILDS

Column 13

9. Into which of the following groups did your total family income, from all sources, fall last year before taxes?

    1. Under $5,000
    2. $5,000 to $9,999
    3. $10,000 to $14,999
    4. $15,000 to $19,999
    5. $20,000 to $24,999
    6. $25,000 to $34,999
    7. $35,000 to $49,000
    8. $50,000 and over
    9. DK
   10. NA

INCOME

[ ]

Column 14

10. On the average day, about how many hours do you personally watch television?

    0–24. Actual number
    98.   DK
    99.   NA

TVHOURS

[|]

Columns 15–16

11. Sex.

    1. Male
    2. Female

SEX

[ ]

Column 17

12. What is your age?

    0–97. Actual age
    98.   DK
    99.   NA

AGE

[ ]

Column 18

13. This is the last question. What do you think you could do to be happier five years from now than you are today?

Thank you for your cooperation.

APPENDIX D
COMPARISON OF SPSS^X
AND SPSS

If you are accustomed to using SPSS, you may ask "Why should I bother to make the transition to SPSS^X?"

As you know, SPSS has been continually improved and expanded. In the future such improvements will be made in SPSS^X but not in SPSS. In fact, there are already many such improvements in SPSS^X, making it easier to use than SPSS. SPSS^X is also capable of doing more than SPSS.

In SPSS^X you do not need to begin command specifications and continuations in column 16. All that is needed is a one-space separation between the command and what follows.

In SPSS^X parentheses are not needed on SELECT IF and IF commands, eliminating the frequently encountered error of unmatched parentheses.

SPSS^X has commands for working with hierarchical files, which are common in government and business data files. For example, many census tapes contain both household and individual records. First there is a household record, followed by one or more records for each individual in the household. Then comes the next household record followed by its individual records. The researcher often wants to combine information from the household record, such as family income or place of residence, with information from the individuals' records.

SPSS^X has advantages over SPSS, and the transition to using SPSS^X is not difficult. There are, however, small but crucial differences between SPSS and SPSS^X in some commands.

Generally, for the commands we covered in Part I of this text, SPSS commands continue to work. Still there are a few changes you must make.

The GET FILE command of SPSS will not work. Use the GET FILE= command of SPSS^X.

The LIST CASES command of SPSS will not work. Use the LIST command of SPSS^X.

In SPSS, blanks are read as zeros. In SPSS^x, they are read as missing unless you use the following RECODE command:

RECODE   (BLANKS=0)

VAR LABELS and VALUE LABELS from SPSS will work if the labels for each variable or each category are not split between two lines.

In SPSS^x a label that extends beyond one line must be indicated by a plus (+) as the first entry on the second line. Both parts of the label are enclosed with apostrophes or quotation marks. The SPSS command would not use the plus or the apostrophes or quotation marks. The following is an SPSS^x example:

VARIABLE LABELS   HAPPY 'TAKEN ALL TOGETHER'
  +'WOULD YOU SAY THAT YOU ARE'
   +'VERY HAPPY, PRETTY HAPPY, OR NOT TOO HAPPY?'

READ INPUT DATA must be replaced with BEGIN DATA, and END INPUT DATA must be replaced with END DATA.

The STATISTICS and OPTIONS for FREQUENCIES, CROSSTABS, and BREAKDOWN from SPSS will work with SPSS^x, but SPSS^x has some STATISTICS and OPTIONS not available in SPSS.

A rather lengthy summary of changes is in Appendix A of the *SPSS^x User's Guide,* pages 749–773.

GLOSSARY OF SPSSˣ COMMANDS

BREAKDOWN examples:

```
DATA LIST    ID 1-2    EDUC 3-4    SEX 5    HAPPY 6
BEGIN DATA
     .
     .
     .
END DATA
MISSING VALUES    EDUC(-9,99)    HAPPY SEX(0)
BREAKDOWN    HAPPY BY SEX

GET   FILE=NORC84
BREAKDOWN    HAPPY BY HEALTH
```

COMPUTE examples:

Mathematical operators—

+	plus
−	minus
*	multiplication
/	division
**	exponention
SQRT	square root

```
COMPUTE    ANSWER1=450+200

COMPUTE    ANSWER2=450-200
```

```
COMPUTE    ANSWER3=450*2

COMPUTE    ANSWER4=450/50

COMPUTE    ANSWER5=5**3

COMPUTE    ANSWER6=SQRT(81)

COMPUTE    TINC=WINC+HINC

COMPUTE    RETIRE=65-AGE

COMPUTE    TPAY=DSALARY*DAYS

COMPUTE    AVESAL=PAYROLL/NEMPLOYS

COMPUTE    DEVIAT=(INC-MINC)**2

COMPUTE    SD=SQRT(SUMDEV)
```

CROSSTABS examples:

```
DATA LIST    ID 1-2   EDUC 3-4   SEX 5   HAPPY 6
BEGIN DATA
    .
    .
    .
END DATA
MISSING VALUES   EDUC(-9,99)   HAPPY SEX(0)
RECODE    EDUC  (0 THRU 11=1) (12 THRU 15=2) (16 THRU 30=3)
CROSSTABS    EDUC BY SEX
OPTIONS   4,13


GET   FILE=NORC84
CROSSTABS    SATFAM SATFRND SATJOB BY INCOME
OPTIONS   4,13
```

DATA LIST examples:

Single record file—

```
DATA LIST    ID 1-2   EDUC 3-4   SEX 5   HAPPY 6
```

Multiple record file—

```
DATA LIST    RECORDS=2/1 ID 1-4   SEX 6
                       /2 MARITAL 5
```

FREQUENCIES examples:

```
GET   FILE=NORC84
FREQUENCIES   VARIABLES=ALL/
            STATISTICS


GET   FILE=NORC84
FREQUENCIES   VARIABLES=ABDEFECT  ABNOMORE  ABHLTH  ABPOOR
                         ABRAPE  ABSINGLE/
            STATISTICS
```

(The VARIABLES subcommand could also be written VARIABLES=ABDEFECT TO ABSINGLE)

IF examples:

EQ	equal
NE	not equal
LT	less than
GT	greater than
LE	less than or equal to
GE	greater than or equal to

```
IF AGE LE 9   AGEGROUP=1
IF AGE GT 9   AND   AGE LE 19   AGEGROUP=2
IF AGE GT 19   AND   AGE LE 29   AGEGROUP=3
IF AGE GT 29   AND   AGE LE 39   AGEGROUP=4
IF AGE GT 39   AND   AGE LE 49   AGEGROUP=5
IF AGE GT 49   AND   AGE LE 59   AGEGROUP=6
IF AGE GT 59   AND   AGE LE 69   AGEGROUP=7
IF AGE GT 69   AND   AGE LE 79   AGEGROUP=8
IF AGE GT 79   AGEGROUP=9


IF   TENURE LT 12   NEWEXEC=1


IF   FAMINCOM GT AVEINCOM   INCOME=1
```

LIST examples:

```
LIST   VARIABLES=ALL
       CASES=15


LIST   VARIABLES=INCOME
       CASES=ALL


DATA LIST   ID 1-2   EDUC 3-4   SEX 5   HAPPY 6
BEGIN DATA
   .
   .
   .
END DATA
SELECT IF  SEX NE 1   OR   SEX NE 2
LIST
```

MISSING VALUES examples:

```
MISSING VALUES   EDUC(-9)

MISSING VALUES   INCOME(-8,-9)

MISSING VALUES   SEX RELIGION PARTY(0)

MISSING VALUES   EDUC(-9,99)   HAPPY SEX(0)


DATA LIST   ID 1-2   EDUC 3-4   SEX 5   HAPPY 6
BEGIN DATA
   .
   .
   .
END DATA
MISSING VALUES   EDUC(-9,99)   HAPPY,SEX(0)
FREQUENCIES   VARIABLES=ALL
```

RECODE examples:

```
RECODE   MARITAL  (2 THRU 4=1)

RECODE   HEIGHT  (LOW THRU 59=1)(60 THRU 70=2)(71 THRU
HI=3)
```

RECODE   CARS (3 THRU HI=2)

RECODE   AGE (LO THRU 15=1) (16 THRU 65=2) (66 THRU HI=3)

SELECT IF examples:

EQ	equal
NE	not equal
LT	less than
GT	greater than
LE	less than or equal to
GE	greater than or equal to

SELECT IF   EDUC GT 15

SELECT IF   SEX EQ 1

SELECT IF   AGE GT 15   OR   AGE LT 66

SELECT IF   EDUC GT 16   OR   INCOME GT 30000

SELECT IF   EDUC GT 12   AND   SEX EQ 2

SELECT IF   SEX EQ 2   AND   (AGE GT 14   AND   AGE LT 45)

(The parentheses in this command are not necessary, but they do make it easier to read. The same cases could be selected by using two SELECT IF commands—one for SEX and one for AGE.)

SELECT IF   SEX EQ 2
SELECT IF   AGE GT 14   AND   AGE LT 45

DATA LIST   ID 1-2   EDUC 3-4   SEX 5   HAPPY 6
BEGIN DATA
   .
   .
   .
END DATA
SELECT IF   SEX EQ 1
FREQUENCIES   VARIABLES=EDUC SEX HAPPY/
            STATISTICS

TEMPORARY examples:

```
DATA LIST   ID 1-2   EDUC 3-4   SEX 5   HAPPY 6
BEGIN DATA
   .
   .
   .
END DATA
TEMPORARY
SELECT IF   SEX EQ 1
FREQUENCIES   VARIABLES=ALL/
            STATISTICS
TEMPORARY
SELECT IF   SEX EQ 2
FREQUENCIES   VARIABLES=ALL/
            STATISTICS


GET   FILE=NORC84
TEMPORARY
SELECT IF   AGE GT 49
FREQUENCIES   VARIABLES=EDUC/
            STATISTICS
TEMPORARY
SELECT IF   AGE GT 24   AND   AGE LT 50
FREQUENCIES   VARIABLES=EDUC/
            STATISTICS
```

ANSWERS TO REVIEW QUESTIONS

Chapter 1

1.1 Column 1

1.2 Any column after column 1 and before column 72

1.3 Column 72

1.4 Column 80

1.5 Column 72

1.6 No. Computer installations do not all use the same operating system language. Even if they did, the components of the system and the names given to accounts, printers, tapes, disks, and so on, would differ.

1.7 Yes

1.8 Cards, tapes, disks, and memory core

1.9 Most likely not. It will probably be one of many terminals communicating with a mainframe central processing unit and its accompanying set of input devices, storage devices, and output devices.

1.10 Program commands instruct the computer about how to obtain, process, and store information about cases in your study. The data are the actual information about the cases.

Chapter 2

2.1 The Hedderson case would be coded 25 in the first two columns to indicate his identification number. The third and fourth columns would be coded 21 to indicate the 21 years of formal education, the fifth column would be coded 1 to indicate his sex, and the sixth column would be coded 1 to indicate that he stated he felt very happy. Thus, the record line for Hedderson would read:

252111

2.2   To code age, researchers usually simply record the respondent's age in years in two columns. Someone who is 19 years old would be given a value of 19. Someone who is 45 years old would be given a value of 45. Grouped intervals could also be used. For example:

AGE	Code
Under 10	1
10–19	2
20–29	3
30–39	4
40–49	5
50–59	6
60–70	7
Over 70	8

2.3   In the United States, political party affiliation might be coded as follows:

Party	Code
Democrat	1
Republican	2
Independent (no affiliation)	3
Other affiliation	4

The code numbers used to indicate the categories of a variable are an arbitrary choice of the researcher. In this example, Republican could just as well be coded 1, and Democrat 2. The code numbers are merely short labels used to save space.

2.4   The simplest way to code annual salary would be to use two columns and code the case's income in thousands of dollars. Thus, someone with an income of $20,000 would be given a value of 20. A value of 99 could be used for people whose annual income is $99,000 or more.

2.5   DATA LIST   EDUC 3-4

2.6   DATA LIST commands are not used with SPSS^x system files. The variable location information is already saved with the file.

2.7   DATA LIST   INCOME 13   SEX 16

2.8   MISSING VALUES   EDUC (-9)

2.9   MISSING VALUES   INCOME (-9, -8)

2.10   MISSING VALUES   SEX RELIGION PARTY (0)

2.11   Nothing. It is treated as missing automatically by the program.

Chapter 3

3.1   DATA LIST   ID 1-2   EDUC 3-4   SEX 5   HAPPY 6
        BEGIN DATA
        010912
        021223
        031521
        041222
        050611
        061612
        071522
        081612
        091821
        101412
        111321
        121611
        130922
        141212
        151221
        161821
        170821
        181222
        191613
        201421
        END DATA
        LIST

3.2   GET   FILE=NORC84
        LIST   VARIABLES=ALL
               CASES=20

3.3   GET   FILE=NORC84
            LIST   VARIABLES=INCOME
                      CASES=ALL

Your commands would be the same as 3.1 except ALL would replace LIST.

3.4   FREQUENCIES   VARIABLES=ZIPCODE

3.5   FREQUENCIES   VARIABLES=AGE SEX MARITAL

3.6   You would need to recode INCOME into a manageable number of categories. Otherwise there would be almost as many income categories in the frequencies table as there are cases, because most people would have a unique income.

3.7   This output indicates that a variable named NEIGHBOR has three categories coded 1, 2, and 3. Category 1 has three cases, or 30.0 percent of the total number of cases for which there are data. Category 2 has five cases, or 50.0 percent of the total number of cases for which there are data. Category 3 has two cases, or 20.0 percent of the total number of cases for which there are data. There is one "missing case," which means there is one case for which we do not have the NEIGHBOR information.

3.8   GET   FILE=NORC84
            FREQUENCIES   VARIABLES=ALL/
                      STATISTICS

3.9   GET   FILE=NORC84
            FREQUENCIES   VARIABLES=ABDEFECT ABNOMORE ABHLTH
                                   ABPOOR ABRAPE ABSINGLE/
                      STATISTICS

(The VARIABLES= subcommand could also be written VARIABLES=ABDEFECT TO ABSINGLE.) See Appendix A.6.

3.10   GET   FILE=NORC84
            FREQUENCIES   VARIABLES=EDUC HEALTH HAPPY/
                      STATISTICS

3.11   SELECT IF   SEX EQ 1

3.12   SELECT IF   AGE GT 65

3.13   SELECT IF   EDUC GT 16   OR   INCOME GT 30000

3.14   SELECT IF   AGE GT 15   OR   AGE LT 66

3.15   SELECT IF SEX EQ 2   AND   (AGE GT 14 AND AGE LT 45)

The parentheses in this command are not necessary, but they do make it easier to read. The same cases could also be selected by using two SELECT IF commands: one for SEX and one for AGE:

```
SELECT IF   SEX EQ 2
SELECT IF   AGE GT 14   AND   AGE LT 45
```

3.16   SELECT IF EDUC GT 15   AND   SEX EQ 2
```
LIST   VARIABLES=ALL
          CASES=25
```

Chapter 4

4.1   RECODE MARITAL (3,4=2)

4.2   RECODE HEIGHT (LOW THRU 59=1) (60 THRU 70=2) (71 THRU HI=3)

4.3   RECODE CARS (2 THRU HI=2)

or

RECODE CARS (3 THRU HI=2)

4.4   RECODE AGE (0 THRU 15=1) (16 THRU 65=2) (66 THRU HI=3)

4.5   COMPUTE FAMILY\$=WIFE\$+HUSBAND\$

4.6   COMPUTE HOURLY\$=SALARY/160

4.7   IF TENURE LT 12 NEWEXEC=1
       IF TENURE GT 11 NEWEXEC=0

4.8   IF FAMINCOM GT AVEINCOM INCOME=1
       IF FAMINCOM LT AVEINCOM INCOME=0

4.9   GET FILE=NORC84
```
TEMPORARY
SELECT IF   SEX EQ 1
FREQUENCIES   VARIABLES=INCOME/
                 STATISTICS
TEMPORARY
SELECT IF   SEX EQ 2
FREQUENCIES   VARIABLES=INCOME/
                 STATISTICS
```

4.10   GET   FILE=NORC84
           SELECT IF   AGE GT 49
           FREQUENCIES   VARIABLES=EDUC/
                          STATISTICS
           TEMPORARY
           SELECT IF   AGE GT 24   AND   AGE LT 50
           FREQUENCIES   VARIABLES=EDUC/
                          STATISTICS

4.11   VARIABLE LABEL   CHILDS "NUMBER OF CHILDREN"

4.12   VARIABLE LABEL   INCOME "GROSS INCOME"
                             NET "NET INCOME"

4.13   VALUE LABELS POLVIEWS 1"LIBERAL"
                                  2"MIDDLE OF THE ROAD"
                                  3"CONSERVATIVE"

4.14   VALUE LABELS OVERDUE   1"LESS THAN 60 DAYS"
                                   2"MORE THAN 60 DAYS"/
                          MILITARY 1"MILITARY PERSONNEL"
                                   2"CIVILIAN PERSONNEL"

Chapter 5

5.1   CROSSTABS   INCOME BY SEX
          OPTIONS   4,13

          (Although a run would occur without the OPTIONS command, the output would be more difficult to understand. It would contain the *number* of cases in each cell rather than the *percent* of cases.)

5.2   CROSSTABS   SALES BY DAY
          OPTIONS   4,13

5.3   DATA LIST   ID 1-2   EDUC 3-4   SEX 5   HAPPY 6
          BEGIN DATA
          010912
          021223
          031521
          041222
          050611
          061612
          071522
          081612

```
        091821
        101412
        111321
        121611
        130922
        141212
        151221
        161821
        170821
        181222
        191613
        201421
        END  DATA
        MISSING  VALUES   EDUC(-9,99)    HAPPY SEX(0)
        RECODE EDUC  (0  THRU  11=1)(12  THRU  15=2)(16  THRU  30=3)
        CROSSTABS   EDUC  BY  SEX
        OPTIONS   4,13
```

5.4   GET   FILE=NORC84
CROSSTABS   POLITICS BY RELIGION
OPTIONS   4,13

5.5   GET   FILE=NORC84
CROSSTABS   HAPPY HEALTH INCOME BY EDUC
OPTIONS   4,13

5.6   GET   FILE=NORC84
CROSSTABS   HAPPY BY MARITAL BY SEX
OPTIONS   4,13

5.7   STATISTICS   1,2

5.8   Cramer's *V* is a transformation of chi-square that ranges from 0.0 for no association to 1.0 for a perfect association. Unlike chi-square, the size of Cramer's *V* is not affected by the number of cases or cells. It is, however, affected by the percentage of cases in each category of the variables being used. For example, if one sample had 20 percent females and a second sample had 60 percent females, this in itself would alter Cramer's *V* involving sex as a variable—even if the associations between sex and the other variables were the same.

Chapter 6

6.1   BREAKDOWN   INCOME BY SEX

6.2   BREAKDOWN   HEALTH BY EDUC INCOME

6.3   DATA LIST   ID 1-2   EDUC 3-4   SEX 5   HAPPY 6
           BEGIN DATA
           010912
           021223
           031521
           041222
           050611
           061612
           071522
           081612
           091821
           101412
           111321
           121611
           130922
           141212
           151221
           161821
           170821
           181222
           191613
           201421
           END DATA
           MISSING VALUES   EDUC(-9,99)   HAPPY SEX(0)
           BREAKDOWN   HAPPY BY EDUC

6.4   GET   FILE=NORC84
           BREAKDOWN   HAPPY BY HEALTH

6.5   The criterion variable in a BREAKDOWN output is the variable whose
           mean score is given for each category of another variable.

6.6   In a BREAKDOWN command, the dependent variable is placed before
           the BY.

6.7   BREAKDOWN   INCOME BY SEX BY EDUC

6.8   BREAKDOWN   INCOME BY EDUC
           STATISTICS   ALL

6.9   SELECT IF   EDUC EQ 12   OR   EDUC EQ 15
         BREAKDOWN   INCOME BY EDUC
         STATISTICS   ALL

Chapter 7

7.1   SCATTERGRAM   INCOME WITH EDUC

7.2   SCATTERGRAM   INCOME EDUC WITH AGE
         STATISTIC   1

7.3   PEARSON CORR   HAPPY HEALTH

7.4   PEARSON CORR   INCOME AGE FAMSIZE CARSIZE
         OPTION   6

7.5   No, there would not be enough variance in the number of cars per family to produce a revealing scattergram. Too many cases would be clustered in the 1-to-3 range.

7.6   There would be too many cases per point in the scattergram. The problem could be solved by using the SAMPLE command to select out a suitable proportion of the cases. (See the discussion of SAMPLE in Section 7.2.)

7.7   Technically, the Pearson correlation coefficient is meant for interval variables that are linearly associated. The technique is robust, however, and will usually produce reasonably accurate estimates for ordinal variables. Nominal variables with only two categories may also be used with the Pearson correlation coefficient. Nominal variables with more than two categories are absolutely inappropriate and produce nonsensical coefficients.

7.8   The Pearson correlation coefficient presumes a linear relationship; therefore, an exponential negative relationship would not be measured accurately. Using a COMPUTE statement to create a new variable, the log of the infant death rate, and then doing the correlation analysis with the new variable would be appropriate. (See the discussion of the COMPUTE statement in Section 4.2.)

7.9   The negative coefficient indicates that, as one variable increases in value, the other variable tends to decrease in value. The positive coefficient indicates that, as one variable increases in value, the other variable tends to increase in value.

7.10   The Pearson correlation coefficient squared is the true measure of the strength of the association; thus, the relative strengths would be $(.20)^2$

to $(.30)^2$, or .04 to .09. The association between HEALTH and EDUC is only four-ninths as strong as the association between HEALTH and IN-COME. (The associations in this question are purely hypothetical.)

Chapter 8

8.1 Theoretically, the dependent and independent variables in a multiple regression analysis should be interval variables. In practice, ordinal variables are often used. Two-category nominal variables, also called dichotomous variables, can be used as well, if neither category has fewer than 20 percent of the cases.

8.2
```
REGRESSION   VARIABLES=HEALTH INCOME EDUC HAPPY
                       AGE SEX
                       DEPENDENT=HEALTH
                       METHOD=ENTER
```

8.3
```
IF   RELIG EQ 1   D1=1
IF   RELIG NE 1   D1=0
IF   RELIG EQ 2   D2=1
IF   RELIG NE 2   D2=0
IF   RELIG EQ 3   D3=1
IF   RELIG NE 3   D3=0
IF   RELIG EQ 4   D4=1
IF   RELIG NE 4   D4=0
REGRESSION
     VARIABLES=HAPPY INCOME HEALTH D1 D2 D3 D4
     DEPENDENT=HAPPY
     METHOD=ENTER
```

8.4 The multiple R is the correlation between the dependent variable and the entire set of independent variables. The multiple R squared is the proportion of variance in the dependent variable associated with variance in the independent variables.

8.5 Multicollinearity problems exist when there are high intercorrelations among the independent variables. Multicollinearity causes unreliable estimates of beta—that is, estimates that fluctuate greatly from one sample to another. The problem can be resolved by dropping one of two highly correlated variables from the set of independent variables or combining them into a composite variable. There is no problem when more than one independent variable is highly correlated with the dependent variable. Only when two or more independent variables are highly correlated with each other do we have multicollinearity problems.

8.6 When the plot of the standardized residuals by the standardized predicted values is not random, the association between the dependent variable and the set of independent variables is not linear. Either the dependent variable or one or more of the independent variables needs to be transformed.

8.7
```
REGRESSION VARIABLES=HEALTH INCOME EDUC HAPPY
                     AGE SEX/
                     DEPENDENT=HEALTH/
                     METHOD=ENTER/
                     SCATTERPLOT  (*RES,*PRE)/
```

Chapter 9

9.1 MANOVA will enable the reader to use a covariate, to obtain significance tests for multiple predictor variables, and to analyze group differences on a set of dependent variables. Other techniques would do a separate analysis for each dependent variable.

9.2 When there is only one dependent variable, MANOVA assumes its variance within each of the groups is normal and the same. For more than one dependent variable, MANOVA requires the additional assumption that the joint distribution of the dependent variables is multivariate normal. The variances of the dependent variables need not equal one another, but the distribution of scores on one dependent variable for all the cases with a particular score on another dependent variable should be normal.

9.3 `MANOVA  EDUC BY MARITAL (1,5) BY SEX (1,2)`

9.4 Yes, MANOVA assumes that there are some cases for each value in the range indicated.

9.5 `MANOVA  EDUC BY MARITAL(1,5) SEX(1,2)  WITH INCOME`

9.6 `MANOVA  CONFINAN TO CONARMY BY RELIG(1,5) SEX(1,2)`

9.7 It would mean that the differences between MARITAL groups, controlling for SEX, would occur from sampling error only 2 times out of 1000.

9.8 It would mean that the differences between the sexes in the effects of marital status would occur less than 1 time out of 1000 owing to sampling error.

9.9   Marital status would be a significant variable in the analysis because of the way it influenced the differences in scores by sex. It would not matter that the effects of marital status alone were not significant.

9.10   Pillai's trace

Chapter 10

10.1   DISCRIMINANT   GROUPS=CLASS(1,4) /
           VARIABLES=SEX RACE AGE INCOME EDUC DEFENSE SPEND

10.2   GET   FILE=NORC84
           SELECT IF   SEX EQ 2
           IF   CHILDS EQ 0   AND   WRKSTAT GE 4   FAMWORK=1
           IF   CHILDS NE 0   AND   WRKSTAT GE 4   FAMWORK=2
           IF   CHILDS EQ 0   AND   WRKSTAT LT 4   FAMWORK=3
           IF   CHILDS NE 0   AND   WRKSTAT LT 4   FAMWORK=4
           DISCRIMINANT   GROUPS=FAMWORK#
            VARIABLES=RACE EDUC INCOME AGE MEMPLOY CLASS

10.3   The primary purpose of a discriminant analysis is to improve our ability to classify cases. Compare the percent of cases that were misclassified by the discriminant analysis to the percent that would be misclassified by chance. The proportion improvement is equal to

$$\frac{\text{Random error proportion} - \text{Discriminant model-error proportion}}{\text{Random error proportion}}$$

10.4   The expected percent of correct classifications is equal to the sum of the squared proportion in each group.

10.5   The statistical significance of a discriminant analysis is produced for the Wilks' lambda statistic in the Canonical Discriminant Functions table of the output.

10.6   Compare the percent of cases classified correctly with that function in the analysis to the percent classified correctly when that function is not in the analysis. This procedure can be done with the FUNCTIONS sub-command. FUNCTIONS 1 will include only the first and most powerful function; FUNCTIONS 2 will include the two most powerful functions, and so forth. The difference between the percent of cases classified correctly with function 2 and with function 1 is the improvement made by the second function. The difference between the percent of cases classified correctly with function 3 and with function 2 is the improvement made by the third function.

10.7 The statistical significance of individual functions can be assessed from the output in the Canonical Discriminant Functions table. The statistical significance is approximated by the drop in the statistical significance after the function's effects are removed. The statistical significance for Wilks' lambda (the ratio of the within-groups sum of squares to the total sum of squares) is used.

10.8 To determine the contribution of a particular variable to the discriminant analysis classification accuracy, redo the analysis, dropping the variable in question from the VARIABLES subcommand. The change in the percent of cases classified correctly when the variable is dropped represents the variable's contribution.

$$\text{Contribution} = \% \text{ correct with variable} - \% \text{ correct without variable}$$

10.9 To approximate the contribution of a particular variable to the statistical significance of a discriminant analysis, drop the variable in question from the analysis and compare the statistical significance of the analysis using the variable to the statistical significance without the variable. Letting P^2 equal the statistical significance without the variable and P^1 equal the statistical significance with the variable, the formula would be

$$\text{Contribution} = \frac{P^2 - P^1}{P^2}$$

This contribution is the proportionate reduction in the likelihood that the group differences are the result of sampling probability error.

10.10 To classify new cases, use the SELECT subcommand to choose the cases used for calculating the discriminant function, and use the command STATISTICS 13,14 to produce for each of the new cases its predicted group membership.

Chapter 11

11.1 Regression analysis assumes that the dependent variable and the predictor variables are interval and that the dependent variable is normally distributed for each value of the predictor variables.

11.2   When a table has three or more variables and many cells, log-linear analysis with the HILOGLINEAR command will allow the user to see more easily what the significant relationships are.

11.3   A log-linear analysis of health (4 categories) by marital (5 categories) by religion (5 categories) would normally require (4*5*5)*5 = 500 cases.

11.4   HILOGLINEAR   HEALTH(1,4) MARITAL(1,5)
                                       RELIGION(1,5) /
                        PRINT ALL

11.5   The first-order effects would indicate whether each cell in the table has the same number of cases. This statistic is uninteresting because we do not expect to have an equal number of cases in each category of these variables.

11.6   The second-order effects would indicate whether any of the bivariate associations controlling for the effects of the third variable were significant—for example, whether the association between HEALTH and MARITAL is significant controlling for the effects of RELIG.

11.7   The third-order effects would indicate interaction effects—for example, whether the association between HEALTH and MARITAL is the same for each value of RELIG.

11.8   The chi-square and probability of the highest-order effects are given in the output in the table entitled TESTS THAT K-WAY AND HIGHER ORDER EFFECTS ARE ZERO.

11.9   The partial chi-square is a measure of the association between HEALTH and MARITAL controlling for the effects of RELIG. A partial chi-square probability of .023 would indicate that an association at least this strong would occur 23 times out of 1000 through sampling error.

11.10   The strength of the association is most easily measured by comparing the observed frequencies in the categories of the dependent variable for the different categories of the predictor variables.

Chapter 12

12.1   A factor is a composite variable underlying the variance in a set of variables.

12.2   A factor loading is a measure of the association between a variable and a factor of which it is one component. Factor loadings range from −1.0 to 1.0. A 0 would indicate no association, and a 1 would indicate a perfect association. The sign of the loading indicates whether the association is positive or negative.

12.3 The eigenvalue is a measure of variance in the set of variables in the factor analysis. The total eigenvalue is equal to the number of variables in the analysis.

12.4 The communality of a variable is the proportion of its variance accounted for by the variables in the analysis. The communality is 0.0 for no association and 1.0 for a perfect association. The communality of all the variables will be 1.0 when the number of factors equals the number of variables.

12.5 A factor score is the value of the factor for a particular case.

12.6 In an orthogonal rotation, the correlation between the factors in the analysis is kept at 0.0. In an oblique rotation, some correlation is permitted among the factors in the analysis. The default level of correlation in an oblique rotation will usually be below an absolute value of 0.30.

12.7 The factor extraction technique used by default for FACTOR is principal components.

12.8 The default rotation technique is a varimax orthogonal rotation.

12.9 The default rotation technique when the ROTATION=OBLIQUE subcommand is given is oblimin.

12.10 `FACTOR   VARIABLES=CONFINAN TO CONARMY/`

Chapter 13

13.1 A PUMS file is a sample of households and individuals. An STF file has as units geographic areas for which aggregate statistics are available.

13.2 Yes

13.3 No. The necessary individual data would be lacking.

13.4 When you want the information on a household record applied to the individuals who reside in the household

13.5 Use a SELECT IF command with the variable SUMRYLV, which indicates geographic level.

13.6 Use a SELECT IF command with the variable RECOIND, which indicates ethnic and racial group.

13.7   There is not a household-value variable for which you can produce a
frequencies table. Rather, each cell in the household value distribution
is a variable that must be named and included in a LIST command.

13.8   In the STF files a 0 value can indicate that the information was suppressed or it can indicate that the coded value was 0. You need to use
an IF statement with the variable that indicates suppression to change
0 to a missing value when suppression is indicated.

Chapter 14

14.1   You would need to add to your system a hard disk with 10 megabytes
of storage, and you would need to upgrade your RAM to 380K.

14.2   CD \SPSS
SPSS/PC

14.3   SPSS/PC+ is waiting for you to finish the command and indicate it is
finished by entering a period or a blank line.

14.4   GET   FILE=DATAFILE

14.5   DISPLAY   DATAFILE

14.6   DISPLAY   EDUC

14.7   INCLUDE   COMMANDS

14.8   Use the command REVIEW to load the on-line editing program. Then, if
you are unfamiliar with REVIEW, press the F1 key to produce an explanation of the commands that operate REVIEW.

14.9   HELP   REGRESSION

14.10   In SPSS/PC+, BREAKDOWN is replaced by MEANS; COMMENT is replaced by *; CONDESCRIPTIVE is replaced by DESCRIPTIVES; MATCH
FILES and ADD FILES are replaced by JOIN; N OF CASES is replaced
by N; and PEARSON CORR is replaced by CORRELATION.

INDEX

Pages on which definitions appear are *italicized*.